Third Canadian Edition

P.O.W.E.R. LEARNING AND YOUR LIFE

ESSENTIALS OF STUDENT SUCCESS

FELDMAN | LAVOIE

McGraw Hill Education

P.O.W.E.R. LEARNING AND YOUR LIFE: ESSENTIALS OF STUDENT SUCCESS
Third Canadian Edition

The Internet addresses listed in the text were accurate at the time of publication. The inclusion of a website does not indicate an endorsement by the authors or McGraw-Hill Ryerson, and McGraw-Hill Ryerson does not guarantee the accuracy of the information presented at these sites.

ISBN-13: 978-1-25-946065-4
ISBN-10: 1-25-946065-7

1 2 3 4 5 6 7 8 9 10 TCP 22 21 20 19 18

Printed and bound in Canada.

Care has been taken to trace ownership of copyright material contained in this text; however, the publisher will welcome any information that enables them to rectify any reference or credit for subsequent editions.

Portfolio Director, Humanities, Social Sciences & Languages, International: *Rhondda McNabb*
Portfolio Manager: *Sara Braithwaite*
Senior Marketing Manager: *Kelli Legros*
Content Developer: *Melissa Hudson*
Senior Portfolio Associate: *Marina Seguin*
Supervising Editor: *Jeanette McCurdy*
Photo/Permissions Editor: *Monika Schurmann*
Copy Editor: *Julia Cochrane*
Plant Production Coordinator: *Michelle Saddler*
Manufacturing Production Coordinator: *Sheryl MacAdam*
Cover Design: *David Montle*
Cover Image: *Rawpixel Ltd / Alamy Stock Photo*
Interior Design: *Jennifer Stimson*
Page Layout: *Laserwords Private Limited*

About the Authors

ROBERT S. FELDMAN

Professor Feldman is a Fellow of both the American Psychological Association and the Association for Psychological Science. He is a winner of a Fulbright Senior Research Scholar and Lecturer award and has written some 100 scientific articles, book chapters, and books. His books include *Improving the First Year of College: Research and Practice*; *Understanding Psychology*, 9th edition; and *Development across the Life Span*, 5th edition. One of his publications, *Psychology and Your Life*, afforded Professor Feldman an opportunity to work closely with returning and commuter students. It was through that experience that he devoted research and development to applying the P.O.W.E.R. Plan.

Professor Feldman's research interests encompass the study of honesty and truthfulness in everyday life, development of non-verbal behaviour in children, and the social psychology of education. His research has been supported by grants from the National Institute of Mental Health and the National Institute on Disabilities and Rehabilitation Research (now known as the National Institute on Disability, Independent Living and Rehabilitation Research).

Professor Feldman occupies his spare time with serious cooking and earnest, but admittedly unpolished, piano playing. He also loves to travel. He lives with his wife, who is an educational psychologist, in a home overlooking the Holyoke mountain range in western Massachusetts.

DANICA LAVOIE

At the age of 17, Danica Lavoie left Dalhousie, a town in northern New Brunswick (population 3600), to attend Humber College in Toronto (population 2 million). It was there that she encountered some remarkable professors—Michael Hatton, Pam Hanft, and Wayson Choy—who inspired her and encouraged her to continue her studies. She went on to complete an Honours Bachelor of Arts in Psychology from the University of Waterloo; a Master of Business Administration from the Schulich School of Business; and, later on, a Teacher of Adults Certificate from Centennial College.

While studying for her MBA, Professor Lavoie was offered the opportunity by one of her former professors to teach part time at Humber College. Though she was only 22 at the time, it was this teaching experience that many years later motivated her to return to the classroom after a successful career in banking and as an entrepreneur. Currently, Professor Lavoie teaches marketing and analytics courses at Centennial College in Toronto, at both the undergraduate and graduate levels. She has never regretted moving from her lucrative business career into teaching, noting that "every semester is different, and every day brings a chance to make a difference in a student's life."

Professor Lavoie lives just outside Toronto with her husband Martin. When she isn't teaching or writing, she enjoys cooking, travelling, playing Scrabble, and catching up with hundreds of her former students on LinkedIn.

Brief Table of Contents

Table of Contents

3 Reading and Remembering 69

4 Taking Notes 96

5 Taking Tests 120

8 Making Decisions and Solving Problems 206

11 Planning Your Career (ONLINE) 298

Preface

What Makes This Textbook Different from Many Others?

Like many students in their first year of post-secondary education, you are probably feeling overwhelmed. You may be on your own for the first time, going back to school after a few years in the working world, or juggling the needs of a family while you further your education. Whether your parents are paying your way, you've saved your own money, or you have a large student loan hanging over your head, the pressure to succeed is always present. That's where this textbook comes in. While most college and university textbooks are designed with a *specific* course in mind, this textbook contains content that you will be able to apply to *all* of your courses. It is a handbook designed to teach you how to be successful—in college, in university, and as a lifelong learner.

I know all about that pressure, because I felt it, too. I only wish back then that I'd been able to take a course on how to be a successful student. So, decades later, when as a professor at Centennial College, I was given the opportunity to design such a course, I jumped at it! And a few years after that, when McGraw-Hill Ryerson came knocking on my door to see if I'd be interested in developing the Canadian edition of a textbook on student success, I jumped at that, too.

You see, it's one thing to learn about nursing or marketing or aviation technology; it's quite another to learn how to be a successful student in any of those disciplines.

Being a successful student means recognizing how you learn, what you value, and what you are striving for. It means knowing how to manage your time and your money. It means learning how to take notes, how to write tests, and how to make good decisions. Being a successful student requires you to learn how to research, how to write, and how to present. It involves collaborating with others and using technology to make your life more effective and efficient. And *that's* what this textbook is all about.

What's New in the Third Canadian Edition?

As with the first and second Canadian editions of *P.O.W.E.R. Learning and Your Life: Essentials of Student Success*, the third Canadian edition continues the tradition of being designed specifically to meet the needs and wants of Canadian educators and their students, while addressing the skills most sought after by Canadian employers. As before, I've drawn on feedback from reviewers, discussions with colleagues, and comments from my own students in developing a text that draws on sound principles of adult education, while emphasizing interactivity, critical thinking, and experiential learning.

Each chapter begins with learning outcomes based on Bloom's taxonomy, and the material within the chapter has been developed and organized around these specific outcomes. This makes it easier for educators to create course outlines based on the text, while giving students a clear sense of what they will learn in each chapter. Hands-on exercises labelled "Try It!", Course and Career Connections, and end-of-chapter cases are included in every chapter. All of these features are designed to promote active learning by encouraging students to engage in the material.

In the third Canadian edition, I've added more Try It! exercises, in keeping with the experiential nature of the text. Try It! exercises that previously referred to group work have been renamed "class discussion" and can be used either in small groups or with participation from the entire class.

Canadian psychotherapist Dr. Anne Dranitsaris's Striving Styles™ continue to appear in the third edition, as do familiar frameworks such as the SMART approach to goal-setting, the Cornell method of note-taking, and the SQ3R approach to reading.

A great deal of research[1] supports the positive impact that reflection has on learning. With that in mind, the "Time to Reflect" feature is back in the third edition, providing students with an opportunity to crystallize their learning. In the words of American philosopher, psychologist, and educational reformer John Dewey: "We do not learn from experience ... we learn from reflecting on experience."[2]

"Did You Know?" is a new section that can be found in every chapter, just before "Looking Back." Intended to spur a lively discussion, this new feature presents students with interesting—and often surprising—data or findings relating to the chapter.

The "Resources" section at the end of every chapter has been updated to reflect the most current print and web-based resources available. Within the "Resources" section, I've also added a feature called "There's an App for That," which is sure to be of interest to today's smartphone-obsessed student.

Chapter 1

- Replaced Employability Skills 2000+ with the more current Nine Essential Skills.

- Added figures on graduate earnings.

- Talked specifically about the cost/benefit of education and provided statistics to support it.

- Included a link to a survey on the five broad personality domains that are part of the Five-Factor model, an approach to personality testing that is gaining widespread support from psychologists. The Five-Factor model, or "Big Five" Dimensions of personality, is sometimes referred by the acronym "OCEAN," which stands for **O**penness to Experience, **C**onscientiousness, **E**xtroversion, **A**greeableness, and **N**euroticism.

- Provided a link to the recently published Angus Reid survey on Canadian values, which complements the discussion about how your values influence your life choices and the Try It! exercise that helps you determine what you value.

- Added the concept of "stretch goals" to the goal-setting section.

- Discussed motivation from the perspective that effort produces success.

- Moved the material on learning disabilities to Chapter 10.

Chapter 2

- Added a new learning outcome on creating timelines.
- Added material on creating timelines and provided a link to some project management templates.
- Added material on priority setting in a professional/working environment.
- Added a Try It! on the Black Holes of Time Management.
- Added a section on taking control of one's technology devices.
- Updated data on the time use of university and college students.
- Discussed the findings on multi-tasking and updated data on time spent on social media and impact of social media on student performance.
- Added identifying what is and isn't controllable to the section on taking control of the environment.

Chapter 3

- Revised and updated the "Reading Goes Digital" section to include recent studies of use of e-books.

Chapter 4

- Added a new section on the value of taking notes on a laptop or tablet versus writing notes the old-fashioned way, with research studies to back up which is most effective.
- Added references to several note-taking apps.
- Removed the section called "Taking Notes on Material You Cannot Write On."

Chapter 5

- Added a section dealing specifically with preparing for multiple-choice questions on a test.
- Added a section on taking online tests.

Chapter 6

Chapter 6, which deals with how to leverage technology and develop information competency, has been updated to include the latest technology tools. The emphasis, as before, is on how technology can be leveraged to make students' lives more effective and efficient. In this chapter, students will find helpful information on a wide range of topics, including what to expect from a distance learning course, how to use citation software, how to deal with anti-plagiarism software, and how to protect their online privacy. Indeed, references to new technologies continue to be woven throughout the text. For example, technologies related to calendars and to-do lists have been moved to Chapter 2, and those relating to online collaboration have been moved to Chapter 9. And, as mentioned previously, a new feature called "There's an App for That" can be found at the end of every chapter.

- Renamed chapter as "Leveraging Technology and Developing Information Competency." Replaced material on organizing one's desktop and folders with specific suggestions for regularly deleting/upgrading technology.
- Moved material on calendars and to-do lists to Chapter 2 and material on online collaboration to Chapter 9. Shortened the section on what can be found in the library. Updated the definition of plagiarism. Removed material on different types of plagiarism.
- Updated material in the section on protecting your privacy online and the information in Table 6.1 (which now goes beyond mobile privacy to laptops, etc.).

Chapter 7

The third Canadian edition continues to include a chapter on Writing and Presenting (Chapter 7). It addresses some of the fundamental skills in Skills Canada's Nine Essential Skills, which are introduced in Chapter 1. In this chapter, students are introduced to the concept of writing as a process and are provided with a framework for case analysis and a format for developing a business report. They are also introduced to how to create and deliver an effective presentation, as well as how to develop presentation slides to complement a presentation.

- Added a sample table of contents.
- Created good slide versus bad slide example.

Chapter 8

- Added material from Charles Duhigg's bestseller *Smarter Faster Better* on information blindness, envisioning multiple futures, and the importance of narrowing down to two or three alternatives.
- Added a section on taking accountability for decisions made and on the need to avoid decision fatigue.
- Added additional items to Try It! 4 (distinguish fact from opinion).
- Added a link to a template for a decision tree.
- Added Suzy Welch's 10-10-10 strategy to "solving life's messier problems."

Chapter 9

- Updated the opening vignette on Naheed Nenshi.
- Expanded to include specific information on how to make group work more effective.
- Put learning outcomes on working in groups and resolving conflict back-to-back. Added a new learning outcome on how to facilitate a group meeting by using an agenda and minutes.
- Added additional information on Emotional Intelligence and some practical considerations when selecting group members.
- Added a section on what to do when group members don't deliver.

Chapter 10

- Added up-to-date information from the ACHA National College Health Assessment (Canadian Reference Group) on the stresses faced by today's college and university students.
- Added a new section called "How Common Is Stress?" along with supporting data.
- Incorporated the Learning Disabilities section that had previously been in Chapter 1 and retitled it "Stress Related to Dealing with Learning Disabilities."
- Added references to vaping and binge drinking and a paragraph on facts related to drinking.
- Continued focus on personal finance, with its emphasis on the uses and abuses of credit, which continues to be a major issue for today's students. Added additional information on credit scoring.
- Updated data in Try It! 3 "Test Your Knowledge of Personal Finance."
- Reduced the number of columns in the budget template from four to three.

Chapter 11

- Remains in an online environment.
- Addresses the use of LinkedIn as a powerful networking tool and the increasing use of e-portfolios as part of ongoing career management.
- Changed content that begins the first learning outcome. It now starts with "Are You in the Right Program?" and deals with articulation agreements and transfers between institutions.
- Added a list of interview questions designed for recent graduates.
- Added a section called "Find Yourself a Mentor."
- Added additional information on how to manage one's online reputation.

I hope you will enjoy not only *reading* this book, but also *using* this book, much as you would a workbook. Complete the surveys in it, highlight it, make notes in the margins, and refer back to it throughout your time as a student. Use it as a *resource* when you find yourself in later years struggling with a course, or studying for a test, or trying to get a group to collaborate on a project. Review it when you have to analyze a case, or write a report, or prepare a presentation. Apply what you've learned in this text to all of the other courses you take, and it will go a long way toward ensuring that you become the very best student and, eventually, the very best employee that you can be.

Features

Student-Friendly Design and Layout: The book has been designed to capture students' attention and enhance student engagement. Students will find images, charts, and photos throughout this innovative learning tool, showcasing the diversity of students as well as the latest in technological aids and devices.

Systematic Framework for Success: Each chapter utilizes the principles of the P.O.W.E.R. system (Prepare, Organize, Work, Evaluate, and Rethink) so students can clearly see how easy it is to incorporate this effective process into their everyday routine. The P.O.W.E.R. plan illustration in each chapter highlights the key steps for the corresponding chapter material.

Reinforced Learning across Chapters: Following their introduction in the first chapter, concepts like multiple intelligences, values, learning styles, and Striving Styles™ are reinforced throughout the book.

Skill-Building Opportunities: Each chapter offers numerous exercises and activities to reinforce key concepts and relate the material to students' other courses.

Connection of Academic and Career Success: Each chapter links the text material to the world of work and demonstrates how the chapter strategies are related to career choices and success.

Development of Critical Thinking Skills: Throughout the text, students are encouraged to assess their skills, reflect on their progress, and think critically about related experiences. Cases in each chapter provide an opportunity for students to consider what they have learned and use critical thinking skills to respond to related questions.

Additional Resources: At the end of each chapter, students are directed to on-campus help, books, smartphone applications, and Web-based resources to advance their learning.

Superior Learning Solutions and Support

The McGraw-Hill Education team is ready to help you, the instructor, assess and integrate any of our products, technology, and services into your course for optimal teaching and learning performance. Whether it's helping your students improve their grades or putting your entire course online, the McGraw-Hill Education team is here to help you. Contact your Learning Solutions Consultant today to learn how to maximize all of McGraw-Hill Education's resources.

For more information, please visit us online: **mheducation.ca/he/ solutions**.

Achieving the Goals of  Learning

Chapter-opening scenarios describe an individual grappling with a situation that is relevant to the subject matter of the chapter. Readers will be able to relate to these vignettes, which feature students running behind schedule, figuring out a way to keep up with reading assignments, or making decisions about what to do after graduation.

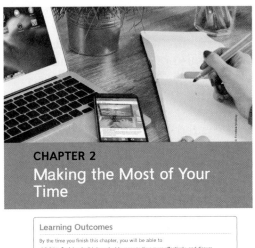

The **Career Connections** feature in every chapter links the material in the chapter to the world of work, demonstrating how the strategies discussed in the chapter are related to career choices and success in the workplace.

Every chapter includes a **Course Connections** box that shows students how to use the chapter's content to maximize their success in particular classes.

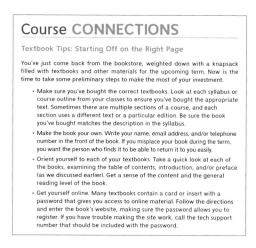

Try It! activities in each chapter provide opportunities for gaining hands-on experience with the material covered in the chapter. These include questionnaires, self-assessments, and group exercises to do with classmates. The Try It! activities, along with other assessment opportunities, are also available on the McGraw-Hill online resource.

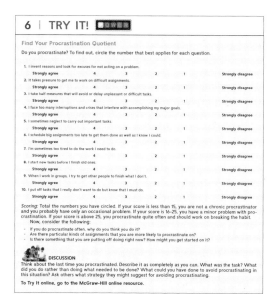

The **Did You Know?** feature provides students with interesting—and often surprising—data that address the chapter's main topic and are sure to spur discussion with their classmates.

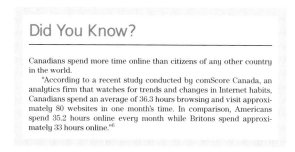

The Time to Reflect feature encourages students to reflect back on what they learned in the chapter and how they will use that information in the future.

Time to Reflect: What **Did I Learn?**

1. Generally speaking, how would you characterize your time management skills?

2. What would be the benefit to you personally if you could manage time more effectively? That is, what goals might you accomplish if you had more time at your disposal?

3. Based on what you learned about time management in this chapter, what do you plan to do differently in the future? Be specific.

The **Looking Back** feature summarizes the main information provided in the chapter and serves as an excellent study tool for tests.

Looking Back

How can I manage my time most effectively?
Decide to take control of your time.
> Become aware of the way you use your time now.
> Set clear priorities.
> Distinguish the important priorities from the not-so-important and the urgent from the not-so-urgent.
> Use time management tools such as a master calendar, a weekly timetable, and a daily to-do list.
> Estimate the time required to complete tasks, and create timelines for complex undertakings.

How can I control my environment?
> Control your environment by saying no, getting away from it all, working in silence, taking control of your devices, and leaving some slack in your schedule to accommodate the unexpected.

How can I work smarter, instead of harder?
> Accomplish tasks in the most efficient way possible, match the amount of effort you expend to the importance of the task, develop a consistent approach to tasks you do regularly, and use device blockers to help you manage your time.

How can I avoid procrastination?
> Avoid procrastination by breaking large tasks into smaller ones, starting with the easiest parts of a task first, working with other people, and calculating the true costs of procrastination.

How can I balance competing priorities?
> Consider how your competing priorities relate to one another.
> Manage work time carefully, use slack time on the job to perform school assignments, use flextime, accept new responsibilities thoughtfully, and assign the proper priority to work.

The **Resources** feature includes an updated list of the types of resources that are useful in finding and utilizing information relevant to the chapter: these may include on-campus resources, books, websites, videos, and smartphone applications.

RESOURCES

ON CAMPUS

The person who determines when classes meet is usually known as the registrar. If you are having difficulty scheduling your classes, the registrar's office may be helpful. In addition, your academic adviser can help you work out problems with enrolling in the classes you want.

For help with such issues as planning a study schedule for the upcoming term, dealing with multiple assignments and obligations on the same date, or dealing with competing academic and work demands, consult your campus learning centre. The staff can help you sort out the options you may have.

Many college and university student associations or Student Services offices provide students with a paper-based agenda free of charge. Stop by and pick one up at the beginning of the school year. And while it might seem obvious, don't forget that your instructors are a great source of information.

IN PRINT

Stephen Covey's classic, the 25th-anniversary edition of *The Seven Habits of Highly Effective People* (Simon & Schuster, 2013), and Alan Axelrod and Brian Tracy's *Eat That Frog! 21 Great Ways to Stop Procrastinating and Get More Done in Less Time* (Berrett-Kohler, 2007) are practical, hands-on guides to time management.

168 Hours: You Have More Time Than You Think (Penguin, 2010), by Laura Vanderkam, focuses on the best time management practices used by ordinary, everyday people like you.

The Willpower Instinct: How Self-Control Works, Why It Matters, and What You Can Do To Get More of It (Avery, 2011), by Kelly McGonigal, comes highly recommended by Carleton University professor and noted expert on procrastination Dr. Timothy A. Pychyl.

ON THE WEB

The McGraw-Hill online resource provides online versions of all the time management forms present in this chapter. You can complete the forms online or download them and print out as many copies as you need. The following websites provide an opportunity to extend your learning about the material in this chapter:

> **The lifehack.org** site offers many tips and tricks for making life easier. For their time management hacks, check out this link: **lifehack.org/articles/technology/top-15-time-management-apps-and-tools.html.**

THERE'S AN APP FOR THAT

Many apps are available to help you manage your time:

> The Google Calendar app is available for both iOS and Android.

> For to-do lists for iOS and Android, try Todoist or Any.DO.

> For apps that allow you to block access to sites from your favourite device, try SelfControl for iOS or Self Control for Study for Android.

> For a multi-platform app that allows you to combine scheduling, homework, and grades, try out istudiez.

> To see just how much time you are spending on your device, download Checky for Android or iOS.

Key terms appear in boldface in the text and are defined in the Glossary at the end of the text.

Taking It to the Web exercises encourage students to use the Internet to build on their understanding of the concepts presented in the chapter and to explore other perspectives.

TAKING IT TO THE WEB

1 Complete a weekly organizer online. Find a site on the Web that offers shareware or freeware featuring a weekly planner (for example, **printablecalendar .ca/** or **studygs.net/schedule/weekly.htm**). Create a weekly schedule sheet for yourself based on this design. Be sure to write in all of your classes, job obligations, and any other regular responsibilities that you have. Be sure to set specific times in your daily schedule to study. (If you already use Google Calendar or Outlook, use its calendar function to do the same thing.)

2 Make a master calendar for the term using the same software you used for the exercise above. If your calendar does not provide this information automatically, you can go to **timeanddate.com/calendar/**. Here you'll find many links to different calendar-related information, such as when holidays occur. Be sure to indicate dates when important assignments are due and when exams occur.

Each chapter ends with a case **(The Case of . . .)** to which the principles described in the chapter can be applied. Cases are based on situations that students might themselves encounter. Each case provides a series of questions that encourage students to consider what they've learned and to use critical thinking skills in responding to these questions.

THE CASE OF . . .
Time Crunched

Paul Misir couldn't believe it. He was working overtime at his delivery job because one of his co-workers was on vacation. During a break from his shift, he got a text message from a classmate asking if he wanted to study the next day for the exam the following Monday. Paul had forgotten all about the exam.

Even worse, Paul couldn't study with his classmate the next day because he'd promised his girlfriend he would join her to visit her grandmother, who lived an hour's drive from the city. Although he wasn't looking forward

to the two-hour round trip, he knew his girlfriend would be furious if he broke his promise. And on top of all that, he also had to find time in the next few days to work on a term paper due in one of his other classes.

As he was driving home thinking about all this, his car started to sputter and then stalled. He was unable to get it started. That was it. He sat there on the side of the road, feeling as if his life had completely fallen apart and wondering how he'd ever get it back together again.

1. What might you tell Paul that could help solve his predicament?

2. What specific time management techniques might Paul have employed in the past to avoid these problems?

3. What strategies might Paul use now to take control of his limited time during the coming days?

4. What advice could you give Paul to try to prevent problems in time management for his next term?

With Gratitude

I want to begin by thanking the mentors whose sage advice helped me forge my life's path: Michael Hatton, Helen K. Sinclair, and Perrin Lewis. Each of you played an important role in making me understand what I could do and who I could become. I also want to thank my husband, Martin Durand, who supported me in so many ways throughout the time it took to complete the third edition of this text. A special thank you also goes out to Dr. Anne Dranitsaris for developing a student version of her Striving Styles™ framework specifically for this textbook.

I would also like to thank the many people in Higher Education at McGraw-Hill Ryerson who helped make this text possible. They include former Sponsoring Editor Lisa Rahn, who first proposed that I get involved with the project; Product Manager Sara Braithwaite; Product Developer Melissa Hudson; Permissions Editor Monika Schurmann; Supervising Editor Jeanette McCurdy; and Copy Editor Julia Cochrane.

And last, but certainly not least, I owe a debt of gratitude to the reviewers who provided feedback on the revision of *P.O.W.E.R. Learning and Your Life*, Third Canadian Edition. Their carefully considered comments and suggestions are reflected in the final version of the text.

Lidia Dorosz	*St. Lawrence College*
Dr. Michael O'Brien Moran	*University of Manitoba*
Laura Norman	*St. Lawrence College*
Catherine Skimson	*Conestoga College*

Danica Lavoie

The Complete Course Solution

We listened to educators from around the world, learned their challenges, and created a whole new way to deliver a course.

Connect2 is a collaborative teaching and learning platform that includes an instructionally designed complete course framework of learning materials that is flexible and open for instructors to easily personalize, add their own content, or integrate with other tools and platforms.

- Save time and resources building and managing a course.
- Gain confidence knowing that each course framework is pedagogically sound.
- Help students master course content.
- Make smarter decisions by using real-time data to guide course design, content changes, and remediation.

MANAGE — Dynamic Curriculum Builder

With one click you can launch a complete course framework developed by instructional design experts. Each Connect2 course is a flexible foundation for instructors to build upon by adding their own content or drawing upon the wide repository of additional resources.

- Easily customize Connect2 by personalizing the course scope and sequence.
- Get access to a wide range of McGraw-Hill Education content within one powerful teaching and learning platform.
- Receive expert support and guidance on how best to utilise content to achieve a variety of teaching goals.

MASTER — Student Experience

Improve student performance with instructional alignment and leverage Connect2's carefully curated learning resources. Deliver required reading through Connect2's award winning adaptive learning system.

- Teach at a higher level in class by helping students retain core concepts.
- Tailor in-class instruction based on student progress and engagement.
- Help focus students on the content they don't know so they can prioritize their study time.

MEASURE — Advanced Analytics

Collect, analyze and act upon class and individual student performance data. Make real-time course updates and teaching decisions backed by data.

- Visually explore class and student performance data.
- Easily identify key relationships between assignments and student performance.
- Maximize in-class time by using data to focus on areas where students need the most help.

Course Map

The flexible and customizable course map provides instructors full control over the pre-configured courses within Connect2. Instructors can easily add, delete, or rearrange content to adjust the course scope and sequence to their personal preferences.

Implementation Guide

Each Connect2 course includes a detailed implementation guide that provides guidance on what the course can do and how best to utilise course content based on individual teaching approaches.

Instructor Resources

A comprehensive collection of instructor resources are available within Connect2. Instructor Support and Seminar Materials provide additional exercises and activities to use for in-class discussion and teamwork.

For more information, please visit www.mheconnect2.com

CHAPTER 1

P.O.W.E.R. Learning: Becoming an Expert Student

Learning Outcomes

By the time you finish this chapter, you will be able to

LO 1.1 Discuss the benefits of a post-secondary education.

LO 1.2 List the nine essential skills valued by Canadian employers.

LO 1.3 Identify the basic principles of P.O.W.E.R. Learning and how expert students use P.O.W.E.R. Learning to set goals and achieve academic success.

LO 1.4 Compare and contrast learning styles, striving styles, and multiple intelligences; identify your own styles; and reflect on how they relate to your values and academic success.

The day has started off with a bang. Literally. As Daniela Oliveira reaches sleepily to turn off the alarm on her cellphone, she knocks it off the table next to her bed and sighs as it hits the wood floor.

Struggling to get out of bed, Daniela reflects on the day ahead. It's the end of the semester and this is one of her most intense days—a final project due, two exams to write, and a six-hour shift at a local restaurant.

After a quick shower, Daniela jumps on the bus and makes her way to school, where she joins her fellow paralegal students on campus. She glances at her paralegal textbook and feels a wave of anxiety flood over her: Will I do well enough on my exam? How will I manage to hold down a demanding job, find time to exercise, and still have enough time to study? Will I find a job as a paralegal after graduation? Will I make my parents proud? . . . And underlying them all is a single challenge: Will I be successful in college and in my career?

Looking Ahead

Whether academic pursuits are a struggle or come easily to you, whether you are returning to post-secondary education or attending for the first time, whether you are gaining new skills for your current job or have been at home caring for your children and are now starting on a whole new career path, or whether you are attending college or university in your own hometown or have travelled from somewhere else to be here—whatever your situation, pursuing post-secondary education is a challenge. All of us have concerns about our own capabilities and motivation, and the excitement and anxiety most of us bring to new situations—like starting college or university—make us wonder whether we'll succeed.

Whether you are majoring in nursing or business, there are some fundamental skills that will help you to achieve your goal of obtaining a post-secondary education. Students who have already graduated clearly understand this. A 2013 survey conducted for Intel Canada found that, if they could go back in time, "27% of college and university students surveyed would tell their younger selves to boost their self-discipline skills, and another 26% would advise improving time management skills in order to be successful beyond high school."[1]

That's where this book comes in. Whether you are a goal-oriented student who knows exactly what you want to study, or you are still searching for a major, it is designed to help you learn the most effective ways to approach the challenges you encounter, not just in college or university, but in your career, too. It will teach you practical strategies, and it will provide hints and tips that can lead you to success, all centred on an approach to achieving classroom and career success. That approach is called P.O.W.E.R. Learning.

This book is designed to be useful in a way that is different from other texts. It presents information in a hands-on format. It's meant to be used, not just read. Write on it, underline words and sentences, use a highlighter, circle key points, and complete the questionnaires right in the book. If you are using the e-book version of this text, be sure to follow the links to the electronic versions of the surveys and exercises. The more exercises you complete, the more useful the content will be to you. The ideas in this book will help you throughout your post-secondary education and throughout your career, so it's a good idea to invest your time here and now. If the techniques you master here become second nature, the payoff will be enormous.

In the first part of this chapter, you'll read about the benefits of post-secondary education and examine the skills, attitudes, and behaviours valued by Canadian employers. After that, you'll be introduced to the basics of the P.O.W.E.R. Learning process, a process that is used throughout the book and is a fundamental building block in achieving academic and career success. Finally, in the last half of the chapter, you'll discover a number of interactive tools that will help you uncover how you learn best; what you truly value; and how you can use your learning style, Striving Style™, and multiple intelligences to become an expert student.

LO 1.1 The Benefits of a Post-secondary Education

Congratulations. You are enrolled in an institution of higher learning. Clearly, you agree with the many Canadians who overwhelmingly believe that adult learning is critical to success in life and to satisfaction with one's life.[2] The reasons that people go to college or university vary from the practical ("I need new skills for my job"), to the noble ("I want to build a better life for my family"), to the vague ("Why not? I don't have anything better to do"). Consider your own reasons for enrolling as you complete **Try It! 1** "Why Are You Going to College or University?"

But is post-secondary education worth the investment of time, money, and lost wages? Let's start by looking at the numbers. On average, according to Statistics Canada, tuition for one year in an undergraduate program

1 | TRY IT! POWER

Why Are You Going to College or University?

Place a 1, a 2, and a 3 next to the three most important reasons that you have for attending college/university:

_____ I want to get a good job when I graduate.

_____ I want to make my family proud.

_____ I couldn't find a job.

_____ I want to try something new.

_____ I want to get ahead at my current job.

_____ I want to pursue my dream job.

_____ I want to improve my reading and critical-thinking skills.

_____ I want to become a more cultured person.

_____ I want to make more money.

_____ I want to learn more about things that interest me.

_____ A mentor or role model encouraged me to go.

_____ I want to prove to others that I can succeed.

Now consider the following:

1. What do your answers tell you about yourself and your likelihood of success in pursuing your education?

2. What reasons besides these did you think about when you were applying to college or university?

3. How do you think your reasons compare with those of your fellow students?

To Try It online, go to the McGraw-Hill online resource.

was $6,191 in 2015,[3] and according to the Canadian University Survey Consortium's 2015 annual report, the average debt-ridden student owes $26,819.[4] In the 2016 version of this same survey, 44 percent of students indicated that preparing them for a specific job or career was the most important reason for going to university.[5]

With an investment like this on the line, you will be relieved to know that the data clearly demonstrate that a post-secondary education helps people find better-paying jobs. College and university graduates earn about 75 percent more than high-school graduates over their working lifetime.[6] Another way of looking at this is that for every $100 earned by a high school graduate in Canada, a college graduate will earn $116 and a university graduate will earn $179. That difference adds up: over the course of their working lifetimes, college graduates earn close to $1 million more than those with only a high-school diploma. That's like winning the lottery just by staying in school! Of course the amount earned will differ by province (see **Figures 1.1** and **1.2**) and by major. But the evidence is clear: more education means a better job.

Of course, making more money is not the only reason to attend college or university. For example, a survey of first-year students found

figure 1.1 | Income Advantage for Canadian College Graduates by Province

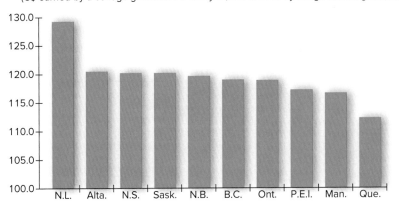

Income Advantage for College Graduates, Full-Time Employees, 2013
(C$ earned by a college graduate for every C$100 earned by a high-school graduate)

© The Conference Board of Canada

figure 1.2 | Income Advantage for Canadian University Graduates by Province

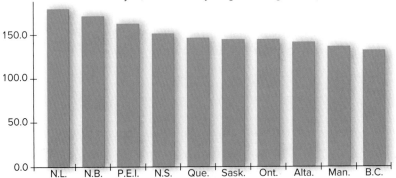

Income Advantage for University Graduates, Full-Time Employees, 2013
(C$ earned by university graduates with a bachelor's degree for every C$100 earned by a high-school graduate)

© The Conference Board of Canada

figure 1.3 | Choosing College

These are the most frequently cited reasons that first-year college students gave when asked in a U.S. survey why they had enrolled in college.[7]

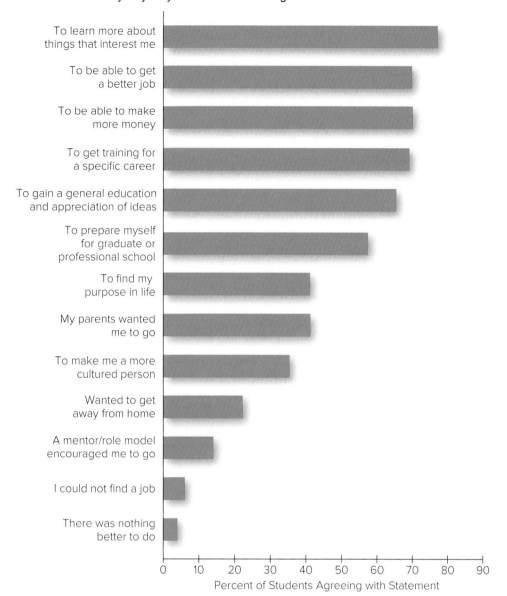

that the number one reason they chose to enroll in college was to learn about things that interest them (see **Figure 1.3**). But no matter what program you choose to pursue, one trend is undeniable: as jobs become increasingly complex and technologically sophisticated, a post-secondary education is becoming an entry-level requirement for many jobs.

Here are some additional reasons the return on investment in your education will likely be life changing:

> **You'll learn to think critically.** Here's what one student said about his college experience after he graduated: "It's not about what you major in or which classes you take. . . . It's really about learning to think. Wherever you end up, you'll need to be able to analyze and solve problems—to figure out what needs to be done and do it."[8] Clearly, potential employers agree. In the 2013 report "It Takes More Than a Major: Employer Priorities for College Learning and Student Success," 93 percent of employers surveyed said that "a demonstrated capacity

to think critically, communicate clearly, and solve complex problems is more important than a candidate's undergraduate major."[9] Education improves your ability to understand the world—to understand it as it now is, and to prepare to understand it as it will be.

> **You'll learn how to communicate better.** Post-secondary institutions provide you with the opportunity to communicate your thoughts and ideas orally and in writing; teachers provide important feedback on how to do this well. As you will learn in the next section of this chapter, communication is a skill that is highly valued by Canadian employers.

> **You'll be able to better deal with advances in knowledge and technology that are changing the world.** Genetic engineering . . . drugs to reduce forgetfulness . . . foods that make us smarter—no one knows what the future will hold. But you can prepare for it through a post-secondary education. Education can provide you with intellectual tools that you can apply regardless of the specific situation in which you find yourself.

> **You'll learn to adapt to new situations.** College and university are different worlds from high school or the workplace. They present new experiences and new challenges. Your adjustment to the culture of your college or university will prepare you for future encounters by helping you deal with the mixture of fear and excitement that often accompanies new situations.

> **You'll be better prepared to live in a world of diversity.** The ethnic composition of Canada is changing rapidly. Whatever your ethnicity, chances are you'll be working and living with people whose backgrounds, lifestyles, and ways of thinking are entirely different from your own. You won't be prepared for the future unless you understand others and their cultural backgrounds, as well as how your own cultural background affects you.

> **You'll make learning a lifelong habit.** Higher education isn't the end of your education. Education will build upon your natural curiosity about the world, and it will make you aware that learning is a rewarding and never-ending journey.

> And, finally, the obvious: **You will boost your career prospects.** Not only will you acquire skills that Canadian employers value, but these skills can also help you find work that interests you and pays you well.

LO 1.2 What Canadian Employers Value

Forging a successful career depends, as much as anything else, on the "fit" between what employers are looking for and what you have to offer. In this section, we focus on uncovering the nine essential skills sought by Canadian employers. Later, we will provide you with an opportunity to examine how you can best harness your talents to offer employers what they are seeking.

Canadian employers are a diverse lot. They span the public and private sectors, large and small businesses, and every industry imaginable. Yet according to Skills Canada, employers pretty much agree on the nine essential skills

ESSENTIAL SKILLS

NUMERACY

Numeracy refers to the workers' use of numbers and their capability to think in quantitative terms. We use this skill when doing numerical estimating, money math, scheduling or budgeting math and analyzing measurements or data.

ORAL COMMUNICATION

Oral Communication pertains primarily to the use of speech to give and exchange thoughts and information by workers in an occupational group. We use this skill to greet people, take messages, reassure, persuade, seek information and resolve conflicts.

WORKING WITH OTHERS

Examines the extent to which employees work with others to carry out their tasks. We use this skill when we work as a member of a team or jointly with a partner, and when we engage in supervisory or leadership activities.

CONTINUOUS LEARNING

We use this skill when we learn as part of regular work or from co-workers and when we access training in the workplace or off-site. All workers must continue learning to keep or to grow with their jobs.

READING TEXT

Reading refers to the ability to understand reading material in the form of sentences or paragraphs. We use this skill to scan for information, skim overall meaning, evaluate what we read and integrate information from multiple sources: forms and labels if they contain at least one paragraph; print and non-print media (for example, text on computer screens and microfiche); and paragraph-length text in charts, tables and graphs

WRITING

The ability to write text and documents; it also includes non paper-based writing such as typing on a computer. We use this skill when we organize, record, document, provide information to persuade, request information from others and justify a request such as writing texts and writing in documents (for example, filling in forms) and/or non-paper- based writing (for example, typing on a computer)

THINKING

Thinking is the ability to engage in the process of evaluating ideas or information to reach a rational decision. Thinking differentiates between six different types of interconnected cognitive functions: problem solving, decision making, critical thinking, job task planning and organizing,significant use of memory and finding information.

DOCUMENT USE

Document Use involves a variety of information displays in which words, numbers, icons, and other visual characteristics (eg. line, colour, shape) are given meaning by their spatial arrangement. We use this skill when we read and interpret graphs, charts, lists, tables, blueprints, schematics, drawings, signs, and labels.

DIGITAL

Digital skills are those needed to understand and process information from digital sources, use digital systems, technical tools, and applications. Digital sources and/or devices include cash registers, word processing software, and computers to send emails and create and modify spreadsheets.

Skills Compétences
Canada

Canada

they are looking for from their employees. They are numeracy, oral communication, working with others, continuous learning, reading text, writing, thinking, document use, and digital skills (see the graphic on page 7).

Acquiring the skills Canadian employers are looking for takes time and effort. Many people think success is a straight upward line, but, in fact, the image above is a better representation of what success *really* looks like.

To help you develop the skills valued by Canadian employers, it's time to introduce you to a fundamental process that will help you achieve success, both in school and in life beyond: P.O.W.E.R. Learning.

LO 1.3 P.O.W.E.R. Learning: Five Key Steps to Achieving Success

P.O.W.E.R. Learning
A system designed to help people achieve their goals, based on five steps: Prepare, Organize, Work, Evaluate, and Rethink

The term **P.O.W.E.R. Learning** is an acronym—it is formed from the first letters of a series of steps—for an approach to learning that will help you take in, process, and make use of the information you'll acquire in college or university. It will help you to achieve your goals, both while you are in school and after you graduate.

Prepare, **O**rganize, **W**ork, **E**valuate, and **R**ethink. That's it. It's a simple framework, but an effective one. Using the systematic framework that P.O.W.E.R. Learning provides (illustrated in the P.O.W.E.R. Plan diagram below) will increase your chances of success at any task, from writing a paper to buying the weekly groceries to filling out a purchase order.

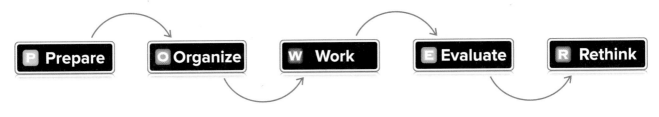

P.O.W.E.R. Plan

Keep this in mind: P.O.W.E.R. Learning isn't a product that you can simply pull down off the shelf and use without thinking. P.O.W.E.R. Learning is a process, and you are the only one who can make it succeed. Without your personal investment in the process, P.O.W.E.R. Learning consists of just words on paper.

Relax, though. You already know each of the elements of P.O.W.E.R. Learning, and you may discover that you are already putting this process, or parts of it, to work for you. You've applied and been accepted at an institution of higher learning. You may have also held down a job, started a family, and paid your monthly bills. Each of these accomplishments required that you use P.O.W.E.R. Learning. What you'll be doing throughout this book is becoming more aware of these methods and how they can be used to help you in situations you will encounter in school and your career.

P Prepare

Chinese philosopher Lao Tzu said that travellers taking a long journey must begin with a single step. But even before they take that first step,

© Design Pics / Don Hammond   © Nick White/Digital Vision/ Getty Images

Students go to school for their own reasons. Gwen recently visited a friend in the hospital and was struck by how much she wanted to be a part of the health-care community. John has survived several rounds of layoffs at his job and wants to make himself more marketable.

travellers need to know several things: what their destination is, how they're going to get there, how they'll know when they reach the destination, and what they'll do if they have trouble along the way. In the same way, you need to know where you're headed as you embark on the academic journeys involved in pursuing a post-secondary education. Whether you are performing a major, long-term task, such as landing a new and better job, or a more limited activity, such as getting ready to complete a paper due in the near future, you'll need to prepare for the journey.

Setting Goals

Before we seek to accomplish any task, all of us do some form of planning. The trouble is that most of the time such planning is done without conscious thinking, as if we are on autopilot. However, the key to success is to make sure that planning is systematic.

The best way to plan systematically is to use goal-setting strategies. In many cases, goals are clear and direct. It's obvious that our goal in washing dishes is to have the dishes end up clean. We know that our goal at the gas station is to fill the car's tank with gas. We go to the post office to buy stamps and mail letters.

Other goals are not so clear cut. In fact, often the more important the task—such as going to college or university—the more complicated our goals may be.

What's the best way to set appropriate goals? Here are some guidelines:

> **Set both long-term and short-term goals. Long-term goals** are aims relating to major accomplishments that take some time to achieve. **Short-term goals** are relatively limited steps you would take

Long-term goals
Aims relating to major accomplishments that take some time to achieve

Short-term goals
Relatively limited steps toward the accomplishment of long-term goals

on the road to accomplishing your long-term goals. For example, one of the primary reasons you're enrolled in a post-secondary institution is to achieve the long-term goal of helping your career. But to reach that goal, you have to accomplish a series of short-term goals, such as completing a set of required courses and earning your diploma or degree. Even these short-term goals can be broken down into shorter-term goals. To complete a required course, for instance, you have to accomplish a series of short-term goals, such as completing papers and taking tests.

SMART approach to goal setting
A framework for goal setting that emphasizes that goals should be specific, measurable, achievable, realistic, and time-bound

The **SMART approach to goal setting** has been around for a long time. The acronym SMART reminds us that goals must be specific, measurable, achievable, realistic, and time-bound. Let's look at each of these in turn.

> **Set goals that are *specific*.** Saying that "someday I'll learn a new language" is not specific enough. When you are setting a goal, make it as specific as possible. Which language? Where will you learn it? How will you learn it? Online? In a classroom setting? When will you learn it? The more specific and vivid the goal, the easier it is to achieve it. A "call to action" is also important; if you want to save for a car, open a separate savings account and arrange for a specific amount to be transferred from your chequing account on the day you get paid. Don't just identify the goal—make it happen!

> **Set goals that are *measurable*.** Goals should represent some measurable change from a current set of circumstances. Your behaviour ought to change in some way that can be expressed in terms of numbers—to show an increase ("raise my grade point average 10 percent"); a decrease ("reduce wasted time by two hours each week"); or a level to be maintained ("keep in touch with my out-of-town friends by writing four email messages each month"), developed ("participate in one workshop on critical thinking"), or restricted ("reduce my phone expenses 10 percent by speaking and texting less").

> **Set goals that are *achievable*.** Antoine de Saint-Exupéry, author of *The Little Prince*, said, "A goal without a plan is just a wish." Everyone would like to win gold medals at the Olympics or star in videos or write best-selling novels. Unfortunately, you are unlikely to achieve such goals. It isn't enough to have a goal. Depending on the goal, you may also need the physical, emotional, or intellectual capacity *and* the motivation and determination required to achieve it.

> **Set goals that are *realistic*.** We all want world peace and an end to poverty. Few of us have the resources or capabilities to bring either about. On the other hand, it is realistic to want to work in small ways to help others, such as by becoming a Big Brother or Big Sister or by volunteering at a local food bank. Be honest with yourself. There is nothing wrong with having big dreams. But it is important to be realistically aware of all that it takes to achieve them. If your long-term goals are unrealistic and you don't achieve them, the big danger is that you may incorrectly conclude that you are inept and lack ability, and you may then use this as an excuse for giving up. If goals are

2 | TRY IT! [POWER]

Turn Goals into Smart Goals

In this **Try It!**, a number of goals are listed that do NOT meet the criteria for SMART goals. Your task is to rewrite the goal so that it does meet the criteria shown.

Goal #1: Make this goal *specific*.
  I want to travel.

_____

Goal #2: Make this goal *measurable*.
  I want to lose weight.

_____

Goal #3: Make this goal *achievable*.
  I want to fly to Mars.

_____

Goal #4: Make this goal *realistic*.
I want to cure cancer.

_____

Goal #5: Make this goal *time-bound*.
  I want to get a degree.

_____

After you complete the exercise, consider how your own goals can be made smarter:

 1. Describe an academic goal in a SMART way.
 2. Describe a personal goal in a SMART way.
 3. Describe a work goal in a SMART way.

To Try It online, go to the McGraw-Hill online resource.

realistic, you can develop a plan to attain them, spurring you on to attain more.

> **Set goals that are *time-bound*.** As mentioned earlier, the more specific the goal, the better. This also applies to timing. When setting a goal, you should have a specific time frame in mind for achieving it—for example, by the time I am 22, I will have enough money to buy a car. Procrastination is all too easy: Before you know it, that goal you set five years ago is pushed far down your priority list, overtaken by more pressing matters and new responsibilities.

For practice in developing SMART goals, complete **Try It! 2** "Turn Goals into Smart Goals."

Recognize that your goals should not be independent of one another. Instead, they should fit together into a larger dream of who you want to be. And don't fall into the trap of setting a lot of easy-to-achieve goals. As former Canadian Psychological Association president Gary P. Latham noted, "you get into this mindset where crossing things off your to-do list becomes more important than asking yourself if you're doing the right things."[10] Instead, do as author Charles Duhigg suggests in his excellent book, *Smarter Faster Better*:[11] add "stretch goals" to your SMART goals—goals that are realistic but not necessarily easy to achieve.

Every once in a while, step back and consider how what you're doing today relates to the kind of career and life that you ultimately want to have. And, finally, if you haven't achieved your goal, revisit it. Reflect on the reasons it wasn't achieved. Was it too ambitious? Was the timing unrealistic? Taking time to figure out why you didn't achieve it will help you when setting goals in the future.

⊙ Organize

By determining where you want to go and expressing your goals in terms that can be measured, you have already made a lot of progress.

The next step in P.O.W.E.R. Learning is to organize the tools you'll need to accomplish your goals. Building upon the goal-setting work you've undertaken in the preparation stage, it's time to determine the best way to accomplish the goals you've identified.

How do you do this? Suppose you've decided to build a set of bookshelves for one room in your house. Let's say that you've already determined the kind of bookshelves you like and you've figured out the basic characteristics of the ones you will build (the preparation step in P.O.W.E.R. Learning). The next stage involves gathering the necessary tools, buying the wood and other building materials, sorting the construction supplies, and preparing the room for your building project—all aspects of organizing for the task.

Similarly, your academic success will hinge to a large degree on the thoroughness of your organization for each academic task that you face. In fact, one of the biggest mistakes that students make is plunging into an academic project—studying for a test, writing a paper, completing an in-class assignment—without being organized.

Course CONNECTIONS

Looking at the Big Picture

It's natural to view college or university as a series of small tasks—classes to attend, a certain number of pages to read each week, a few papers due during the term, quizzes and final exams to study for, and so on.

But such a perspective may lead you to miss what college and university, as a whole, are all about. Using the P.O.W.E.R. Learning framework can help you take the long view of your education, considering how it helps you achieve your long- and short-term goals for your professional and personal life (the *prepare* step) and what you'll need to do to maximize your success (the *organize* step). By preparing and organizing even before you set foot in the classroom for the first time, you'll be able to consider what it is that you want to get out of your post-secondary experience and how it fits into your life as a whole.

Two Kinds of Organization: Physical and Mental

Physical organization involves the mechanical aspects of task completion. For instance, you need to ask yourself if you have the appropriate tools, such as pens, paper, and a calculator. If you're using a computer, do you have access to a printer? Do you have a way to back up your files? Do you have the books and other materials you'll need to complete the assignment? Will the campus bookstore be open if you need anything else? Will the library be open when you need it? Do you have a comfortable place to work?

Mental organization is even more critical. Mental organization is accomplished by considering and reviewing the academic skills that you'll need to complete the task at hand successfully. You are an academic general in command of considerable forces—the basic skills, knowledge, and resources that you have at your command. You will need to make sure your forces are at their peak of readiness. For example, if you're working on a math assignment, you'll want to consider the basic math skills that you'll need and brush up on them. Thinking about these skills actively will help you organize mentally. Similarly, you'll want to mentally review your knowledge of engine parts before beginning car repair work (either for a class project or at the side of the road!).

Why does mental organization matter? The answer is that it provides a context for when you actually begin to work. Organizing paves the way for better subsequent performance.

Too often, students or workers on the job are in a hurry to meet a deadline and figure they had better just dive in and get it done. Organizing can actually save you time, because you're less likely to be anxious and end up losing your way as you work to complete your task.

Much of this book is devoted to strategies for determining—*before* you begin work on a task—how to develop the mental tools for completing an assignment. However, as you'll see, all of these strategies have a common theme: that success comes not from a trial-and-error approach but from following a systematic plan for achievement. Of course, this does not mean that there will be no surprises along the way, nor that simple luck is never a factor in great accomplishments. But it does mean that we can often make our own luck through careful preparation and organization.

W Work

You're ready. The preliminaries are out of the way. You've prepared and you've organized. Now it's time to start actually doing the work.

In some ways, work is the easy part. If you have conscientiously carried out the preparation and organization stages, you should know exactly where you're headed and what you need to do to get to where you want to be.

It's not always easy to get down to work, of course. How effectively you'll get down to the business at hand depends on many factors. Some may be out of your control. There may be a power outage that closes down the library or a massive traffic jam that delays your getting to the office. But most factors should be under your control. If you keep your goals front and centre, then effort will produce the success you are looking for.

Effort Produces Success

In Canadian writer Malcolm Gladwell's book *Outliers*, for example, Gladwell notes that to become a true master in a field—the Penny Oleksiak of swimming or the Measha Brueggergosman of opera, for example—requires about 10,000 hours of concentrated effort. Ten thousand hours is the equivalent of spending 1,000 days (or a little over 3 years), 10 hours a day, pursuing our goal. While most of us would not want to devote this much time to any one goal, that doesn't mean we can't lead a balanced life where our passions and interests receive the time they deserve. It's all about making an effort, i.e., doing the work, something over which you DO have control.

A great deal of psychological research has shown that thinking you have no control over what happens to you sends a powerful and damaging message to your self-esteem—that you are powerless to change things. Just think of how different it feels to say to yourself, "Wow, I worked at it and I did it," as compared with "I lucked out" or "It was so easy that anybody could have done it."

In the same way, we can delude ourselves when we try to explain our failures. People who see themselves as the victims of circumstance may tell themselves, "I'm just not smart enough," when they don't do well on an academic task. Or they might give an excuse: "My co-workers don't have children to care for." The way we view the causes of success and failure is, in fact, directly related to our success. Students who generally see effort and hard work as the reason behind their performance usually do better in college and university. Workers who see their job performance in this way usually do better in their careers. It's not hard to see why: When such individuals are working on a task, they feel that the greater the effort they put forth, the greater their chances of success. So they work harder. They believe that they have control over their success, and, if they fail, they believe they can do better in the future.

The following quote, attributed to various people, says it best: "The more I practise, the luckier I get." Here are some tips for keeping your motivation alive, so you can work with your full energy behind you:

> **Take responsibility for your failures—and successes.** When you do poorly on a test, don't blame the teacher, the textbook, or a job that kept you from studying. When you miss a work deadline, don't blame your boss or your incompetent co-workers. Analyze the situation, and see how you could have changed what you did to be more successful in the future. At the same time, when you're successful, think of the things you did to bring about that success.

It's all too easy to make excuses for our own failures. Can you think of a time when you shifted blame away from yourself for a failure? Was it a reasonable course of action? Why or why not?

© Frizzantine/Getty Images

> **Think positively.** As Indian civil rights leader Mahatma Gandhi once said: "Keep your thoughts positive, because your thoughts become your words. Keep your words positive, because your words become your behaviour. Keep your behaviour positive, because your behaviour becomes your habits. Keep your habits positive, because your habits become your values. Keep your values positive, because your values become your destiny." Assume that the strengths that you have will allow you to succeed and that, if you have difficulty, you can and will figure out what to do.

> **Accept that you can't control everything.** Seek to understand which things can be changed and which cannot. You might be able to get an extension on a paper due date, but you are probably not going to be excused from an institution-wide requirement.

> **Accept that there will be missteps.** Success is not a straight upward-sloping line, as comedian Demetri Martin captures in his simple sketch of what success *really* looks like. Sometimes you will find yourself taking one step forward and two steps back. Learn from your mistakes and keep moving forward and upward!

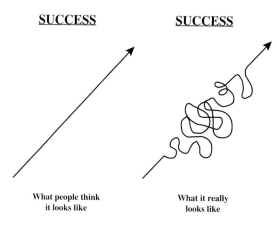

SUCCESS   **SUCCESS**

What people think it looks like   What it really looks like

To further explore the causes of academic success and failure, consider the questions in **Try It! 3** "Examine the Causes of Success and Failure," and discuss them with your classmates.

3 | TRY IT!

 DISCUSSION

Examine the Causes of Success and Failure

Consider the following situations:

1. Although he researched his report thoroughly, Ali is told by his professor that he has not referenced it properly. Ali is disappointed with himself and says, "I'll never be good at writing research reports. I might as well give up trying."

2. Coretta's English professor suggested that she apply for a scholarship offered to first-year students. She wins the scholarship but later finds out that only five people applied for it. She decides she only succeeded because she had no real competition.

3. Usually an A student, Alicia's grades this semester are lower than she expected. Her financial circumstances have forced her to take a part-time job, and while she no longer worries about money, she is disappointed with her performance at school. Distressed, she considers quitting school entirely, because she thinks that she'll never be able to achieve the high marks she is accustomed to.

Now consider the following questions about each of the situations:

1. What did each person conclude was the main cause of their performance?
2. What effect does this conclusion seem to have on the person?
3. Taking an outsider's point of view, what do you think is probably the main cause of each person's performance?
4. What advice would you give to each?

(*continued*)

(continued)

Now consider these broader questions:

1. What are the most important reasons some people are more successful than others?
2. How much does ability determine success? How much does luck determine success? How much do circumstances determine success?
3. If someone performs poorly at a job, what are the possible reasons for his or her performance? If someone performs well, what are the possible reasons for his or her performance? Is it harder to find reasons for good performance or for poor performance? Why?

To Try It online, go to the McGraw-Hill online resource.

E Evaluate

"Great! I'm done with the work. Now I can move on."

It's natural to feel relief when you've finished the work necessary to fulfill the basic requirements of a task. After all, if you've written the five double-spaced pages required for an assignment or balanced a complicated office budget, why shouldn't you heave a sigh of relief and just hand in your work?

The answer is that if you stop at this point, you'll be almost guaranteed a mediocre result. Did Shakespeare dash off the first draft of *Hamlet* and, without another glance, send it off to the Globe Theatre for production? Do professional athletes just put in the bare minimum of practice to get ready for a big game? Think of one of your favourite songs. Do you think the composer wrote it in one sitting and then performed it in a concert?

In every case, the answer is no. Even the greatest creation does not emerge in perfect form, immediately meeting all the goals of its producer. Consequently, the fourth step in the P.O.W.E.R. process is **evaluation**, which consists of determining how well the product or activity we have created matches our goals for it. Let's consider some steps to follow in evaluating what you've accomplished:

Evaluation

An assessment of the match between a product or activity and the goals it was intended to meet

> **Take a moment to congratulate yourself and feel some satisfaction.** Whether studying for a test, writing a paper, completing a report, or drafting a memo, you've done something important. You've moved from square one to a spot that's closer to your goal.

> **Compare what you've accomplished with the goals you're seeking to achieve.** Think back to the goals, both short-term and long-term, that you're seeking to achieve. How closely does what you've done match what you're aiming to do? For instance, if your short-term goal is to complete a math problem set with no errors, you'll need to check over the work carefully to make sure you've made no mistakes.

> **Evaluate your accomplishments as if you were a respected mentor from your past.** If you've written a paper, reread it from the perspective of a favourite teacher. If you've prepared a report, imagine you're presenting it to a boss who taught you a lot. Think about the comments you'd give if you were this person.

> **Evaluate what you've done as if you were your current instructor or supervisor.** This time, consider what you're doing from the perspective of the person who gave you the assignment. How would they react to what you've done? Have you followed the assignment to the letter? Is there anything you've missed?

> **Based on your evaluation, revise your work.** If you're honest with yourself, it's unlikely that your first work will satisfy you. So go back to the Work stage and revise what you've done. But don't think of it as a step back: Revisions you make as a consequence of your evaluation bring you closer to your final goal. This is a case where going back moves you forward.

R Rethink

They thought they had it perfect. But they were wrong.

In fact, it was a $1.5 billion mistake—a blunder on a grand scale. The finely ground mirror of the Hubble space telescope, designed to provide an unprecedented glimpse into the vast reaches of the universe, was not so finely ground after all.

Despite an elaborate system of evaluation designed to catch any flaws, there was a tiny blemish in the mirror that was not detected until the telescope had been launched into space and started to send back blurry photographs. By then, it seemed too late to fix the mirror.

Or was it? NASA engineers pondered the problem for months, devising and discarding one potential fix after another. Finally, after bringing a fresh eye to the situation, they formulated a daring solution that involved sending a team of astronauts into space. Once there, a space-walking Mr. Goodwrench would install several new mirrors in the telescope, which could refocus the light and compensate for the original flawed mirror.

Although the engineers could not be certain that the $629 million plan would work, it seemed like a good solution, at least on paper. It was not until the first photos were beamed back to Earth, though, that NASA knew their solution was A-OK. These photos were spectacular.

It took months of reconsideration before NASA scientists could figure out what had gone wrong and devise a solution to the problem they faced. Their approach exemplifies—on a grand scale—the final step in P.O.W.E.R. Learning: rethinking.

Rethinking what you've accomplished earlier means bringing a fresh—and clear—eye to what you've done. It involves using **critical thinking**, thinking that involves reanalyzing, questioning, and challenging our underlying assumptions. While evaluation means considering how well what we have done matches our initial goals, rethinking means reconsidering not only the outcome of our efforts, but also our goals and the ideas and process we've used to reach them. Critically rethinking what you've done involves analyzing and synthesizing ideas and seeing the connections between different concepts.

Rethinking involves considering whether your initial goals are practical and realistic or if they require modification. It also requires asking yourself what you would do differently if you could do it over again.

Critical thinking
A process involving reanalysis, questioning, and challenge of underlying assumptions

Career CONNECTIONS

P.O.W.E.R. Learning and the World of Work

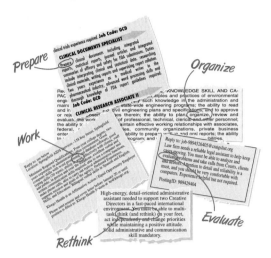

As we've discussed, the P.O.W.E.R. Learning process has applications both in the classroom and on the job. In **Career Connections** boxes, we'll highlight the ways the principles we're discussing can help you excel in the workplace. These "help wanted" advertisements and online postings illustrate the importance of the components of P.O.W.E.R. Learning in a wide variety of fields.

We'll be considering critical thinking throughout this book, examining specific strategies in every chapter, but the following steps provide a general framework for using critical thinking to rethink what you've accomplished:

> **Reanalyze, reviewing how you've accomplished the task.** Consider the approach and strategies you've used. What seemed to work best? Does your answer to that question suggest any alternatives that might work better the next time?

> **Question the outcome.** Take a big-picture look at what you have accomplished. Are you pleased and satisfied? Is there something you've somehow missed?

> **Identify your underlying assumptions; then challenge them.** Consider the assumptions you made in initially approaching the task. Are these underlying assumptions reasonable? If you had used different assumptions, would the result have been similar or different?

> **Consider alternatives rejected earlier.** You've likely discarded possible strategies and approaches before completing your task. Now's the time to think about those approaches once more and determine if they might have been more appropriate than the road you've followed.

> **What would you do differently if you had the opportunity to try things again?** It's not too late to change course.

> **Finally, reconsider your initial goals.** Are they achievable and realistic? Do your goals, and the strategies you used to attain them, need to be modified? Critically rethinking the objectives and goals that underlie your efforts is often the most effective route to success.

Completing the Process

The rethinking step of P.O.W.E.R. Learning is meant to help you understand your process of work and improve the final product if necessary. But mostly it is meant to help you grow, to become better at whatever it is you've been doing. Like a painter looking at a finished work, you may see a spot here or there to touch up, but don't destroy the canvas. Perfectionism can be as paralyzing as laziness. Keep in mind these key points:

> **Know that there's always another day.** Your future success does not depend on any single assignment, paper, or test. Don't fall victim to self-defeating thoughts such as "If I don't do well on this particular assignment, I'll never graduate" or "Everything is riding on this one project." Nonsense. In school, on the job, and in life, there is almost always an opportunity to recover from a failure.

> **Realize that deciding when to stop work is often as hard as getting started.** Knowing when you have put in enough time studying for a test, revising a paper, or reviewing your figures on an estimate is as much a key to success as preparation. If you've carefully evaluated what you've done and if you've seen that there's a close fit between your goals and your work, it's time to stop work and move on.

> **Use the strategies that already work for you.** Although the P.O.W.E.R. Learning framework provides a proven approach to attaining success, employing it does not mean that you should abandon strategies that have brought you success in the past. Using multiple approaches, and personalizing them, is the surest road to success.

LO 1.4 Learning More about Yourself

Consider what it would be like to be a member of the Trukese people, a small group of islanders in the South Pacific. Trukese sailors often sail hundreds of kilometres on the open sea. They manage this feat with none of the navigational equipment used by Western sailors. No compass. No chronometer. No sextant. They don't even sail in a straight line. Instead, they zigzag back and forth, at the mercy of the winds and tides. Yet they make few mistakes. Almost always they are able to reach their destination with precision. How do they do it?

They can't really explain it. They say it has to do with following the rising and setting of the stars at night. During the day, they take in the appearance, sound, and feel of the waves against the side of the boat. But they don't really have any idea of where they are at any given moment, nor do they care. They just know that ultimately they'll reach their final destination.

It would be foolhardy to suggest that the Trukese don't have what it takes to be successful sailors. The fact that they don't use traditional Western navigational equipment when they're sailing does not mean that they are any less able than Western navigators.

What about academic or career success? Isn't it reasonable to assume that there are different ways to reach academic goals and professional goals? Wouldn't it be surprising if everyone learned in exactly the same way?

Doing well in college or university and, ultimately, on the job, depends on an awareness of yourself. How do you learn? What are your strengths? What are your weaknesses? What do you value? What do you do better than most people, and what are your areas for improvement? If you can answer such questions, you'll be able to harness the best of your talents and anticipate challenges you might face. The interactive tools provided in this section of the chapter will go a long way toward helping you better understand what makes you unique and how to make the most of your potential.

Each of us has preferred ways of learning, approaches that work best for us either in the classroom or on the job. And our success doesn't just depend on how well we learn, but on how we learn.

Learning style
One's preferred manner of acquiring, using, and thinking about knowledge

A **learning style** reflects a person's preferred manner of acquiring, using, and thinking about knowledge. We don't have just one learning style, but a variety of styles. Some involve our preferences regarding the way information is presented to us, some relate to how we think and learn most readily, and some relate to how our personality traits affect our performance. An awareness of your learning styles will help you in college or university by allowing you to study and learn course material more effectively. On the job, knowing your learning styles will help you master new skills and techniques, ensuring you can keep up with changing office practices or an evolving industry.

We'll start by considering the preferences we have for how we initially perceive information.

What Is Your Preferred Learning Style?

One of the most basic aspects of learning styles concerns how we initially receive information from our sense organs. People have different strengths in terms of how they process information and which of their senses they prefer to use in learning. Specifically, there are four different types of learning styles:

Read/write learning style
A style that involves a preference for written material, favouring reading over hearing and touching

Visual/graphic learning style
A style that favours material presented visually in a diagram or picture

> **Read/write learning style.** If you have a **read/write learning style**, you prefer information that is presented visually in a written format. You feel most comfortable reading, and you may recall the spelling of a word by thinking of how the word looks. You probably learn best when you have the opportunity to read about a concept rather than listening to a teacher explain it.

> **Visual/graphic learning style.** Those with a **visual/graphic learning style** learn most effectively when material is presented visually in a diagram or picture. You might recall the structure of an engine or a part of the human body by reviewing a picture in your mind, and you might benefit from instructors who make frequent use of visual aids in

class, such as videos, maps, and models. Students with visual learning styles find it easier to see things in their mind's eye—to visualize a task or concept—than to be lectured about them.

> **Auditory/verbal learning style.** Have you ever asked a friend to help you put something together by having them read the directions to you while you worked? If you did, you may have an **auditory/verbal learning style.** People with auditory/verbal learning styles prefer listening to explanations rather than reading them. They love class lectures and discussions, because they can easily take in the information that is being talked about.

> **Tactile/kinesthetic learning style.** Those with a **tactile/kinesthetic learning style** prefer to learn by doing—touching, manipulating objects, and doing things. For instance, some people enjoy the act of writing because of the feel of a pencil or a computer keyboard—the tactile equivalent of thinking out loud. Or they may find that it helps them to make a three-dimensional model to understand a new idea.

Learning styles have implications for effective studying or for learning new skills on the job:

> If you have a **read/write style**, consider writing out summaries of information, highlighting and underlining written material, and using flash cards. Transform diagrams and math formulas into words.

> If you have a **visual/graphic style**, devise diagrams and charts. Translate words into symbols and figures.

> If you have an **auditory/verbal style**, recite material out loud when trying to learn it. Work with others in a group, talking through the material, and consider recording lectures, with your professor's approval, of course.

> If you have a **tactile /kinesthetic style**, incorporate movement into your study. Trace diagrams, build models, arrange flash cards, and move them around. Keep yourself active when learning, taking notes, drawing charts, and jotting down key concepts.

Table 1.1 summarizes the features of these learning styles, and **Try It!** 4 "What Is Your Learning Style?" will help you figure out which of the four is your preferred learning style.

Steven Spielberg, an award-winning filmmaker, is a self-admitted visual learner. How can you use your own learning style to influence your career decisions?
© AF archive / Alamy Stock Photo

table 1.1 The Four Learning Styles

Learning Style	Description	Using the Style
Read/write	A style that involves a preference for material in a written format, favouring reading over hearing and touching	Read and rewrite material; take notes and rewrite them; organize material into tables; transform diagrams and math formulas into words.
Visual/graphic	A style that favours material presented visually in a diagram or picture	Use figures and drawings; replay classes and discussions in your mind's eye; visualize material; translate words into symbols and figures.
Auditory/verbal	A style in which the learner favours listening as the best approach	Recite material out loud; consider how words sound; study different languages; record lectures or training sessions; work with others, talking through the material.
Tactile/kinesthetic	A style that involves learning by touching, manipulating objects, and doing things	Incorporate movement into studying; trace figures and drawings with your finger; create models; make flash cards and move them around; keep active during classes and meetings, taking notes, drawing charts, and jotting down key concepts.

4 | TRY IT! P O W E R

PERSONAL STYLES

What Is Your Learning Style?

Read each of the following statements and rank them in terms of their usefulness to you as learning approaches. Base your ratings on your personal experiences and preferences, using the following scale:

1 = Not at all useful
2 = Not very useful
3 = Neutral
4 = Somewhat useful
5 = Very useful

	1	2	3	4	5
1. Studying alone					
2. Studying pictures and diagrams to understand complex ideas					
3. Listening to class lectures					
4. Performing a process myself rather than reading or hearing about it					
5. Learning a complex procedure by reading written directions					
6. Watching and listening to film, computer, or video presentations					
7. Listening to a book or lecture on tape					
8. Doing lab work					
9. Studying teachers' handouts and lecture notes					
10. Studying in a quiet room					
11. Taking part in group discussions					

(continued)

12. Taking part in hands-on demonstrations					
13. Taking notes and studying them later					
14. Creating flash cards and using them as a study and review tool					
15. Memorizing how words are spelled by spelling them "out loud" in my head					
16. Writing down key facts and important points as a tool for remembering them					
17. Recalling how to spell a word by seeing it in my head					
18. Underlining or highlighting important facts or passages in my reading					
19. Saying things out loud when I'm studying					
20. Recalling how to spell a word by "writing" it invisibly in the air or on a surface					
21. Learning new information by reading about it in a book					
22. Using a map to find an unknown place					
23. Working in a study group					
24. Finding a place I've been to once by just going there without directions					

Scoring: The statements cycle through the four learning styles in this order: (1) read/write; (2) visual/graphic; (3) auditory/verbal; and (4) tactile/kinesthetic.

To find your primary learning style, **disregard your 1, 2, and 3 ratings**. Add up your 4 and 5 ratings for each learning style (i.e., a "4" equals 4 points and a "5" equals 5 points). Use the following chart to link the statements to the learning styles and to write down your summed ratings:

Learning Style	Statements	Total (Sum) of Rating Points
Read/write	1, 5, 9, 13, 17, and 21	
Visual/graphic	2, 6, 10, 14, 18, and 22	
Auditory/verbal	3, 7, 11, 15, 19, and 23	
Tactile/kinesthetic	4, 8, 12, 16, 20, and 24	

The total of your rating points for any given style will range from a low of 0 to a high of 30. The highest total indicates your main learning style. Don't be surprised if you have a mixed style, in which two or more styles receive similar ratings.

To Try It online, go to the McGraw-Hill online resource.

What Is Your Striving Style™?

Figuring out how best to leverage your college or university education begins with understanding who you are meant to be. Investing several years of your life in study only to find out that the work you have studied for does not align with your needs and values is a depressing thought. No matter which diploma or degree you want to pursue, what you strive to be influences how you learn and achieve. The Striving Styles™ Personality Assessment, developed by Canadian psychotherapist Dr. Anne Dranitsaris, helps you understand how to best approach learning by identifying what Dranitsaris calls your **Striving Style™** and what is the predominant need that must be met for you to feel confident and secure. **Try It! 5** "What Is Your

Striving Style™
A mode of thought and behaviour driven by a predominant need that directs how we seek satisfaction from our lives

5 | TRY IT!

PERSONAL STYLES ○ ○ ○ ◐ ○

What Is Your Striving Style?

STRIVING STYLES™ SELF-ASSESSMENT—Student Version

Rate how *often* the description in each of the following sentences applies to you.	
Section A Never = 0; Rarely = 1; Infrequently = 2; Frequently = 4; Always = 5	
1. I prefer to have the choice and responsibility for making my own decisions.	
2. Others turn to me to know what to do in most situations.	
3. I look for chances to be in charge of people and activities.	
4. I usually know what is best for my friends and expect them to listen to my advice.	
5. I find it hard to see the point of people getting emotional or creating drama.	
6. I like to have goals for myself for school and my future.	
7. For me, doing my school work and projects is more important than my social life.	
8. I am uncomfortable when I have to let others be in charge.	
Section A Total	
Section B Never = 0; Rarely = 1; Infrequently = 2; Frequently = 4; Always = 5	
1. I like being with people and easily make friends with others.	
2. I have many friends and I enjoy introducing people to each other.	
3. When I am involved in group activities, I tend to talk a lot and get others involved.	
4. I have a hard time saying no to invitations from friends. My social calendar is usually pretty full.	
5. I like to see the positive in people and have a hard time understanding when they hurt my feelings.	
6. I can sometimes get so involved with my friends and their problems that I forget about my own chores or homework.	
7. I like giving compliments to people and letting my friends know how special they are to me.	
8. I see everyone I meet as a potential friend.	
Section B Total	
Section C Never = 0; Rarely = 1; Infrequently = 2; Frequently = 4; Always = 5	
1. I enjoy being the centre of attention and look for chances to be there.	
2. I have many talents and do lots of things well.	
3. I am very conscious of how I look and work hard to make sure I look good.	
4. I often try to act like other people tell me I should act.	
5. I believe I am meant to do something important.	
6. I like to let people know what I can do and special things I have done.	
7. When I'm having fun, I will lose track of time and force myself to stay awake even if I'm tired so I don't miss anything.	

(continued)

(continued)

8. I often end up doing things that make others notice me.	
Section C Total	
Section D Never = 0; Rarely = 1; Infrequently = 2; Frequently = 4; Always = 5	
1. I like to be involved in a lot of activities most of the time.	
2. I have a strong need for adventure, excitement, and new and different experiences.	
3. I don't like having to do the same thing the same way twice.	
4. I tend to be outgoing, friendly, and sociable with many friends and acquaintances.	
5. I like to be where the action is.	
6. I am good when a problem needs to be solved or when there is trouble happening.	
7. I don't really think about how what I do might make other people feel.	
8. I need a lot of freedom and don't like it when people try to make me follow rules.	
Section D Total	
Section E Never = 0; Rarely = 1; Infrequently = 2; Frequently = 4; Always = 5	
1. I seek beauty, originality, and creativity in all I do.	
2. Others describe me as being moody and emotional.	
3. I tend to have only a few friends, but I am very close with them.	
4. I don't feel it is important to conform to what others or society thinks I should do.	
5. I tend to be a perfectionist and am self-critical.	
6. I feel that most people do not understand me.	
7. I look calm on the outside even though there is a lot going on inside of me.	
8. I enjoy spending time alone in nature.	
Section E Total	
Section F Never = 0; Rarely = 1; Infrequently = 2; Frequently = 4; Always = 5	
1. I get absorbed in things that interest me, spending hours alone with them.	
2. I like to know as much as I can about how things work. I also like to do things well.	
3. When I am tired or feel pressure, I tend to withdraw from others and spend a lot of time alone.	
4. I believe I'm different than others and I don't like it when others try to make me conform.	
5. I will challenge people in authority (such as teachers or parents) by disagreeing with or questioning them.	
6. I don't like to talk about myself, and others find me difficult to know.	
7. I am not naturally curious about what I feel or how others feel.	
8. I say what's on my mind and sometimes people think I'm being critical, even when I'm not.	
Section F Total	
Section G Never = 0; Rarely = 1; Infrequently = 2; Frequently = 4; Always = 5	
1. My friends often come to me for my opinions on things.	
2. I enjoy schoolwork where I can independently research, investigate, or create new ideas about how things might be in the future.	
3. I try to understand the deeper meaning of things.	

(continued)

(*continued*)

4. I prefer to figure out how something works than to ask for help.	
5. I sometimes know things are going to happen before they do.	
6. I am talented at solving problems and dealing with things that are complicated.	
7. I sometimes focus too much on little, unimportant things and avoid what I really need to do.	
8. When I am tired or stressed I tend to overindulge in food, alcohol, or other things that aren't really good for me.	
Section G Total	
Section H Never = 0; Rarely = 1; Infrequently = 2; Frequently = 4; Always = 5	
1. Others would describe me as loyal, hardworking, and predictable.	
2. I don't like change because it's more comfortable when things stay the same.	
3. I try to do what is expected of me and am respectful of authority.	
4. I tend to say no when asked to try new things, preferring to stay with what I am familiar with.	
5. I have a hard time saying no when people ask me to do important things for them.	
6. I prefer to be with the friends I know well rather than meeting new people.	
7. I sometimes worry and can imagine terrible things when I think about the future.	
8. I tend to focus more on doing things with people and less on getting to know who those people are (what they like, what they think about things, etc.).	
Section H Total	

Overall Totals

Once you have answered the questions in each of the sections, place your scores in the <u>first column below</u>. Your striving style is the style in which you have scored highest. If you have two similar scores, read the descriptions of each of the striving styles and determine which most accurately describes how you see yourself.

Total Scores	Striving Style	Predominant Need	Key Characteristics
Section A Total _____	Leader	To Be in Control	Analytical, driven, goal oriented; implements; organizes others
Section B Total _____	Socializer	To Be Connected	Sociable, outgoing, sentimental; seeks personal and social success
Section C Total _____	Performer	To Be Recognized	Extroverted, innovative; seeks novelty; goal and achievement driven
Section D Total _____	Adventurer	To Be Spontaneous	Adventurous, hands-on, impulsive, pleasure-seeking, straightforward
Section E Total _____	Artist	To Be Creative	Inaccessible, holistic, enigmatic, self-contained; seeks inner intensity
Section F Total _____	Intellectual	To Be Knowledgeable	Solitary, introspective; seeks knowledge; expert, aloof
Section G Total _____	Visionary	To Be Perceptive	Idealistic, creative thinker, futuristic revolutionary, discovering
Section H Total _____	Stabilizer	To Be Secure	Intense, obsessive, detached, authoritarian, dutiful

Adapted from the Striving Styles Personality System™ Level I Assessment, developed by Anne Dranitsaris, Ph.D. and published by Sage, Kahuna Enterprises (2010).

To Try It online, go to the McGraw-Hill online resource.

Striving Style?" will help you determine your striving style. For a more in-depth report on your striving style, go to the McGraw-Hill online resource. or **whoareyoumeanttobe.com/striving-styles**. **Table 1.2** summarizes each striving style and describes how people of each style learn best.

Multiple Intelligences: Showing Strength in Different Domains

Do you feel much more comfortable walking through the woods than navigating city streets? Are you an especially talented musician? Is reading and using a complicated map second nature to you?

If so, in each case you may be demonstrating a special and specific kind of intelligence. According to psychologist Howard Gardner, rather than asking "How smart are you?" we should be asking "How are you smart?" To answer the latter question, Gardner has developed a theory of multiple intelligences that offers a unique approach to understanding learning styles and preferences.

The multiple intelligences view says that we have eight different forms of intelligence, each relatively independent of the others and linked to a specific kind of information processing in our brains:

> **Logical-mathematical intelligence** involves skills in problem solving and scientific thinking.

> **Linguistic intelligence** is linked to the production and use of language.

> **Spatial intelligence** relates to skills involving spatial configurations, such as those used by artists and architects.

table 1.2 The Eight Striving Styles

Striving Style	Description	How You Learn
Leader	Self-directed, can experience difficulty accepting opinions of others	Enjoy logical discussions in study groups, but dislike tangents; have high expectations of yourself and others, including the teacher
Socializer	Skillful communicator, tend to take criticism personally	Learn best in structured settings where you can discuss with your peers
Performer	Success-oriented, enthusiastic, and like recognition	Engage in learning through discussions with teacher and other students
Adventurer	Spontaneous, enjoy constant activity, enjoy group work	Learn by doing; like to challenge teachers
Artist	Diligent, motivated to learn mainly about subjects that interest you	Struggle to assess quality of your own work; learn best when you get to know and can consult with the teacher
Intellectual	Enjoy the learning process	Need to have respect for the teacher; prefer to learn at your own pace
Visionary	Strong work ethic; dislike memorization	Learn through interaction with others, whether in person or through reading
Stabilizer	Tenacious and persistent with your studies; need to master fundamentals before moving on	Learn best in well-structured environment with clear, precise assignments

Adapted from the Striving Styles Personality System™ Learning Styles Reports written by Anne Dranitsaris, Ph.D. and published by Sage, Kahuna Enterprises (2011).

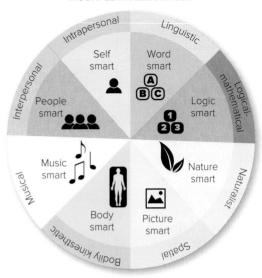

MULTIPLE INTELLIGENCES

Intrapersonal
Linguistic
Self smart
Word smart
Logical-mathematical
Interpersonal
People smart
Logic smart
Musical
Music smart
Nature smart
Naturalist
Body smart
Picture smart
Bodily kinesthetic
Spatial

> **Interpersonal intelligence** is found in learners with particularly strong skills involving interacting with others, such as sensitivity to the moods, temperaments, motivations, and intentions of others.

> **Intrapersonal intelligence** relates to a particularly strong understanding of the internal aspects of oneself and having access to one's own feelings and emotions.

> **Musical intelligence** involves skills relating to music.

> **Bodily kinesthetic intelligence** relates to skills in using the whole body or portions of it to solve problems or to construct products or displays, exemplified by dancers, athletes, actors, and surgeons.

> **Naturalist intelligence** involves exceptional abilities in identifying and classifying patterns in nature.

All of us have the same eight kinds of intelligence, although to varying degrees, and they form the core of our learning styles and preferences (see **Try It! 6** "Multiple Intelligences: How Are You Smart?"). While relatively independent of one other, these separate intelligences do not operate in isolation. Instead, any activity involves several kinds of intelligences working together. **Table 1.3** describes each type of intelligence and shows how each is used. Later on in this book, we'll also introduce you to the notion of "emotional intelligence," which, while not part of Howard Gardner's model, is a valuable addition to the work done in this area.

What Do You Value?

Values
What you judge to be important in life

In addition to understanding how you learn, what motivates you, and the ways in which you are smart, it is important to reflect on how all of these intersect with your value system. **Values** are what a person thinks is important in life; your values are reflected in your beliefs, your attitudes, and your behaviours. For example, the Canadian Index of Wellbeing identified the following values that are important to Canadians: fairness, diversity, equity, inclusion, health, safety, economic security, democracy, and sustainability.[12] The Angus Reid Institute, in collaboration with the CBC, polled thousands of Canadians to identify what they value.[13] The five resulting "mindsets" they identified are shown in **Table 1.4**.

To complete a quiz that identifies *your* mindset using the Canadian Values Index, visit **angusreid.org/canadian-values-index/**. To learn more

---

6 | TRY IT!

PERSONAL STYLES ⚪⚪⚪⚫⚪

Multiple Intelligences: How Are You Smart?

To complete the Multiple Intelligences test, go to the website **businessballs.com** and type "multiple intelligences test" in the search field. Once the options come up, click on the link to select the Multiple Intelligences Test based on Howard Gardner's MI Model, and select the pdf or Excel version.

To Try It online, go to the McGraw-Hill online resource.

about the results found in the study that underlies the Canadian Values Index, visit **cbc.ca/news/canada/british-columbia/which-type-of-canadian -are-you-answer-these-questions-to-find-out-1.3786252**.

Your personal values likely reflect your upbringing, your culture, and your education and experiences thus far. When you examine the lives of well-known people, it is relatively easy to identify the values they hold. For example, one might expect that Bill Gates, co-founder of Microsoft and noted philanthropist, would feel that the following values were important: ambition, hard work, and making a difference. The values of socialite and reality TV star Kim Kardashian, on the other hand, would probably look more like this: status, extravagance, and celebrity. For more opportunities to identify your values and create a list of core values, visit **mindtools .com/pages/article/newTED_85.htm**.

What Is Your Personality Type?

In recent years, one of the most popular measures of personality type is rooted in an approach known as the Big Five inventory of personality traits.[14] This model measures scores on five dimensions of personality: extroversion, agreeableness, conscientiousness, neuroticism, and openness. To see how you score on each of these dimensions, take the 46-question survey at **outofservice.com/bigfive/.**

table 1.3 Multiple Intelligences

Multiple Intelligences	Description	Using the Intelligence
Logical-mathematical	Strengths in problem solving and scientific thinking	Express information mathematically or in formulas.
Linguistic	Strengths in the production and use of language	Write out notes and summarize information in words; construct stories about material.
Spatial	Strengths involving spatial configurations, such as those used by artists and architects	Build charts, graphs, and flowcharts.
Interpersonal	Found in learners with particularly strong skills involving interacting with others, such as sensitivity to the moods, temperaments, motivations, and intentions of others	Work with others in groups.
Intrapersonal	Strengths in understanding your internal aspects and having access to your own feelings and emotions	Build on your prior experiences and feelings about the world; use your originality.
Musical	Strengths relating to music	Write a song or lyrics to help you remember material.
Bodily kinesthetic	Strengths in using the body or parts of it to solve problems or to construct products or displays, exemplified by dancers, athletes, actors, and surgeons	Use movement in studying; build models.
Naturalist	Exceptional strengths in identifying and classifying patterns in nature	Use analogies based on nature.

table 1.4   Canadian Mindsets

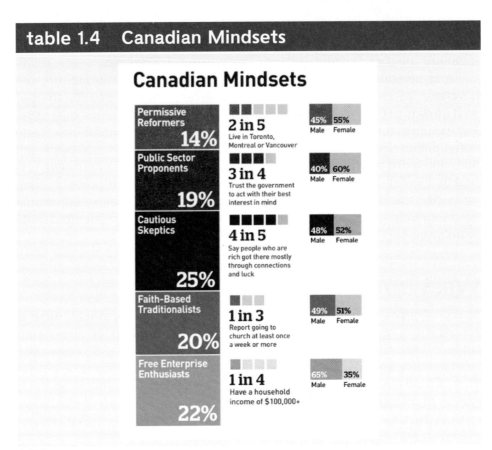

Putting It All Together

So what did you discover about yourself? Summarize your survey findings in the box below:

What You Are Looking For:	Where to Find It:	Your Answer:
What is your preferred learning style?	Try It! 4	
What is your Striving Style™?	Try It! 5	
What is your primary multiple intelligence?	Try It! 6	
What are your core values and what is your "mindset"?	**mindtools.com** and **angusreid.org /canadian-values-index/**	
How did you score on each of the five personality traits?	**www.outofservice .com/bigfive/**	

Here are some key facts to remember about learning styles, Striving Styles™, multiple intelligences, your value system, and your personality type:

> **You have a variety of styles.** As you can see in the summaries in Tables 1.1, 1.2, and 1.3, there are several types of learning styles, Striving Styles™, and intelligences. For any given task or challenge, some may be more relevant than others. Furthermore, success is possible

even when there is a mismatch between what you need to accomplish and your own pattern of preferred styles. It may take more work, but learning to deal with situations that require you to use less-preferred styles is important for college or university and for your career.

> **Your style reflects your preferences regarding which abilities you** *like* **to use—not the abilities themselves.** Styles are related to our preferences and the mental approaches we like to use. You may prefer to learn in a tactile way, but that in and of itself doesn't guarantee that the products you create in that way will be good. You still have to put in work! Conversely, you can produce very good results using approaches that are difficult and uncomfortable for you.

> **Your style and your values may change over the course of your life.** You can learn new styles and expand the range of learning experiences in which you feel perfectly comfortable. In fact, you can conceive of this book as one long lesson in learning styles because it provides you with strategies for learning more effectively in a variety of ways. You may also find that your values change over time as you are exposed to post-secondary education, where perspectives may be different from those you grew up with.

> **You should work on improving your less-preferred styles.** Although it may be tempting, don't always make choices that increase your exposure to preferred styles and decrease your practice with less-preferred styles. The more you use approaches for which you have less of a preference, the better you'll be at developing the skills associated with those styles.

> **Work cooperatively with others who have different styles or values.** If your instructor or supervisor asks you to work cooperatively, seek out classmates or co-workers who have styles or values that are different from yours. Working with people with differing styles and/or values will help you to achieve collective success, and you can also learn from observing others' approaches to tackling tasks.

Time to Reflect: What **Did I Learn?**

1. Look back at the Nine Essential Skills List, which describes the skills valued by Canadian employers. Which of these skills do you already possess? Which need more work?

2. Before reading this chapter, had you ever considered the fact that there are many different kinds of intelligences? How can knowing this affect how you see other people?

3. In his book *Outliers*, Canadian writer Malcolm Gladwell put forth the notion that to be a true master in any field requires about 10,000 hours of concentrated effort, which translates into about 3 hours a day, every day, for 10 years. What do you enjoy doing that would make you want to put in that kind of effort? Could you see yourself committing to that amount of time and effort? Why or why not?

Did You Know?

You've completed a lot of surveys in this chapter that have hopefully made you more aware of yourself and what makes you similar to or different from others. But did you know that having a high degree of self-awareness also affects how well people work together on tasks? In an article published in *Harvard Business Review*, researchers found that teams composed of people with a high degree of self-awareness outperformed teams with low self-awareness on decision quality, coordination among team members, and conflict management.[15] Knowing more about yourself and understanding differences that exist between team members are important factors in working well with others. Take the time to learn more about your classmates and how they scored on their surveys—it could have an important impact on your grades!

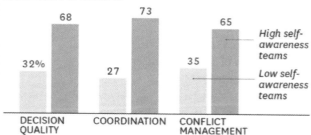

HIGH SELF-AWARENESS LEADS TO BETTER TEAM PERFORMANCE
A simulation shows that it affects decision-making, coordination, and conflict management.

PROBABILITY OF SUCCESS

DECISION QUALITY: 32%, 68
COORDINATION: 27, 73
CONFLICT MANAGEMENT: 35, 65

High self-awareness teams
Low self-awareness teams

From "Research: We're Not Very Self-Aware, Especially at Work" by Erich C. Dierdorff and Robert S. Rubin. March 12, 2015 © Harvard Business Review

Looking Back

What are the benefits of a post-secondary education?

> College and university graduates can earn close to a million dollars more than a high-school graduate over a lifetime of work.

> A post-secondary education provides many benefits in addition to improved career prospects. These include becoming well educated, learning to think critically and communicate effectively, understanding the interconnections among different areas of knowledge and our place in history and the world, and understanding diversity.

What do Canadian employers value in a potential employee?

> Canadian employers are seeking nine essential skills from their potential employees: numeracy, oral communication, working with others, continuous learning, reading text, writing, thinking, document use, and digital skills.

What are the basic principles of P.O.W.E.R. Learning?

> P.O.W.E.R. Learning is a systematic approach people can easily learn, using abilities they already possess, to acquire successful habits for learning and achieving personal goals.

> P.O.W.E.R. Learning involves **p**reparation, **o**rganization, **w**ork, **e**valuation, and **r**ethinking.

How do expert students use P.O.W.E.R. Learning?

> To prepare, learners set both long-term and short-term goals, making sure that their goals are realistic, measurable, and under their control and will lead them toward their final destination.

> They organize the tools they will need to accomplish these goals.

> They get down to work on the task at hand. Using their goals as motivation, expert learners also understand that success depends on effort.

> They evaluate the work they've done, considering what they have accomplished in comparison with the goals they set for themselves during the preparation stage.

> Finally, they rethink, reflecting on the process they've used, taking a fresh look at what they have done, and critically reassessing their goals.

How can I use knowledge about my learning styles and Striving Styles™, multiple intelligences, and values to be more successful?

> People have patterns of diverse learning styles—characteristic ways of acquiring and using knowledge.

> Learning styles include read/write, visual/graphic, auditory/verbal, and tactile/kinesthetic styles.

> Striving Styles™ include leader, socializer, performer, adventurer, artist, intellectual, visionary, and stabilizer.

> The multiple intelligences view suggests that we have eight different forms of intelligence, each relatively independent of the others: logical-mathematical, linguistic, spatial, interpersonal, intrapersonal, musical, bodily kinesthetic, and naturalist.

> Knowing more about how you learn, how you are smart, how you like to interact with the world around you, and what you think is important in life can help you identify the specific techniques that will allow you to master material in class and on the job more effectively.

RESOURCES

ON CAMPUS

Every college and university provides a significant number of resources to help its students succeed and thrive, ranging from the activities coordination office to a multicultural centre to writing labs to career centres. You can check them out on your institution's website, or in the calendar or phone directory.

Here's a list of some typical campus resources, many of which we'll be discussing in future chapters:

> Activities/clubs office
> Adult and re-entry centre
> Advising centre
> Alumni office
> Art gallery
> Bookstore
> Career centre
> Chaplain/religious services
> Childcare centre
> Cinema/theatre
> Computing centre/ computer labs
> Continuing education
> Disability centre (learning or physical disabilities)

> Financial aid office
> Fitness centre/ gymnasium
> Health centre
> Honours program
> Housing centre
> Information centre
> Intramural sports
> Language lab
> Lost and found
> Mathematics lab
> Multicultural centre
> Museum
> Online education (distance learning) office
> Off-campus housing and services

> Ombudsperson/ conflict resolution
> Photography lab
> Police/campus security
> Post office
> Printing centre
> Registration office
> Residential life office
> School newspaper
> Student affairs office
> Student government office
> Study abroad/ exchange programs
> Testing centre
> Volunteer services
> Work-study centre
> Writing lab

If you are commuting to school, your first "official" encounters on campus are likely to be with representatives of the college or university's Student Affairs Office or its equivalent. The Student Affairs Office has the goal of maintaining the quality of student life, helping to ensure that students receive the support they need. Student Affairs personnel are often in charge of student orientation programs that help new students familiarize themselves with their new institution.

Whatever representatives you deal with during your first days on campus, remember that their job is to help you. Don't be shy about asking questions about what you may expect, how to find things, and what you should be doing. And it goes without saying that your instructors are a great source of information.

Above all, if you are experiencing any difficulties, be certain to make use of your institution's resources. Success in post-secondary education does not come easily for anyone, particularly when it demands juggling responsibilities of work and family. You should make use of whatever supports your college or university offers.

IN PRINT

For a variety of views of what it takes to be a successful college or university student, read *How to Survive Your Freshman Year: By Hundreds of College Sophomores, Juniors, and Seniors Who Did,* 5th edition, published by Hundreds of Heads Books (2013).

Sue Teele's *Rainbows of Intelligence: Exploring How Students Learn* (2015) introduces learning styles, offering tips and suggestions for making use of the way people learn.

To learn more about Canadian writer Malcolm Gladwell and the 10,000-hour theory, take a look at his fascinating book, *Outliers: The Story of Success* (Little, Brown and Company, 2008).

ON THE WEB

The following websites provide an opportunity to extend your learning about the material in this chapter:

- Macleans.ca's on-campus website (**macleans.ca/education-hub/**) offers students university and program rankings and information on student finance and scholarships.
- To examine each of the Striving Styles™ in more depth, visit **strivingstyles.com /ssps/striving-styles-personality-system.**
- New to Canada? Check out **cic.gc.ca/english/study/** for information on studying and working in Canada.

THERE'S AN APP FOR THAT

- For a SMART goal-setting app, available on both iOS and Android, you'll want to check out goalmap.

TAKING IT TO THE WEB

1 For a web-based solution to tying your core values to SMART goals, take a look at **lifetick.com/index.html.**

2 Do you control your destiny, or are you controlled by it? This *Psychology Today* "Locus of Control" test assesses how you view the relative impact of hard work versus luck on achieving success: **psychologytoday.tests.psychtests.com/take _test.php?idRegTest=1317.**

THE CASE OF . . .
Vexed in Vancouver

It was during the second week of classes that the questioning started. Until then, Jian Chung had been fairly confident in his decision to enrol at a college in the Vancouver suburbs to gain training to be a medical technician. He had been excited to try something new and to start a new career, but more and more he was wondering if he'd made the right choice.

To get to campus, Jian had to take a 45-minute bus ride, because his girlfriend needed the car to get to her office in downtown Vancouver. Jian was also keeping his part-time job as an executive assistant at a doctor's office, a job that meant another long commute. On top of that, Jian needed to find time between work, classes, and studying to visit his ailing grandmother, who lived in a seniors' residence in Burnaby.

Maybe, Jian was beginning to think, college hadn't been such a good idea. True, he could earn more money as a medical technician and begin a more promising career. But was it really worth all this added time and stress? Plus, Jian had never done very well academically. Why would college be any different? If he wanted to make more money, he could just add more shifts at his current job.

Why bother with college? Jian thought to himself. What an expense, and what a hassle. For what?

1. What arguments could you use to convince Jian of the value of a college education?

2. Do you think that Jian's doubts are common?

3. What might you suggest that Jian do to help deal with his doubts about the value of college?

4. Why might a student's doubts about the value of college be especially strong during the beginning weeks of college?

5. Do you share any of Jian's concerns about the value of a college education? Do you have additional concerns?

© FirmBee/pixabay

CHAPTER 2
Making the Most of Your Time

Learning Outcomes

By the time you finish this chapter, you will be able to

LO 2.1 Explain why it is important to manage time more effectively, and discuss techniques that can help you better manage your time.

LO 2.2 Analyze how to handle competing priorities.

LO 2.3 Estimate how much time various tasks will take, and create a timeline.

LO 2.4 Identify strategies for dealing with surprises and distractions.

As Jen Wong waits in line for her morning cup of coffee, she mentally goes over the things she needs to get done during the day: *Get to the gym at 8:00 a.m. for her morning yoga class . . . study for her anatomy quiz over lunch at 12:30 . . . from 1:30 to 4:30, go to classes at the college where she's studying for her massage therapist diploma . . . meet her boyfriend at 5:00 to watch his son's soccer game . . . go home, make dinner, finish an assignment, and spend some time catching up with her friends on Facebook.* She has the nagging feeling that there's something else she needs to do, but she can't put her finger on it.

Jen finally gets to the head of the line to pay for her double-double. Glancing at a clock as she leaves the Tim Hortons, she gives up the thought of getting in some additional last-minute studying for her anatomy quiz before her yoga class. It will be a minor miracle if she even makes it to the gym on time.

Jen has been up less than an hour, and already she is running behind schedule.

Looking Ahead

Are your days like Jen's? Are you constantly trying to cram more activities into less time? Do you feel as if you never have enough time?

You're not alone: Most of us wish we had more time to accomplish the things we need to do. However, some people are a lot better at juggling their time than others. What's their secret?

There is no secret. No one has more than 24 hours a day and 168 hours a week. The key to success is figuring out our priorities and making better use of the time we do have.

Time management is like juggling a bunch of tennis balls: For most of us, juggling doesn't come naturally, but it is a skill that can be learned. Not all of us will end up perfect jugglers (whether we are juggling tennis balls or time), but, with practice, we can become a lot better at it.

The P.O.W.E.R Plan in this chapter starts where every P.O.W.E.R. Plan starts—with *preparation*—where you learn to account for the ways you currently use—and misuse—time. Then, it helps you *organize*, by providing you with tools to help you track your time and strategies to help you manage your priorities and competing goals. After that comes *work*—where you implement the tools and give the strategies a try. Then it's time to *evaluate*—how are the tools and strategies working for you? How are you dealing with the inevitable interruptions and counterproductive personal habits that can sabotage your best intentions? And, finally, it's time to *rethink*—to reflect on how your personal style of time management affects you and others in your life, and to examine some of the special challenges involved in juggling the priorities of school and work with other aspects of life, such as child rearing or hobbies. The P.O.W.E.R. Plan in this chapter will provide you with skills that are important for success not only in post-secondary education and on the job but in your personal life as well.

LO 2.1 Managing Your Time Effectively

Without looking up from the page, answer this question: What time is it?

Most people are pretty accurate in their answer. And if you don't know for sure, it's very likely that you can find out. Your cellphone may display the time; there may be a clock on the wall, desk, or computer screen; maybe you're riding in a car that shows the time in the instrument panel; or perhaps you're wearing a watch. Time is something from which we can't escape. Even if we ignore it, it's still going by, ticking away, second by second, minute by minute, hour by hour. In Laura Vanderkam's book *168 Hours:*

You Have More Time Than You Think, she writes about "how different people spend the 168 hours we all have per week."[1] We all have the same 168 hours to work with. So the main question is this: How are YOU using YOUR 168 hours? We can allow time to slip by and let it be our enemy. Or we can take control of it and make it our ally.

By taking control of how you spend your time, you'll increase your chances of becoming more successful in your post-secondary education and in your career. Here's another way to look at it: The better you are at managing the time you devote to your studies and your job, the more time you will have to spend on your outside interests. How you approach time and time management will undoubtedly be a reflection of the learning style, Striving Style™, and multiple intelligences you uncovered in Chapter 1. You can get a sense of your own personal "time style" by completing **Try It! 1** "Find Your Time Style."

1 | TRY IT!

PERSONAL STYLES ○ ○ ○ ● ○

Find Your Time Style

Rate how well each of the statements below describes you. Use this rating scale:

1 — Doesn't describe me at all

2 — Describes me only slightly

3 — Describes me fairly well

4 — Describes me very well

	1	2	3	4
1. I often wake up later than I should.				
2. I am usually late for classes and appointments.				
3. I am always in a rush getting places.				
4. I put off big tasks and assignments until the last minute.				
5. My friends often comment on my lateness.				
6. I am easily interrupted, putting aside what I'm doing for something new.				
7. When I look at a clock, I'm often surprised at how late it is.				
8. I often forget appointments and have to reschedule them.				
9. When faced with a big task, I feel overwhelmed and turn my mind away from it until later.				
10. At the end of the day, I have no idea where the time went.				

Rate yourself by adding up the points you assigned. Use this scale to assess your time style:

10–15 — Very efficient time user

16–20 — Efficient time user

21–30 — Time use needs work

31–40 — Victim of time

To Try It online, go to the McGraw-Hill online resource.

all your regularly scheduled activities, as well as one-time appointments when they arise. A blank weekly timetable is provided in **Figure 2.6.** You can also find it on the McGraw-Hill online resource, or use the one that comes with your calendar software.

Remember the priorities you identified in Try It! 3 and Try It! 4? You can map these priorities to the tasks and reminder functions available in most online calendars. These functions keep track of what you need to do and automatically remind you before you need to do it. The reminder function can—and should—be used for report due dates, tests, and so forth,

4 | TRY IT! POWER

Urgent? Important?

Fill in the quadrants in **Figure 2.3** to help you figure out what is truly urgent and what is just really important. Revisit the priorities you identified in Try It! 3, but this time distinguish the important priorities from the less important and the urgent from the not-so-urgent, taking into account *what* and *who* will be affected if a priority is not addressed in time.

figure 2.3 | Priority Setting: The Importance of Distinguishing What Is Important and What Is Urgent

Urgent and Important

Important but Not Urgent

Urgent but Not Important

Not Important and Not Urgent

To Try It online, go to the McGraw-Hill online resource.

figure 2.4 | A Sample Master Calendar

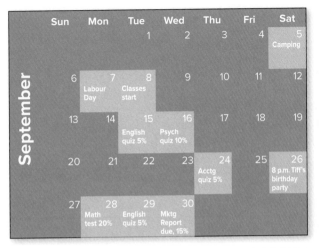

September

Sun	Mon	Tue	Wed	Thu	Fri	Sat
		1	2	3	4	5 Camping
6	7 Labour Day	8 Classes start	9	10	11	12
13	14	15 English quiz 5%	16 Psych quiz 10%	17	18	19
20	21	22	23	24 Acctg quiz 5%	25	26 8 p.m. Tiff's birthday party
27	28 Math test 20%	29 English quiz 5%	30 Mktg Report due, 15%			

October

Sun	Mon	Tue	Wed	Thu	Fri	Sat
				1	2 9 a.m. Dentist	3 Study Group Mtg
4	5	6	7	8 English quiz 5%	9	10
11	12 Thanks-giving	13 English midterm 20%	14 Mktg midterm 25%	15 Acctg midterm 20%	16 Psych midterm 20%	17
18 Brunch with Maria	19	20	21	22 Acctg quiz 5%	23	24 Study Group Mtg
25	26	27 English quiz 5%	28 Mktg Report Due 15%	29	30	31 Halloween party at Pierre's

November

Sun	Mon	Tue	Wed	Thu	Fri	Sat
1	2	3	4	5 Acctg quiz 5%	6	7 Weekend in Montreal
8 Montreal	9	10 English quiz 5%	11 Mktg test 25%	12	13	14 Study Group Mtg
15	16	17	18	19 Acctg quiz 5%	20 Psych quiz 10%	21
22	23	24	25	26	27	28
29	30					

December

Sun	Mon	Tue	Wed	Thu	Fri	Sat
		1	2 Mktg Report due, 15%	3 Acctg quiz 5%	4 Psych quiz 10%	5 Study Group Mtg
6	7 Martin's Birthday	8	9 Group Report Due, 30%	10	11	12
13	14 Final Exam Week	15	16	17	18	19 Xmas Shopping
20	21	22	23	24	25 Christmas	26 Boxing Day
27	28	29	30	31		

figure 2.5 | A Weekly Timetable Showing Both Calendar and Tasks

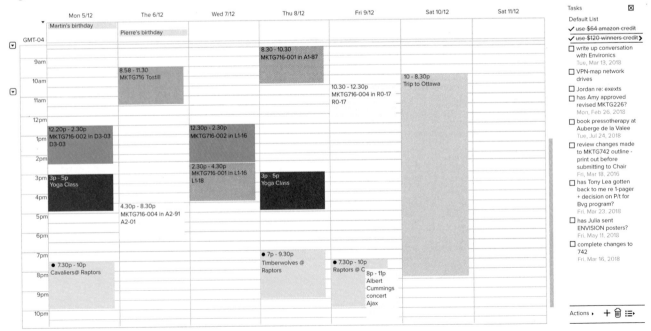

figure 2.6 | A Weekly Timetable Template

Week #

	14 Sunday	15 Monday	16 Tuesday	17 Wednesday	18 Thursday	19 Friday	20 Saturday
7 am							
8 00							
9 00							
10 00							
11 00							
12 pm							
1 00							
2 00							
3 00							
4 00							
5 00							
6 00							
7 00							
8 00							
9 00							
10 00							
11 00							

but in these cases, it can remind you not only that you are having a test but also that it's time to start studying. Why keep all of this in your head when it is so easy to use technology to track it for you?

Daily to-do list
A schedule showing the tasks, activities, and appointments due to occur during the day

A **daily to-do list** can be integrated into your online calendar program; it can be written on a small, portable calendar that includes a separate page for each day of the week; or it can simply be a small notebook, with a separate sheet of paper for every day of the week. Whatever form your daily to-do list takes, make sure it's portable, because you'll need to keep it with you all the time.

The basic organizational task you face is filling in these three schedules. You'll need at least an hour to do this, so set the time aside—time management takes time! In addition, there will be some repetition across the three schedules, and the task may seem a bit tedious. But every minute you invest now in organizing your time will pay off in hours that you will save in the future. Obviously, your task will be much simpler if you choose to use a digital calendar!

Follow these steps to complete your schedule. The steps are similar, whether you track your appointments on paper or digitally:

> **Start with the master calendar, which shows all the weeks of the term on one page.** Input to the master calendar every class assignment, quiz, or test you have for the entire term, noting it on the date that it is due. Use your course outline or syllabus as your guide. Where due dates are not provided, ask your professor for guidance. Also include major events at work, such as days when you might need to work overtime. In addition, include important activities from your personal life and student activities, drawn from your list of priorities. For instance, if your spouse or child has a performance or your college or university has a sporting event you want to attend, be sure to mark it down.

Finally, schedule some free time—time when you promise yourself you will do something that is just plain fun. Consider these times to be written in stone, and promise yourself that you won't use them for anything else except for something enjoyable. Just knowing that you have some downtime planned will help you to throw yourself into more demanding tasks. In addition, getting into the habit of allowing yourself time to relax and reflect on your life is as important as any other time management skill you may learn.

You now have a good idea of what the next few weeks have in store for you. You can identify just by looking at your master calendar the periods when you are going to be especially busy. You can also note the periods when you will have less to do.

Use the off-peak periods to get a head start on future assignments! In this way, your master schedule can help you head off disaster before it occurs.

© Photodisc/Getty Images
Short- and long-term priorities may not always match. What would you do if your buddies wanted you to shoot hoops, but you had to study for an important test?

> **Now move to the blank weekly timetable provided in Figure 2.6.**
Input the times for all your fixed, prescheduled activities—the times
when your classes are scheduled, when your study groups meet, when
you have to be at work, or when you have to pick up your child at day-
care, as well as any other regularly recurring appointments. In electronic calendars like Google Calendar, it is very easy to schedule any
type of repeating appointment—whether it occurs weekly, biweekly,
monthly, or even annually—the latter being particularly useful
for remembering birthdays, anniversaries, or your annual medical
checkup.

Once you've filled in the weekly timetable, as in the sample version provided in **Figure 2.7**, you get a bare-bones picture of the average week. You will still need to take into account the specific activities
required to complete the assignments on the master calendar.

If you are not using a digital calendar, you will now have to move
from your "average" week to specific weeks. To do this, make photo-
copies of the weekly timetable that now contains your fixed appointments. Make enough copies for every week of the term. On each copy,
write the week number of the term and the specific dates it covers.

Using your master calendar, add assignment due dates, tests, and
any other activities on the appropriate days of the week. Then put in
the blocks of time necessary to prepare for those events. See the next
section for help with estimating timelines.

> **If you've taken each of the previous steps, you're now in a posi-
tion to work on the final step of organization for successful time
management: completing your daily to-do list.** Unlike the master
calendar and weekly timetable—both of which you develop weeks or
even months in advance—complete your daily to-do list just one day
ahead of time, preferably at the end of the day.

List all the things that you intend to do the next day, and their
level of priority. Start with the things you know you *must* do and that
have fixed times, such as classes, work schedules, and appointments.
These are your first-priority items. Then add in the other things that
you *should* accomplish, such as an hour of study for an upcoming test
or a trip to the garage to have the oil changed in your car. Finally, list
things that are lower priority but still desirable—setting aside time for
a run or a walk, for example. If you use a digital to-do list, like the one
in Microsoft Outlook, turn on the auditory reminder function to remind
you when a task is scheduled to begin.

Don't schedule every single minute of the day. That would be
counterproductive, and you'd end up feeling as if you'd failed if
you deviated from your schedule. Instead, think of your daily to-do
list as a path through a forest. If you were hiking, you would allow
yourself to deviate from the path, occasionally venturing onto side
tracks when they looked interesting. But you'd also be keeping tabs
on your direction so you would end up where you needed to be at the
end of the hike, rather than several kilometres away from your car
or home.

Like the sample daily to-do list in **Figure 2.8**, include a column to check or cross off after you've completed an activity.
There's something very satisfying in acknowledging what you have
accomplished.

figure 2.7 | A Sample Weekly Timetable

Week

	14 Sunday	15 Monday	16 Tuesday	17 Wednesday	18 Thursday	19 Friday	20 Saturday
7 am							
8 00							
9 00		Economics Room D3-02		Economics Room D3-02	Study Group Meeting MKTG Library	Work Tim Hortons	
10 00							
11 00			Statistics Room B1-02	Study Group Meeting ECON Library	Statistics Room B1-02		
12 pm							
1 00		Lunch	Lunch with Drew	Lunch	Lunch		Yoga Class Hot Yoga Centre
2 00		Human Resources D3-06	Marketing C3-26	Human Resources D3-06	Marketing C3-26		
3 00							
4 00							
5 00			Soccer Practice Recreation Centre				
6 00		Supper		Supper			
7 00		Work Tim Hortons	Supper	Work Tim Hortons	Supper	Supper out with friends Restaurant	
8 00			Volunteer Work Community Centre		Finance-Night course A2-15		
9 00							
10 00							
11 00							

figure 2.8 | Sample Daily To-Do List

To-Do List for

Fri 19/10/2018

☐ ! ⓘ Task Subject	Status	Due Date	Priority	% Complete	Done
☑ Call Navendra about quiz	Not Started	Fri 19/10/2018	■ 2	0 %	
☑ Finish Marketing Assignment	In Progress	Fri 19/10/2018	1	60 %	
☑ Call dentist for appt	Not Started	Fri 19/10/2018	■ 3	0 %	
☑ Meet with Prof. Lavoie	Done	Fri 19/10/2018	1	100 %	✔
☑ Pick up Megan at school	Done	Fri 19/10/2018	1	100 %	✔
☑ Bring book to library	Done	Fri 19/10/2018	■ 2	100 %	✔
☑ Do laundry	Not Started	Fri 19/10/2018	■ 3	0 %	
☑ Work on outline Economics	In Progress	Fri 19/10/2018	▨ 2	30 %	

LO 2.3 Creating Timelines

How much time should you allocate for schoolwork? One very rough rule of thumb holds that every one hour that you spend in class requires, on average, two hours of study outside of class to earn a B and three hours of study outside of class to earn an A. Do the arithmetic: If you are taking five three-hour courses weekly or 15 credits (with each credit equivalent to an hour of class per week), you'll need to plan for 30 hours of studying each week to earn a B average—an intimidating amount of time. Of course, the amount of time you must allocate to a specific class will vary from week to week, depending on what is happening in the class.

What about assignments and projects? Has your professor assigned a major project that isn't due until the end of the term? Unfortunately, many students assume that they can pull off a major project by turning their attention to it a few days before it is due. This is *not* the best way to approach a major project. Like anything else that takes a lot of effort, time for a major project should be planned out and inserted into your weekly timetable.

Whether it's a group or individual project, you should begin by breaking up any major project into its component parts and identifying a reasonable amount of time required for completion of each task. Keep in mind that estimates are just that: estimates. Don't think of them as set in stone, but don't deliberately under- or overestimate the amount of work required either.

A major group research project might involve, for example, four group meetings of one hour each, ten hours of research, five hours of writing, three hours of editing, one hour of proofreading, and one hour to put together an integrated bibliography. Once you've identified the tasks and the time they require, put the tasks in the logical order in which they must be accomplished, noting which tasks involve time overlap. If it's a group project, allocate the tasks by putting a group member's name beside each one.

Now, starting with the *last* task, and taking into account how long each task takes, work your way *backwards* from the project due date. Do this with the next-to-last task, and so on, until you've worked your way back to the very first task. You will now know the very latest date

Workback

A plan of when to start an assignment, report, or project set up by working your way back from its due date

on which work on the project must begin. You have just created a **workback** from the project's due date and can transfer your tasks into your weekly timetable.

While you are at it, you can use the same information that you used to create your workback to create a project timeline that can be used by all group members. A free Microsoft Excel template is one of four project management templates that can be found online at **wordstemplatespro.com/project-timeline-excel-template.html**. To make it work for your group, add a column showing who is responsible for each task and replace the months and weeks with specific dates.

And, finally, remember: It's crucial not to over-schedule yourself. You'll still need time to eat, to talk with your friends, to spend time with your family, and to enjoy yourself in general. If you find that your life is completely filled with things that you feel you must do to survive and that there is no room for fun, then take a step back and cut out something to make some time for yourself in your daily schedule. Finding time for yourself is as important as carving out time for what others want you to do. Besides, if you are overworked, you're likely to "find" the time by guiltily goofing off without really setting aside the time and enjoying it.

LO 2.4 W Work Dealing with Surprises and Distraction

We've now reached step 3 of the P.O.W.E.R. Plan for managing your time: *work*. The good news is that you've already done a lot of the work, because much of the work in time management is preparation and organization. The work involved in time management is to follow the schedules and to-do lists that you've prepared and organized. But it won't be easy. Our lives are filled with surprises. Things take longer than we've planned. A friend we haven't spoken to in a while calls to chat, and it seems rude to say that we don't have time to talk. Crises occur; buses are late; computers break down; kids get sick.

The difference between effective and ineffective time management lies in (1) how well you take control of your environment, (2) how efficiently you work, (3) how well you deal with procrastination, and (4) how well you balance competing responsibilities.

Take Control of Your Environment

It is up to you to take active control of your environment and not let it take control of you. Here are a few suggestions to help you do just that:

> **Identify the controllable and uncontrollable problems that prevent you from getting this done.** Identify the problems you face that are getting in your way in **Try It! 5** "The Black Holes of Time Management." Once you've identified the problems and which ones are proving to be the biggest obstacles to managing your time, identify which are controllable and which are uncontrollable and discuss with your classmates how you can address the controllable items.

> **Just say no.** You don't have to agree to every request and every favour that others ask of you. You're not a bad person if you refuse

5 | TRY IT! POWER

The Black Holes of Time Management

The items on this list are common problems that prevent us from getting things done. Check off the ones that are problems for you, and indicate whether you have control over them (controllable problems) or they are out of your control (uncontrollable problems). There is space to add two more items that are not on this list, but that affect you.

1 — Big problem for me　　　　　　3 — Seldom or not a problem for me

2 — Often a problem for me

Indicate C for controllable or U for uncontrollable.

	1	2	3	U or C
1. Phone calls				
2. Texting or email				
3. Playing games online				
4. Spending time on social networking sites				
5. Surfing the Internet				
6. Drop-in visitors				
7. Socializing				
8. Errands and shopping				
9. Family or personal appointments				
10. Children's interruptions				
11. Snacking				
12. Making meals and mealtime				
13. Perfectionism				
14. Inability to say no				
15. Looking for lost items				
16. Correcting errors or mistakes				
17. Jumping from task to task				
18. Waiting for transit				
19. Car trouble				
20. Binge-watching TV series				
21. Other: _____				
22. Other: _____				

 DISCUSSION

Discuss the "big" or "often" items you've identified with your classmates, and answer the following: Do your time management problems follow a specific pattern; for instance, are they all related to technology? Are there problems that at first seemed uncontrollable that can actually be controlled? What strategies for dealing with these problems have you or your classmates successfully used in the past?

To Try It online, go to the McGraw-Hill online resource.

to do something that will eat up your time and prevent you from accomplishing your goals. And if you do decide to do someone else a time-consuming favour, try to come up with the most efficient way of accomplishing it. Don't let all your time get taken up by the priorities of others. This advice is especially important for those of you with strong interpersonal intelligence, because you tend to put the needs of others ahead of your own.

> **Respect others' time as well.** If you agree to meet up with someone, whether it is a peer, a family member, or a professor, remember that they, too, are setting aside valuable time to see you, so show up when you said you would, and if you are going to be a few minutes late, either call or text the person to let them know. Similarly, if you agree to meet a particular deadline either at work or at school, respect that deadline, as others in your office or project group are counting on you, and they may have made commitments of their own that depend on you delivering on time.

> **Get away from it all.** Go to the library. Lock yourself in your bedroom. Find a quiet, out-of-the-way coffee shop. Any of these places can serve to isolate you from everyday distractions and thereby permit you to work on the tasks that you wish to complete. Try to adopt a particular spot as your own, such as a corner desk in a secluded nook in the library. If you use it enough, your body and mind will automatically get into study mode as soon as you seat yourself there.

> **Make an appointment with yourself.** Set aside time each week—or even every day—when no one is allowed to interrupt you. Use the time to address some of your priority-1 items, to reflect, or simply to daydream.

> **Enjoy the sounds of silence.** Although many people insist they accomplish more when the television or radio is on or while music is playing in the background, scientific studies suggest otherwise: We are able to concentrate best when our environment is silent. So even if you're sure you work best with a soundtrack playing, experiment and work in silence for a few days. Even those of you with strong musical intelligence may be surprised to find out that you get more done in less time than you would in a more distracting environment.

> **Expect the unexpected.** Interruptions and crises, minor and major, can't be eliminated. However, they can be prepared for. How is it possible to plan for surprises? Though it may still be too early in the term to get a clear picture of what sorts of unanticipated events you'll encounter, you should keep an eye out for patterns. Perhaps one instructor routinely gives surprise assignments. Maybe you're asked to work extra hours on the weekends because a certain co-worker doesn't show up for their shift.

You'll never be able to escape the interruptions and surprises that will require your attention. But by trying to anticipate them, and by thinking about how you'll react to them, you'll be positioning yourself to react more effectively when they do occur. Another way to prepare for the unexpected is to stick to your to-do list as best you can; that way, the time that you need to deal with the unexpected will be available to you.

Take Control of Your Devices

Manage e-distractions. Snapchat, Instagram, Vine, Facebook, Twitter, phone calls, email. Who doesn't love to connect with other people? But the impact on your success as a student can be alarming. For example, CBC News reported that engineering students at Dalhousie University were blaming Facebook and other forms of social media for failing courses.[3] Ask yourself, is knowing what your best friend ate for dinner really worth risking a failing grade?

Remember Try It! 4, where you were encouraged to distinguish between what is urgent and what is important? If you were honest with yourself—and I hope you were—you probably described the vast majority of the texts you receive on a daily basis as not important and not urgent, particularly when taken in the context of your long-term goals. Knowing this, taking control of your devices becomes an important part of your time management strategy *and* your strategy for reaching your goals.

We may not control when communications arrive, but we *can* make the message wait until we are ready to receive it. Take a break and shut down your communication devices for a period of time. When it comes to notifications from social networking sites or emails, set aside a specific time each day to deal with them, rather than looking at your phone every time a friend posts on Instagram. Consider turning off audible or visual notifications entirely, so you won't be distracted by them. This is especially important during class and when you are trying to get some sleep!

Avoid multitasking. A 2013 York University study published in *Computers and Education* found that students who use a laptop to take notes while listening to a lecture are more likely to multitask and less likely to understand the content than students who use pen and paper. Surprisingly, the study found that even sitting near someone else who was multitasking had a negative effect.[4]

If you need a more heavy-handed approach to avoiding distractions, consider a program like Cold Turkey, a free download, or the more full-featured Freedom, available for Windows, Mac, and iOS, which allow you to block access to social networking sites and any other sites you would like to see blocked. According to the Freedom website, studies show that it takes 23 minutes to refocus your mind on a task after you've been distracted, so it's *not* just about the time it takes to click "Like"! The site also indicates that multitasking makes you 40 percent less productive—can you really afford that?

Work Smarter, Not Harder

Thanks to smartphones, computers, and the Internet, you are never more than a click away from a massive encyclopedia of the world's knowledge. Learning to leverage this knowledge is one of the most important investments you can make. Here are some additional strategies for working smarter rather than harder:

> **Accomplish the task in the most efficient way possible.** We tend to do things the way we've always done them, without considering whether there might be a more efficient way to accomplish what we've set out to do. For example, you may consider heading out to your local bookstore to see whether they have a particular book. Why not check online first or phone ahead? You'll save time and gas, and you'll also avoid the possibility of wasting even more time browsing once you reach the bookstore!

> **Match the amount of effort you expend to the importance of the task.** You probably wouldn't spend just 10 minutes deciding which car to buy, but you might spend 10 minutes selecting a pair of shoes. The same goes for schoolwork. The amount of time you put into a report worth 25 percent of your mark should differ significantly from the time you spend studying for a weekly 1 percent quiz.

> **Develop a consistent approach to tasks you do regularly.** Whether it's folding towels or developing a business presentation, there are efficiencies to be gained by approaching tasks that you do regularly in the same way each time. When it comes to your schoolwork, reuse presentation or report templates that have worked well for you in the past. Examine some of the templates available in Microsoft Word or PowerPoint to get ideas. Why reinvent the wheel if someone else has already put time and effort into developing something that you can use as a foundation?

> **Use electronic devices to help you manage your time—and your life—more effectively.** Use your smartphone or computer calendar's "reminder" functions whenever it makes sense to do so. Input due dates for upcoming assignments and then ask to be reminded about the task a few days and/or hours in advance. Invest an hour of your life putting important birthdays and anniversaries into your electronic calendar; use the "recurring annually" function with no end date, and you will never forget these dates again. Add in a reminder a week in advance of the date to prepare an e-card and purchase a gift online, a time saver if ever there was one. And if you are an auditory/verbal learner, go one step further by making that reminder an auditory one.

Deal with Procrastination

Procrastination

The habit of putting off tasks that need to be accomplished

Procrastination, the habit of putting off tasks that need to be accomplished, is like a microscopic parasite. It is invisible to the naked eye, but it eats up your time nonetheless. You can't control interruptions and crises that are imposed on you by others. But even when no one else is throwing interruptions at us, we make up our own.

Ever wonder how much time the average Canadian spends consuming media in an average day? The figures are startling. No wonder we feel we never have time to do anything else. The latest figures show that Canadians spent an average of 65.25 hours every week consuming media in 2016, according to a report prepared by PHD Canada.[5] Check out **Figure 2.9** to see which media are being consumed and how this has changed over time.

The problem with procrastinating is that you are merely delaying the inevitable. Eventually, the task *must* get done, and you *know* it must get done. The longer you delay, the more stressed you get, and the more you open yourself up to any number of potential problems: not finding the information you are looking for, running out of printer ink, not having time to ask the professor for clarification, and so forth. Procrastinating when working on a group project is even more stressful—perhaps not for you, but certainly for the people you are working with. Instructors usually expect group projects to have a unified look and to read as though they were written by one person. To accomplish this requires careful editing and proofreading—tasks that take time and that cannot wait for procrastinators to get their act together!

To identify whether you are a procrastinator, check out **Try It! 6** "Find Your Procrastination Quotient."

figure 2.9 | Canadians' Average Daily Media Consumption

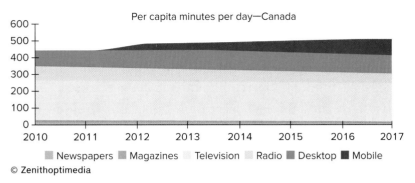

Per capita minutes per day—Canada

■ Newspapers ■ Magazines ■ Television ■ Radio ■ Desktop ■ Mobile

© Zenithoptimedia

6 | TRY IT! [P O W E R]

Find Your Procrastination Quotient

Do you procrastinate? To find out, circle the number that best applies for each question.

1. I invent reasons and look for excuses for not acting on a problem.

| Strongly agree | 4 | 3 | 2 | 1 | Strongly disagree |

2. It takes pressure to get me to work on difficult assignments.

| Strongly agree | 4 | 3 | 2 | 1 | Strongly disagree |

3. I take half-measures that will avoid or delay unpleasant or difficult tasks.

| Strongly agree | 4 | 3 | 2 | 1 | Strongly disagree |

4. I face too many interruptions and crises that interfere with accomplishing my major goals.

| Strongly agree | 4 | 3 | 2 | 1 | Strongly disagree |

5. I sometimes neglect to carry out important tasks.

| Strongly agree | 4 | 3 | 2 | 1 | Strongly disagree |

6. I schedule big assignments too late to get them done as well as I know I could.

| Strongly agree | 4 | 3 | 2 | 1 | Strongly disagree |

7. I'm sometimes too tired to do the work I need to do.

| Strongly agree | 4 | 3 | 2 | 1 | Strongly disagree |

8. I start new tasks before I finish old ones.

| Strongly agree | 4 | 3 | 2 | 1 | Strongly disagree |

9. When I work in groups, I try to get other people to finish what I don't.

| Strongly agree | 4 | 3 | 2 | 1 | Strongly disagree |

10. I put off tasks that I really don't want to do but know that I must do.

| Strongly agree | 4 | 3 | 2 | 1 | Strongly disagree |

Scoring: Total the numbers you have circled. If your score is less than 15, you are not a chronic procrastinator and you probably have only an occasional problem. If your score is 16–25, you have a minor problem with procrastination. If your score is above 25, you procrastinate quite often and should work on breaking the habit.

Now, consider the following:

· If you do procrastinate often, why do you think you do it?
· Are there particular kinds of assignments that you are more likely to procrastinate on?
· Is there something that you are putting off doing right now? How might you get started on it?

 DISCUSSION

Think about the last time you procrastinated. Describe it as completely as you can. What was the task? What did you do rather than doing what needed to be done? What could you have done to avoid procrastinating in this situation? Ask others what strategy they might suggest for avoiding procrastinating.

To Try It online, go to the McGraw-Hill online resource.

If you find yourself procrastinating, several strategies can help you:

> **Break large tasks into small ones.** People often procrastinate because a task they're seeking to accomplish appears overwhelming. If writing a 15-page paper seems nearly impossible, think about writing a series of five 3-page papers. If reading a 750-page book seems impossible, think of it as reading three 250-page books.

> **Start with the simplest part of a task, and then do the harder parts.** Succeeding initially on the easy parts can make the harder parts of a task less daunting and make you less apt to procrastinate in completing the task.

> **Just begin!** Sometimes the hardest part of an activity is simply getting started. So take the leap and begin the task, and the rest may follow easily.

> **Work with others.** Just being in the same physical location with others can motivate you sufficiently to accomplish tasks that you consider unpleasant and on which you might be tempted to procrastinate. For instance, filling out tedious order forms can be made easier if you collaborate with co-workers. Beware, though: If you spend too much time socializing, you lower the likelihood of success.

> **Keep the costs of procrastination in mind.** Procrastination doesn't just result in delay; it may also make the task harder than it would have been if you hadn't procrastinated. Not only will you ultimately have less time to complete the task, but you also may have to do it so quickly that its quality may be diminished. In the worst-case scenario, you won't be able to finish it at all. And if others are involved in the task, you will be making their lives difficult as well, something they will remember the next time you are looking to work in their group.

Balance Competing Responsibilities

Balance School and Work Demands

Juggling school and a job can be a real challenge. Not only must you manage your time to complete your school work, but in many cases you'll also face time management demands while you are on the job. Here are some tips to help you keep everything in balance:

> **If you have slack time on the job, get some studying done.** Try to keep at least some of your textbooks, class notes, or notecards with you so you can refer to them. Of course, you should never do school work without your employer's prior agreement. If you don't get permission, you may jeopardize your job.

> **Use your lunch hour effectively.** Although it's important to eat a nutritious lunch and not wolf your food down, you may be able to use some of the time allotted to you for lunch to fit in some studying.

> **Ask your employer about flextime.** If your job allows it, you may be able to set your own hours, within reason, as long as the work gets done. If this is an option for you, use it. Although it may create more time management challenges for you than would a job with set hours, it also provides you with some flexibility.

> **Accept new responsibilities carefully.** If you've barely been keeping up with the demands of work and school, don't automatically accept new job responsibilities without carefully evaluating how they

fit with your long-term priorities. If your job is temporary and you're not planning to stay, you might want to respectfully decline substantial new duties or an increase in the number of hours you work. On the other hand, if you plan to continue in the job once you're done with school, accepting new responsibilities may be more reasonable.

Balance School and Work Obligations with Family Demands

If you have a job and are a student and you also have caregiver responsibilities for children or other family members, time management is especially challenging. Your family demands—and deserves—substantial quantities of your time, and juggling school and work along with family obligations can prove to be exhausting. However, there are some specific strategies that can help.

> **Dealing with child-care demands:**

Provide activities for your children. Kids enjoy doing things on their own for part of the day. Plan activities that will keep them happily occupied while you're doing schoolwork.

Make spending time with your children a priority. Carve out "free-play" time for your kids. Even 20 minutes of good time devoted to your children will give all of you—you *and* them—a lift. No matter how busy you are, you owe it to your children, and to yourself, to spend time as a family.

Enlist your child's help. Children love to play adult, and, if they're old enough, you can ask them to help you study. Maybe they can help you clear a space to study. Perhaps you can give them "assignments" that they can work on while you're working on your assignments.

Encourage your child to invite friends over to play. Some children can remain occupied for hours if they have a playmate.

Use television appropriately. Television viewing is not all bad, and some shows and DVDs can be not just engaging, but educational. The trick is to pick and choose what your children watch.

Find the best child care or babysitters that you can. The better the care your children are getting, the better you'll be able to concentrate on your classes or your job. You may still feel guilty that you're not with your children as much as you'd like, but accept that guilt. Remember, your attendance in class and good performance at work build a better future for your children.

Use your children's "downtime" effectively. If your children are young, use their nap time as a chance to catch up on work or chores. Or consider getting up early, before your children wake up, for a period in which you will have fewer interruptions than later in the day.

> **Dealing with the elder-care demands:**

Encourage as much independence as possible on the part of older adults for whom you are responsible. Not only will it take some of the pressure off you, but it will be helpful to the older adult.

Ask for support from your siblings and other family members. Caring for an ill or aging parent should be a family affair, not a burden that falls on any one individual.

© George Doyle & Ciaran Griffin/Stockbyte/
Getty Images

Determine what community resources are available. Local centres for the aged may provide assistance not only to the elderly but also to their caregivers.

Respect your own needs. Remember that your own priorities are important. Elders for whom you are responsible will understand that you will sometimes need to put yourself first.

Career CONNECTIONS

On-the-Job Time Management

In the business world, schedules are unpredictable. Crises occur, perhaps due to manufacturing problems or client demands, which require sudden flurries of work. Perhaps you have a demanding boss who may, without warning, give you an urgent assignment due the next morning. Time is always at a premium. You may be forced to drop everything you normally work on and pitch in on a sudden new task. As a result, your plans to complete your everyday work may be disrupted completely.

Simply put, time management is an essential survival skill when developing your career. Learning the basic principles of time management now will help you well beyond your years in college or university, throughout your later career. You'll also want to learn new time management strategies specific to the working world. For instance, if you supervise other employees, it may be possible to delegate some work to them, allowing them to help you complete assignments on time. Or sometimes it may be possible to deflect assignments brought to you by a boss to some other unit or department. Always keep in mind what you can do alone and what you cannot complete without the aid of co-workers. Don't be afraid to ask for help. In the working world, the end result is what counts above all.

▣ Evaluate Check Your Use of Time

Your time management P.O.W.E.R. Plan is on track. Now it's time to *evaluate* your progress. Evaluating how you use your time is pretty straightforward: You either accomplished what you intended to do in a given period, or you didn't. Did you check off all the items on your daily to-do list? If you go over your list at the end of every day, you will know how successful your time management efforts have been, and you will be able to incorporate any activities you missed into the next day's to-do list.

Checking off the completed items on your to-do list is important because it provides an objective record of what you have accomplished on a given day. Just as important, it provides you with concrete reinforcement for completing the task. There are few things more satisfying than gazing at a to-do list with a significant number of check marks.

Of course, you won't always accomplish every item on your to-do list. That's not surprising, or even particularly bad, especially if you've included some second- and third-level priorities that you don't absolutely have to accomplish anyway.

Give yourself a pat on the back for completing the things that you've accomplished. Successful time management is not easy, and if you've improved at all, you deserve to feel some personal satisfaction.

R Rethink | Reflect on Your Personal Style of Time Management

At the end of the day, after you've evaluated how well you've followed your time management plan and how much you've accomplished, it's time to *rethink* where you are. Maybe you've accomplished everything you set out to do. Every task for the day is completed, and every item on your to-do list has a check mark next to it.

Or maybe you have the opposite result. Your day has been a mess, and you feel as if nothing has been accomplished. Because of a constant series of interruptions and chance events, you've been unable to make headway on your list.

Or—most likely—you find yourself somewhere between these two extremes. Some tasks got done, while others are still hanging over you. Now is the time to rethink in a broad sense how you manage your time by doing the following:

> **Reassess your priorities.** Are your long- and short-term goals appropriate? Are you expecting too much of yourself, given the constraints in your life? Reassess your priorities to be sure you're attempting to do what is most important to you.

> **Reconsider your personal style of time management.** We've outlined one method of time management. Although it works well for most people, it isn't for everyone. Some people just can't bring themselves to be so structured and scheduled. They feel hemmed in by to-do lists.

> If you're one of those people, fine. You don't need to follow the suggestions presented in this chapter exactly. In fact, if you go to your campus bookstore or any office supply store, you'll find lots of other aids to manage your time. Publishing companies produce elaborate planners, such as Daytimers. The Student Services office will often provide students with a paper-based planning agenda free of charge. In addition, software companies produce computerized time management software, such as Microsoft Outlook or Novell GroupWise, that reside on computers and on wireless handheld devices such as the BlackBerry or iPhone. Many cellphones contain a calendar system and alarm, and they can be set to provide periodic reminders.

However you choose to manage your time, the important thing is to do so consistently. And remember that whatever approach to time management you take, it will work best if it is compatible with your own personal values and strengths. Keep experimenting until you find an approach that works for you.

> **Consider doing less.** If you keep falling behind, do less. There are only 24 hours in the day, and we need to sleep for about a third of the time. In the remaining hours, it is impossible to carry a full load of classes and work full time and care for a child and still have some time left to have a normal life.

Consequently, if you consistently fall behind in your work, it may be that you are just trying to do too much. Reassess your goals and your priorities, and make choices. Determine what is most important to you. It's better to accomplish less, if it is accomplished well, than to accomplish more, but poorly.

> **Use your free time well.** Although it is a problem that many of us would envy, some people have too much time on their hands. Their classes may not be too demanding, or work demands may suddenly slacken off. If this happens to you, take advantage of it. For example, you might use the extra time to simply relax and enjoy your more unhurried existence. There is a lot to be said for having time to let your thoughts wander. We need to take time out to enjoy our friends, admire the flowers in the park, exercise, and consider the spiritual side of our lives.

On the other hand, if you consistently have more time than you know what to do with, reflect on what you want to accomplish and add some activities that help you reach your goals. For example, consider becoming involved in an organization on campus. Volunteer your time to the community. Think about taking an extra course during the next term.

But whatever you decide to do, make a real decision. Don't let the time slip away. Once it's gone, it's gone forever.

Time to Reflect: What **Did I Learn?**

1. Generally speaking, how would you characterize your time management skills?

2. What would be the benefit to you personally if you could manage time more effectively? That is, what goals might you accomplish if you had more time at your disposal?

3. Based on what you learned about time management in this chapter, what do you plan to do differently in the future? Be specific.

Did You Know?

Canadians spend more time online than citizens of any other country in the world.

"According to a recent study conducted by comScore Canada, an analytics firm that watches for trends and changes in Internet habits, Canadians spend an average of 36.3 hours browsing and visit approximately 80 websites in one month's time. In comparison, Americans spend 35.2 hours online every month while Britons spend approximately 33 hours online."[6]

Looking Back

How can I manage my time most effectively?

Decide to take control of your time.

> Become aware of the way you use your time now.
> Set clear priorities.
> Distinguish the important priorities from the not-so-important and the urgent from the not-so-urgent.
> Use time management tools such as a master calendar, a weekly timetable, and a daily to-do list.
> Estimate the time required to complete tasks, and create timelines for complex undertakings.

How can I control my environment?

> Control your environment by saying no, getting away from it all, working in silence, taking control of your devices, and leaving some slack in your schedule to accommodate the unexpected.

How can I work smarter, instead of harder?

> Accomplish tasks in the most efficient way possible, match the amount of effort you expend to the importance of the task, develop a consistent approach to tasks you do regularly, and use device blockers to help you manage your time.

How can I avoid procrastination?

> Avoid procrastination by breaking large tasks into smaller ones, starting with the easiest parts of a task first, working with other people, and calculating the true costs of procrastination.

How can I balance competing priorities?

> Consider how your competing priorities relate to one another.
> Manage work time carefully, use slack time on the job to perform school assignments, use flextime, accept new responsibilities thoughtfully, and assign the proper priority to work.

RESOURCES

ON CAMPUS

The person who determines when classes meet is usually known as the registrar. If you are having difficulty scheduling your classes, the registrar's office may be helpful. In addition, your academic adviser can help you work out problems with enrolling in the classes you want.

For help with such issues as planning a study schedule for the upcoming term, dealing with multiple assignments and obligations on the same date, or dealing with competing academic and work demands, consult your campus learning centre. The staff can help you sort out the options you may have.

Many college and university student associations or Student Services offices provide students with a paper-based agenda free of charge. Stop by and pick one up at the beginning of the school year. And while it might seem obvious, don't forget that your instructors are a great source of information.

IN PRINT

Stephen Covey's classic, the 25th-anniversary edition of *The Seven Habits of Highly Effective People* (Simon & Schuster, 2013), and Alan Axelrod and Brian Tracy's *Eat That Frog! 21 Great Ways to Stop Procrastinating and Get More Done in Less Time* (Berrett-Kohler, 2007) are practical, hands-on guides to time management.

168 Hours: You Have More Time Than You Think (Penguin, 2010), by Laura Vanderkam, focuses on the best time management practices used by ordinary, every-day people like you.

The Willpower Instinct: How Self-Control Works, Why It Matters, and What You Can Do To Get More of It (Avery, 2011), by Kelly McGonigal, comes highly recom-mended by Carleton University professor and noted expert on procrastination Dr. Timothy A. Pychyl.

ON THE WEB

The McGraw-Hill online resource provides online versions of all the time management forms present in this chapter. You can complete the forms online or download them and print out as many copies as you need. The following websites provide an oppor-tunity to extend your learning about the material in this chapter:

> **The lifehack.org** site offers many tips and tricks for making life easier. For their time management hacks, check out this link: **lifehack.org/articles/technology/top-15-time-management-apps-and-tools.html.**

THERE'S AN APP FOR THAT

Many apps are available to help you manage your time:

> The Google Calendar app is available for both iOS and Android.

> For to-do lists for iOS and Android, try Todoist or Any.DO.

> For apps that allow you to block access to sites from your favourite device, try SelfControl for iOS or Self Control for Study for Android.

> For a multi-platform app that allows you to combine scheduling, homework, and grades, try out istudiez.

> To see just how much time you are spending on your device, download Checky for Android or iOS.

TAKING IT TO THE WEB

1 Complete a weekly organizer online. Find a site on the Web that offers share-ware or freeware featuring a weekly planner (for example, **printablecalendar.ca/** or **studygs.net/schedule/weekly.htm**). Create a weekly schedule sheet for yourself based on this design. Be sure to write in all of your classes, job obliga-tions, and any other regular responsibilities that you have. Be sure to set specific times in your daily schedule to study. (If you already use Google Calendar or Outlook, use its calendar function to do the same thing.)

2 Make a master calendar for the term using the same software you used for the exercise above. If your calendar does not provide this information automati-cally, you can go to **timeanddate.com/calendar/**. Here you'll find many links to different calendar-related information, such as when holidays occur. Be sure to indicate dates when important assignments are due and when exams occur.

THE CASE OF . . .
Time Crunched

Paul Misir couldn't believe it. He was working overtime at his delivery job because one of his co-workers was on vacation. During a break from his shift, he got a text message from a classmate asking if he wanted to study the next day for the exam the following Monday. Paul had forgotten all about the exam.

Even worse, Paul couldn't study with his classmate the next day because he'd promised his girlfriend he would join her to visit her grandmother, who lived an hour's drive from the city. Although he wasn't looking forward to the two-hour round trip, he knew his girlfriend would be furious if he broke his promise. And on top of all that, he also had to find time in the next few days to work on a term paper due in one of his other classes.

As he was driving home thinking about all this, his car started to sputter and then stalled. He was unable to get it started. That was it. He sat there on the side of the road, feeling as if his life had completely fallen apart and wondering how he'd ever get it back together again.

1. What might you tell Paul that could help solve his predicament?

2. What specific time management techniques might Paul have employed in the past to avoid these problems?

3. What strategies might Paul use now to take control of his limited time during the coming days?

4. What advice could you give Paul to try to prevent problems in time management for his next term?

© Chris Noble | Dreamstime.com

CHAPTER 3
Reading and Remembering

Learning Outcomes

By the time you finish this chapter, you will be able to

LO 3.1   Identify the essential elements of successful reading, and explain how to improve concentration when reading.

LO 3.2   Demonstrate the use of techniques for remembering large amounts of information.

LO 3.3   Analyze how best to retain what you have read.

"Read the next chapter in the textbook by Tuesday." "Read the first two articles in the course pack by next class." "The test will cover the first hundred pages in your book, so be sure you've read them."

One day, three different reading assignments, Jesse Knowles thought, as the instructor of his last class of the day delivered this last instruction. It would be hard enough for Jesse to complete all this reading during an ordinary week. But this week he had to finish painting his bedroom and he had volunteered to help his brother move. On top of that, there was his part-time job as a cashier—and, Jesse suddenly remembered, he'd agreed to work overtime on Friday.

Still, Jesse figured that even with all his work, family, and household obligations, he could still find time to do all his reading—except Jesse believed he was an unusually slow reader. When he pushed himself to read more quickly and absorb more, he actually read and retained less. For Jesse, the problem wasn't just completing the reading—it was remembering it when test time rolled around.

Looking Ahead

For people like Jesse, reading assignments are the biggest challenge in college or university. The amount of required reading is often enormous. Even skilled readers may find themselves wishing they could read more quickly and effectively. On the job, too, many people struggle with all the memos, emails, manuals, and other documents that they need to read.

Fortunately, there are ways to improve your reading skills. In this chapter, we'll go over a number of strategies to make your reading more effective.

We'll also discuss ways to improve memory skills, not just as they relate to reading, but in general. Most of us have experienced the challenge of memorizing a seemingly impossible amount of information, and we tend to focus on our failures far more than on our successes. But the truth is that our memory capabilities are truly astounding. For instance, if you are like the average college or university student, your vocabulary contains some 50,000 words, you know hundreds of mathematical facts, and you can recall detailed images from events you witnessed years ago. In this chapter, you'll learn how to harness the power of your memory.

LO 3.1 Sharpening Your Reading Skills

One of the reasons many people struggle with reading, especially in college or university, is they feel they *shouldn't* have to struggle with it. Reading, after all, is something almost all of us master as children, right?

In fact, it's not so simple. Reading, as we will see in this chapter, involves more than just recognizing words. The skill of reading large amounts of information and remembering the essential points takes time to master.

To begin, consider the way you read now. In other words, what kind of reader are you? Ask yourself first of all about your reading preferences: What do you *like* to read, and why? What makes you pick up a book and start reading—and what makes you put one down?

Before going any further, reflect on your Striving Style™ and how it might affect how you read and remember material. Then, examine the suggestions and recommendations provided below.

Reading and Remembering and Striving Styles™

Leaders	Try not to get impatient with reading. Set up reading and memorizing challenges to stay engaged. Reading out loud helps focus.
Socializers	Passive learning, such as reading, is de-energizing. Use of visual tools and acronyms is helpful. Helping others helps reinforce learning.
Performers	Read, then review, and talk with others about the subject. Use a visual organizer. Start well in advance and take plenty of breaks.
Adventurers	Try reading while walking (be careful!) or on a treadmill to increase focus. Reading and discussing can help, as can having fun with acronyms and word games.
Artists	Take lots of time and space to read and reflect. Use memory cards and repetition to help with rote learning. Connect reading to something personal.
Intellectuals	Checking for inconsistencies when reading is a time-consuming distraction. Use a timer to keep track of time. Make lots of notes.
Visionaries	Read where there are no distractions. Difficulty with rote memory can cause anxiety about remembering. Make plenty of notes and use visual aids.
Stabilizers	Have others help with theory and complex subjects. Take plenty of time to absorb. Check to ensure understanding of exactly what is expected.

Read for Retention, Not Speed

You may have come across advertisements on the Web promoting reading "systems" that promise to teach you to read so quickly that you'll be reading entire books in an hour and whizzing through assigned readings in a few minutes.

Unfortunately, that's not going to happen. Research has shown that claims of speed-reading are simply groundless. But even if it were physically possible to read a book in an hour, it probably wouldn't matter very much. If we read too quickly, comprehension and ultimately retention plunge. Reading is not a race, and the fastest readers are not necessarily the best readers.

The act of reading is designed to increase our knowledge and open up new ways of thinking. It can help us achieve new levels of understanding and get us to think more broadly about the world and its inhabitants. Speed matters far less than what we take away from what we've read. That's not to say we shouldn't try to become more efficient readers who comprehend and recall more effectively. Ultimately, though, the key to good reading is comprehension, not speed.

In describing how you can use the principles of P.O.W.E.R. Learning to become a better reader with a more complete memory of what you read, we'll focus on the types of reading that are typically called for in academic pursuits—textbook chapters, articles, handouts, and the like. However, the same principles will help you get more benefit and enjoyment out of your recreational reading as well. In addition, the reading skills you learn and employ in the classroom will help you read more efficiently and effectively on the job.

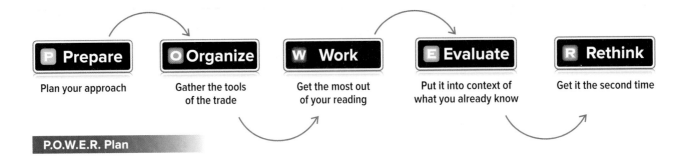

P Prepare Plan Your Approach

Preparation for reading isn't difficult, and it won't take very long; but it's a crucial first step in applying P.O.W.E.R. Learning (summarized in the P.O.W.E.R. Plan below). In fact, preparation is the first step in the **SQ3R approach** to reading, a model developed during World War II by Professor Francis Robinson, a psychology professor at Ohio State University. His SQ3R model—an acronym for **S**urvey, **Q**uestion, and the three Rs, which in this case stand for **R**ead, **R**ecite, and **R**eview—was developed in response to an urgent need to train soldiers to read and understand thousands of pages of complicated technical manuals in preparation for war. **Table 3.1** outlines the main points of the model, which we discuss in more detail throughout the chapter.

The "S" in SQ3R is for surveying, or familiarizing yourself with the materials that surround the core text. These **advance organizers**—which include prefaces, chapter previews, outlines and overviews, learning outcomes, and other clues to the meaning and organization of new material—are built into most textbooks; for example, every chapter in this book includes a Learning Outcomes list and a Looking Ahead section. You can also create your own advance organizers by skimming material to be read and sketching out the general outline of the material you'll be reading. Another tip is to examine end-of-chapter review material before reading the chapter, as it will point you toward what is most important in the chapter.

Advance organizers pave the way for subsequent learning. They help you tie information that you already know to new material you're about to encounter. This connection between old and new material is crucial in helping build memories of what you read. If you approach each new reading task as something entirely new and unrelated to your previous knowledge, you'll have enormous difficulty recalling it. On the other hand, if you connect it to what you already know, you'll be able to recall it far more easily.

SQ3R approach
A model for reading and comprehension based on these five steps: Survey, Question, Read, Recite, and Review

Advance organizers
Broad, general ideas or materials related to what is to about to be read or heard, which pave the way for subsequent learning

table 3.1		SQ3R
S	Survey	Familiarize yourself with the materials that surround the core text.
Q	Question	Question the point of view of the material you are reading *and* the credibility of the person writing it.
R	Read	Read the material.
R	Recite	Recite the material aloud as you read it.
R	Review	Go back and review what you've read, along with any notes you've taken.

In short, the more we're able to make use of advance organizers and our own prior knowledge and experiences, the better we can understand and retain new material. (To prove the value of advance organizers to yourself, complete **Try It! 1** "Discover How Advance Organizers Help.")

Identify the Purpose of the Reading Assignment

The "Q" in SQ3R involves questioning the purpose of the material you are about to read, and your goal in reading it. Will you be reading a textbook on which you'll be thoroughly tested? Is your reading supposed to provide background information that will serve as a context for future learning but that won't itself be tested? Will the material be useful to you personally? Realistically, how much time can you devote to the reading assignment?

Your goal for reading will help you determine which reading strategy to adopt. You aren't expected to read everything with the same degree of intensity. Some material you may feel comfortable skimming; for other material you'll want to put in the maximum effort.

Understand the Author's Point of View

The "Q" in SQ3R also extends to questioning the point of view of the material you are reading and the credibility of the person writing it. What are you reading? Is it a textbook, an essay, an article, a blog? If it is an essay, article, or blog, why was it written? To prove a point? To provide information? To express the author's personal feelings? Knowing the author's purpose (even if the specific point and message aren't yet clear) can help you put the material in context. Knowing something about the author can help you determine if the material is based purely on the author's own

---

1 | TRY IT! POWER

Discover How Advance Organizers Help

Read this passage. What do you think it means?

> The procedure is actually quite simple. First you arrange items into different groups. Of course, one pile may be sufficient, depending on how much there is to do. If you have to go somewhere else due to lack of facilities, that is the next step; otherwise, you are pretty well set. It is important not to overdo things. That is, it is better to do too few things at once than too many. In the short run, this may not seem important; but complications can easily arise. A mistake can be expensive as well. At first, the whole procedure will seem complicated. Soon, however, it will become just another facet of life. It is difficult to foresee any end to the necessity for this task in the immediate future, but then one can never tell. After the procedure is completed, one arranges the materials into different groups again. Then they can be put into their appropriate places. Eventually, they will be used once more and the whole cycle will then have to be repeated. However, this is a part of life.[1]

Bransford, J.D., & Johnson, M.K. (1972). Contextual prerequisites for understanding: Some investigations of comprehension and recall. Journal of Verbal Learning and Verbal Behavior, 11, 722.

If you're like most people, you don't have a clue about what this all means and you won't be able to remember anything about it in five minutes. Now, suppose you have been given some context in advance, and you know before reading it that the description has to do with doing laundry. Now does it all fall into place? Do you think it will be easier to remember? Read the passage once more, and see how having an advance organizer (in this case, *doing laundry*) helps out.

To Try It online, go to the McGraw-Hill online resource.

experience and, therefore, might suffer from an inherent bias, or whether it is drawn from a broad body of professional research.

Start with the Frontmatter

Frontmatter

The preface, introduction, and table of contents of a book

If you'll be using a text or other book extensively throughout the term, start by surveying the preface and/or introduction and scanning the table of contents—what publishers call the **frontmatter**. Instructors often don't formally assign the frontmatter, but reading it can be a big help because it is there that the author has a chance to step forward and explain, often more personally than elsewhere in an academic book, what he or she considers important. Knowing this will give you a sense of what to expect as you read. If you haven't yet done so, take a look at the preface to *this* book. What can you learn from it?

Create Advance Organizers

To provide a context for your reading, you can create your own advance organizers by skimming through the table of contents, which provides the main headings of what you will be reading. Textbooks often have chapter outlines, listing the key topics to be covered, and these also provide a way of previewing the chapter content. As you read over the outline, you can begin to consider how the new material in the book may relate both to what you know and to what you expect to learn—from the reading assignment itself and from the course.

Textbooks also often have end-of-chapter summaries, and many articles include a final section in which the author states their conclusions. Take a look at these ending sections as well. Even though you haven't read the material yet and the summary probably won't make complete sense to you, by reading the summary, you'll get an idea of what the author covers and what is important.

Your instructor may also provide an advance organizer for readings. Sometimes instructors will mention things to pay particular attention to or to look for, such as, "When you read Thomas Paine's *Common Sense*, notice how he lays out his argument and what his key points are." Sometimes they will tell you why they assigned a particular reading. Such information provides clues that can help you develop a mental list of the reading's key ideas.

However you construct or use advance organizers, be sure they provide a framework and context for what you'll be reading; this framework and context can spell the difference between fully comprehending what you read and misunderstanding it.

Now it's time to put all these ideas to good use. Create an advance organizer for a textbook chapter by working through **Try It! 2** "Create an Advance Organizer."

Peanuts by Charles Schultz © United Feature Syndicate, Inc. Reprinted by permission.

2 | TRY IT! POWER

Create an Advance Organizer

Use any information you have available to create an advance organizer for a chapter in a text that you are using this term. Skim the section headings in the chapter, read the chapter summary, consult the book's frontmatter, and recall anything your instructor may have said about the chapter.

Complete the following statements to prepare your organizer:

1. The general topics covered in the chapter are . . .

2. The most critical topics and concepts in the chapter are . . .

3. The most difficult material in the chapter includes . . .

4. Words, phrases, and ideas that are unfamiliar to me include . . .

5. Ways that the material in this chapter relates to other material that I've previously read in the text include . . .

Use this Try It! as a starting point for advance organizers for future chapters in the book.

To Try It online, go to the McGraw-Hill online resource.

Identify What You Need to Remember

No matter how important a reading assignment is to a course, you will not be expected to remember every word of it—nor should you try! The average textbook chapter has something like 20,000 words. Recalling every word of the chapter would be nearly impossible. Furthermore, no matter how much of a perfectionist you are, memorizing every word is a waste of your valuable time. Being able to spew out paragraphs of material is quite different from the more important ability to recall and deeply understand material in meaningful ways.

Within those 20,000 words, there may be only 20 different concepts that you need to learn. And perhaps there are only 10 keywords. *These* are the pieces of information that should be the focus of your efforts to memorize.

How do you know what's so important that you need to recall it? One way is to use the guides built into most textbooks. Key concepts and terms are often highlighted or in boldface type. Chapters often have summaries that recap the most important information. Use such guideposts to understand what's most critical in a chapter. Another approach is to use the journalist's trick of asking the five Ws—who, what, when, where, and why.

Write down what you determine is important. Putting critical information in writing helps you manage what you need to remember, and the very act of writing it down makes it easier to memorize the information later.

In short, the first step in building a better memory of what you read is to determine just what it is that you wish to recall. By extracting what is important from what is less crucial, you'll be able to limit the amount and extent of the material that you need to recall. You'll be able to focus on what you need to remember.

🔘 Organize Gather the Tools of the Trade

It's obvious that the primary item you'll need to complete a reading assignment is the material that you're reading. But there are other essential tools you should gather, potentially including the following:

> Pencils or pens to write notes in the margin.

> Highlighters to indicate key passages in the text.

> A copy of the assignment, so you'll be sure to read the right material.

> A pad of paper and/or index cards for note-taking if the material is particularly complex. If you routinely use a laptop to take notes, get it ready.

> A dictionary. You never know what new words you'll encounter while you're reading. If a dictionary is not handy, you'll be tempted to skip over unfamiliar words—a decision that may come back to haunt you. Note that some word-processing software includes a dictionary; there are also many good dictionaries available online (e.g., Merriam-Webster, at **m-w.com**, where you will also find an online thesaurus). The point is to use what's available—but use something!

Give Yourself Time

There's one more thing you need to prepare successfully for a reading assignment: enough time to complete it. The length of reading assignments is almost never ambiguous. You will typically be given a specific page range, so you will know just how much material you need to cover.

Now get a watch and time yourself as you read the first three pages of your assignment, being sure to pay attention to the material, not the time! Timing how long it takes to read a representative chunk of material provides you with a rough measure of your reading speed for the material—although it will vary even within a single reading assignment, depending on the complexity of the material.

You'll also need to consider an aspect of your personal learning style: your reading attention span. **Attention span** is the length of time that a person is usually able to sustain attention. People with a long attention span can read for relatively lengthy periods without getting jumpy, while those with a shorter attention span can only maintain attention for a short while. Get a general sense of your own attention span by completing **Try It! 3** "Discover Your Attention Span."

You can use the three pieces of information you now have—the length of the assignment, your per-page reading speed at full attention, and your typical attention span—to estimate roughly how long it will take you to complete the reading assignment. For example, if you are asked to read

Attention span
The length of time that attention is typically sustained

3 | TRY IT! [P O W E R]

Discover Your Attention Span

You should be aware of your attention span, the length of time you are usually able to sustain attention to a task, as you prepare for reading assignments. To get an idea of the length of your current attention span for reading, perform this exercise over the next few days.

1. Choose one of the textbooks that you've been assigned to read this semester.

2. Start reading a chapter, without any preparation, noting in the chart below the time that you start reading.

3. As soon as your mind begins to wander and think about other subjects, stop reading and note the time on the chart below.

4. Using the same textbook, but not the same passage, repeat this process four more times over the course of a few days, entering the data on the chart below.

5. To find your reading attention span, calculate the average number of minutes across the five trials.

Trial #1   Starting time: _____   Ending time: _____

Number of minutes between start and end times: _____

Trial #2   Starting time: _____   Ending time: _____

Number of minutes between start and end times: _____

Trial #3   Starting time: _____   Ending time: _____

Number of minutes between start and end times: _____

Trial #4   Starting time: _____   Ending time: _____

Number of minutes between start and end times: _____

Trial #5   Starting time: _____   Ending time: _____

Number of minutes between start and end times: _____

Reading attention span (the average of the number of minutes in the last column, found by adding up the five numbers and dividing by 5) = _____ minutes

---

Ask yourself these questions about your reading attention span:

1. Are you surprised by the length of your reading attention span? In what way?

2. Does any number in the set of trials stand out from the other numbers? For instance, is any number much higher or much lower than the average? If so, can you account for this? For example, what time of day was it?

3. Do the numbers in your trials show any trend? For instance, did your attention span tend to increase, decrease, or stay the same over the course of the trials? Can you explain any trends you may have noted?

4. Do you think your attention span times would be very different if you had chosen a different textbook? Why or why not?

5. What things might you do to improve your attention span?

To Try It online, go to the McGraw-Hill online resource.

12 pages; you have found that you need approximately 4 minutes to read a page; and your reading attention span is, on average, 25 minutes long, you can expect your reading to take at least 60 minutes, assuming you'll take a short break when your attention begins to fade after 25 minutes.

In addition, you may need to interrupt your reading to look up words in the dictionary, get a drink, stretch, or answer the phone. You may also decide to break your reading into several short sessions, in which case your total reading time may be greater since you will have to get re-acquainted with the reading assignment each time you approach it.

You can use this strategy to estimate the amount of time you will need for reading tasks outside the classroom, too. If your employer asks you to read a set of customer feedback forms, for example, you can figure out how much time in your day you'll need to block off to complete the work by factoring in the total length of all the forms, your per-page reading speed, and your attention span. Remember, though, that reading on the job is different from reading in a college or university library or at your desk at home. You can expect many more distractions as you try to read—co-workers asking questions, texts and emails coming in, the phone ringing. Take into account these inevitable workplace distractions when making your reading time estimate.

W Work Get the Most out of Your Reading

Once you've familiarized yourself with the material as a whole and gathered the necessary tools, it's time to get down to work and start reading. Here are several things that will help you get the most out of the reading process.

Stay Focused

The TV show you watched last night . . . your husband forgetting to meet you at the bus stop . . . the new toothbrush you need to buy for your daughter . . . your grumbling stomach. A million and one distractions can invade your thoughts as you read. Your job is to keep distracting thoughts at bay and focus on the material you are supposed to be reading. It's not easy, but the following are things you can do to help yourself stay focused:

> **Read in small bites.** If you think it is going to take you four hours to read an entire chapter, break up the four hours into more-manageable time periods. Promise yourself that you'll read for one hour in the afternoon, another hour in the evening, and the final two hours spaced out during the following day. One hour of reading is far more manageable than a four-hour block.

> **Take a break.** Plan to take several short breaks to reward yourself while you're reading, whether you are reading print material or online. During your breaks, do something enjoyable—eat a snack, watch a bit of a ball game on television, send a text message to a friend. Just try not to get drawn into your break activity to the point that it takes over your reading time.

> **Deal with mental distractions.** Sometimes problems have a way of popping into our minds and repeatedly distracting us. If a particular problem keeps interrupting your concentration—such as a difficulty you're having on the job—try to think of an action-oriented strategy

to deal with it. You might even write your proposed solution down on a piece of paper. Putting it down on paper can get the problem off your mind, making it less intrusive.

> **Manage interruptions.** There are some things you can do to reduce interruptions and their consequences. For instance, you can schedule reading to coincide with periods when you know you'll be alone. You can also plan to read less critical parts of assignments (such as the summaries or book frontmatter) when distractions are more likely, saving the heavier reading for later. Or, if you are a parent with small children, you can get your children involved in an activity that they can perform independently so you'll be free to concentrate.

If you are reading a long assignment, taking a break can be a reward and can reinvigorate you.
© Ian Shaw/Alamy

Write and Recite While You Read

For those of you who are avid readers or who have a read/write learning style, simply reading the material, which is the first "R" in SQ3R, might be enough to help you remember it. But if you lean more toward a visual/graphic or tactile/kinesthetic learning style, the physical act of writing as you read will actually be an important part of your approach to remembering what you read. If you haven't underlined, jotted notes to yourself, placed check marks on the page, drawn arrows, constructed diagrams, and otherwise defaced and disfigured your book while you're reading, you're not doing your job as a P.O.W.E.R. reader.

The idea of writing on a book page may go against everything you've been taught in the past. (And, of course, you should never write on a library book or one that you've borrowed.) However, once you've bought your book, you own it and you should make it your own. Don't keep your textbooks spotless so they will fetch a higher price if you sell them later. Instead, think of textbooks as documents recording your active learning and engagement in a field of study. In addition, you should look at your textbooks as the foundation of your personal library, which will grow throughout your lifetime. In short, writing extensively in your book while you're reading is an important tactic for achieving success. (For more on using textbooks, see the **Course Connections** feature on the next page.)

If you have an auditory/verbal learning style, an effective technique is to recite the material aloud as you read it—and recite, coincidentally, is the second "R" in SQ3R. As you learned in Chapter 1, auditory learners prefer to listen to material aloud or hear explanations rather than read them. For this type of learner, it is worth the extra effort to locate an audiobook version of the novel you are reading in English class, or search for a podcast on a particular topic you are discussing in class to reinforce your learning.

The ability to add your own personal notes, underline, and make other annotations to a clean text while you're reading is one of the reasons it usually pays to buy new, rather than used, textbooks. Why would you want a stranger's comments on something you own? Can you really trust that person's judgment over your own regarding what's important enough to underline? You can mark up new books in your own personal style, without the distraction of competing voices.

What should you be writing while you are reading? There are several things you should write down:

> **Rephrase key points.** Make notes to yourself, in your own words, about what the author is trying to get across. Don't just copy what's been said. Think about the material, and rewrite it in words that are your own.

Writing notes to yourself in your own words has several consequences, all good. First, you make the material yours; it becomes something you now understand and part of your own knowledge base. This is an aid to memorization. When you try to recollect your reading, you won't be trying to summon the thoughts of someone else; rather, you'll be trying to remember *your own* thinking.

Second, trying to summarize a key point in your own words will clarify for you whether you truly understand it. It's easy to be fooled into thinking we understand something as we're reading along. But the true test is whether we can explain it to ourselves (or someone else) on our own, without referring to the book or article.

Third, the very act of writing engages an additional type of perception, involving the physical sense of moving a pen or pressing the keys on a keyboard. This will help you learn the material in a more active way.

Finally, writing notes and phrases will help you study the material later. The key points will be highlighted, and your notes will also quickly bring you up to speed regarding your initial thoughts and impressions.

> **Highlight or underline key points.** Very often, the first or last sentence in a paragraph, or the first or last paragraph in a section, will

present a key point. Before you highlight anything, though, read the whole paragraph through. Then you'll be sure that what you highlight is, in fact, the key information. Topic sentences do not always fall at the beginning of a paragraph.

Be selective in your highlighting and underlining. A page covered in yellow highlighter may be artistically appealing, but it won't help you understand the material any better. Highlight only the key information. You might find yourself highlighting only one or two sentences or phrases per page. That's fine. In highlighting and underlining, less is more. One guideline: No more than 10 percent of the material should be highlighted or underlined.

Keep in mind as you highlight and underline that the key material you are marking is the material you will likely need to remember for exams or assignments. To aid in your recall of such material, read it over a time or two after you've marked it, and consider reading it aloud as well. This will reinforce the memories you are building of the essential points in the assignment.

> **Use arrows, diagrams, outlines, tables, timelines, charts, and other visuals to help you understand and later recall what you are reading.** If there are three examples given for a particular point, number them. If a paragraph discusses a situation in which an earlier point does not hold, link the original point to the exception by an arrow. If a sequence of steps is presented, number each step.

For example, if **Figure 3.1** (on the next page) were a single page of *P.O.W.E.R. Learning*, the annotations might look something like the handwritten notes in the left margin.

Particularly if your learning style is a visual one, representing the material graphically will get you thinking about it—and the connections and points in it—in new and different ways. Rather than considering the material solely in verbal terms, you now add visual images. The act of creating visual annotations will help you to both understand the material better and recall it later. Practise this technique on the sample textbook page in **Try It! 4** "Mark Up a Book Page" (pages 83–84)

> **Look up unfamiliar words in a dictionary.** Even though you may be able to figure out the meaning of an unfamiliar word from its context, use a dictionary anyway. This way you can be sure that what you think it means is correct. A dictionary will also tell you what the word sounds like, which may be important if your instructor uses the word in class.

Reading Goes Digital

"According to Maxwell Nicholson, the director of campaigns and community relations for the University of Victoria Student Society, over the last ten years, prices have risen four times the rate of inflation in the textbook industry."[2] For the 2016–2017 school year, Simon Fraser University in Burnaby, British Columbia, suggested that incoming students with a typical five-course load should budget around $1,020 for textbooks and supplies, more than 10 percent of their expected overall expenses for the year.[3] E-texts would seem to be the obvious answer to the rising cost of textbooks. They are less expensive than physical textbooks, and many e-reading devices incorporate features that make remembering material even easier. Yet when author of *Words Onscreen: The Fate of Reading in a Digital World* Naomi

figure 3.1 | Sample of Annotated Page

Highlight or underline key points.

Topic sentence ① **Highlight or underline key points.** Very often the first or last sentence in a paragraph, or the first or last paragraph in a section, will present a key point.

Read whole paragraph before highlighting Before you highlight anything, though, read the whole paragraph through. Then you'll be sure that what you highlight is, in fact, the key information. Topic sentences do not always fall at the beginning of a paragraph.

Be selective in your highlighting and underlining. A page covered in yellow highlighter may be artistically appealing, but it won't help you understand the material any better. Highlight only the key information. You might find yourself highlighting only one or two sentences or phrases per page. That's fine. In highlighting and underlining, less is more. One guideline: **No more than 10 percent of the material should be highlighted or underlined.**

Reread key points to help memory Keep in mind as you highlight and underline that the key material you are marking is the material you will likely need to remember for exams or class discussions. To aid in your recall of such material, read it over a time or two after you've marked it, and consider also reading it aloud. This will reinforce the memories you are building of the essential points in the assignment.

② **Use arrows, diagrams, outlines, tables, timelines, charts, and other visuals to help you understand and later recall what you are reading.** If there are three examples given for a particular point, number them. If a paragraph discusses a situation in which an earlier point does not hold, link the original point to the exception by an arrow. If a sequence of steps is presented, number each step.

Use visuals →

For example, if **Figure 3.1** were a single page of *P.O.W.E.R. Learning,* the annotations might look something like the handwritten notes in the left margin.

Particularly if your learning style is a visual one, representing the material graphically will get you thinking about it—and the connections and points in it—in new and different ways. Rather than considering the material solely in verbal terms, you can now add visual images. The act of creating visual annotations will both help you to understand the material better and help you to recall it later. Practise this technique on the sample textbook page in **Try It! 4,** "Mark Up a Book Page."

Look up words in dictionary **Look up unfamiliar words in a dictionary.** Even though you may be able to figure out the meaning of an unfamiliar word from its context, use a dictionary anyway. This way you can be sure that what you think it means is correct A dictionary will also tell you what the word sounds like, which may be important if your instructor uses the word in class.

Baron surveyed students on their choice of media for serious reading, she found that 92 percent preferred hard copy:[4] "Digital reading is increasingly popular and reading onscreen has many virtues, including convenience, potential cost-savings, and the opportunity to bring free access to books and other written materials to people around the world. Yet, Baron argues, the virtues of eReading are matched with drawbacks. Users are easily distracted by other temptations on their devices, multitasking is rampant, and screens coax us to skim rather than read in-depth."[5]

An academic research study concluded much the same thing: "participants identified several reasons for preferring print—mostly objecting to the e-textbook option, however: eyestrain from looking at the screen too long, difficulty reading on a small device such as a smartphone or tablet, limited attention span, and technical shortcomings ('I like paper books, they don't crash')."[6]

But like it or not, the trend toward owning tablets or e-readers is still on the upswing. By 2018, nearly half of all Canadians are expected to own a tablet,[7] and the Pew Internet Center in the United States found that 51 percent of adults owned a tablet by the end of 2016.[8] And while the vast majority of students still prefer print books, this is gradually changing.

4 | TRY IT! POWER

Mark Up a Book Page

DISCUSSION

First, working alone, read the excerpt in **Figure 3.2**. Then use the techniques we've discussed for marking up a page to highlight its key points.

figure 3.2 | Sample Page to Annotate

26 • **PART TWO:** *Social Thinking*

world, not … put our foot in our mouths every chance we get." Although a TV ad and commentary from a few politicians do not define the Canadian identity, the flavour of these does reflect distinctions within regional cultures in Canada.

The Self and Culture

So, imagine we replaced the word "Canadian" in the scale we did with some other word from our earlier list (maybe Catholic, or Muslim, or Aboriginal, or any other word that describes a group you belong to). Most of us have multiple identities (e.g., male, Muslim, Canadian and gay; Female, Baptist, Black, and straight), However, can these different identities cause conflict? Do you see conflict in the multiple identities that define who you are? Many immigrants, or children of recent immigrants, report high levels of inter-role conflict. Often, their life satisfaction and well-being is related to their ability to balance the values of their traditional culture with their new language and cultural reality (Lee & Chen, 2000; Liebkind & Jasinskaja-Lhati, 2000; Sam, 2000).

Culture The enduring behaviours, attitudes, and traditions shared by a large group of people and transmitted from one generation to the next.

Culture can be defined as the enduring behaviours, attitudes, and traditions shared by a large group of people and transmitted from one generation to the next For some people, especially those in industrialized Western cultures, individualism prevails as the self-concept. The psychology of Western culture assumes that your life will be enriched by defining your possible selves (that is, the person you could be) and believing in your power of personal control. By the end of the 20th century, individualism had become the dominant voice in Western culture.

Individualism The concept of giving priority to one's own goals over group goals and defining one's identity in terms of personal attributes rather than group identifications.

Cultures native to Asia, Africa, and Central and South America place a greater value on collectivism. They nurture what Shinobu Kitayama and Hazel Markus (1995) call the *interdependent self*. People are more self-critical and have less need for positive self-regard (Heine et al., 1999). Identity is defined more in relation to others. Malaysians, Indians, Japanese, and traditional Kenyans such as the Maasai, for example, are much more likely than Australians, Americans, and the British to complete an "I am…" statement with their group identities (Bochner, 1994; Dhawan et al., 1995; Ma & Schoeneman, 1997; Markus & Kitayama, 1991).

Collectivism Giving priority to the goals of one's groups (often one's extended family or work group) and defining one's identity accordingly.

However, making general statements about a culture's individualistic or collectivist orientations is oversimplified. Even within Canada, there are regional and ethnic differences as well. For example, people in Québec and Ontario tend to be more liberal, whereas people in Western Canada (particularly Alberta) tend to be more individualistic. Conservatives tend to be economic individualists ("don't tax or regulate me") and moral collectivists ("do legislate against immorality"). Liberals tend to be economic collectivists and moral individualists.

With an *inter*dependent self, one has a greater sense of belonging. Uprooted and cut off from family, colleagues, and loyal friends, interdependent people would lose the social connections that define who they are. They have not one self but many selves: self-with-parents, self-at-work, self-with-friends (Cross et al., 1992). As Figure 3-1 suggests, the interdependent self is embedded in social memberships. Conversation is less direct and more polite (Holtgraves, 1997). The goal of social life is not so much to enhance one's individual self as to harmonize with and support one's communities.

(continued)

(continued)

Next, compare and contrast your annotations with those of some classmates, and answer the following questions:

1. How do others' annotations differ from yours?

2. Why did they use the annotations they did?

3. Which annotation techniques worked best for you? Which did others prefer? Why?

4. How might these annotations help you remember what is important?

5. If there were different sorts of material presented on the page, such as mathematical formulas, would you use different kinds of annotations?

To Try It online, go to the McGraw-Hill online resource.

Add to this the fact that some programs in colleges and universities are now mandating that students buy their texts in digital form. For example, at Algonquin College in Ottawa, 10,000 students enrolled in the college's eTextbook programs in Fall 2014 were required to buy e-textbooks.[9]

So why else should you consider getting your textbooks on a digital device? Well, aside from e-texts being 40 to 50 percent cheaper than the list price of physical texts,[10] these devices offer features that can help you engage more with the material you are reading. The iPad, for instance, incorporates features that allow you to change font size, highlight and search text, and bookmark specific sections that you can return to later. For auditory learners, there is a built-in screen reader that will read you the page aloud. E-readers offer many of the same features, but at a lower price. **Figure 3.3** lists some advantages of using e-textbooks.

figure 3.3 | Advantages of E-textbooks

1. **Speed of delivery.** An e-textbook can be downloaded immediately as soon as the book is ordered. It is no longer necessary to wait for physical delivery of the books, which is a bonus if you need them in a hurry.

2. **Easily portable.** Published textbooks in physical form can be bulky and heavy. If you take several classes in a day, carrying half a dozen textbooks around campus can become cumbersome. Digital textbooks, on the other hand, can be carried on a small laptop or e-reader, enabling you to carry hundreds of them.

3. **Easy search.** The search functions make finding any information in the e-textbook quickly and easily. There is no need to go through the index pages or search for a specific paragraph. Most e-readers allow you to tag notes to specific words or paragraphs of a book. This helps you take clear notes in your digital textbooks.

4. **Highlighting.** The highlighting function allows you to mark important parts of the e-textbook for easy study later.

5. **Copy and paste.** The copy and paste functions allow you to quote sections of textbooks in your references, without having to re-type them.

6. **Audio.** E-textbooks can be easily converted to audio files, so you can listen to your lessons when driving or walking to school.

7. **Cheaper.** Digital textbooks are cheaper than traditional textbooks, sometimes as much as 50 to 70 percent cheaper than first edition print texts.

8. **Environmentally friendly.** Environmentally conscious students prefer leaving a smaller carbon footprint.

9. **Quick updates.** Traditional textbooks become obsolete quickly, while e-textbooks can be updated with current information.

10. **Font adjustments and nighttime reading.** E-readers make it convenient to adjust the size of the text and come with back lighting or built-in reading lights, making nighttime reading easy.

LO 3.2 Remembering Key Material

Many of the reading strategies discussed earlier will help fix key material in your mind. Rephrasing key points, highlighting or underlining essential material and then rereading it, and creating visuals will all help you recall the information you've read.

Sometimes, though, these strategies are not enough. You may need to remember a great deal of information, more than you'll be able to recall just through the process of reading, underlining, and so forth. Many people find this daunting. But one of the good things about the work of memorization is that you have your choice of literally dozens of techniques. Depending on the kind of material you need to recall and how much you already know about the subject, you can turn to any number of methods.

In his book *Smarter Faster Better*, Charles Duhigg recommends that "when we encounter new information, we should force ourselves to do something with it. Write a note explaining what you have just learned, or figure out a small way to test an idea, or graph a series of data points onto a piece of paper, or force yourself to explain an idea to a friend."[11] Engaging with the material leads to remembering it—and understanding it! As we sort through the various methods, keep in mind that no one strategy works by itself. (And some strategies don't seem to work at all; for example, forget about supplements like ginkgo biloba—there's no clear scientific evidence that they are effective.[12]) Instead, try the following proven strategies and find those that work best for you. Feel free to devise your own strategies or add those that have worked for you in the past.

Rehearsal

Say it aloud: rehearsal. Think of it in terms of the three syllables that make up the word: re–hear–sal. OK, one more time—say the word "rehearsal."

If you're scratching your head over the last paragraph, it's to illustrate the point of **rehearsal**: to transfer material that you encounter into memory. If you don't rehearse information in some way, it will end up like most of the information to which we're exposed—on the garbage heap of lost memory.

Rehearsing is the equivalent of **R**eciting in SQ3R. To test if you've succeeded in transferring the word "rehearsal" into your memory, put down this book and go off for a few minutes. Do something entirely unrelated to reading this book. Have a snack, catch up on the latest sports scores, or read the front page of the newspaper.

Are you back? If the word "rehearsal" popped into your head when you picked up this book again, you've passed your first memory test. You can be assured that the word "rehearsal" has been transferred into your memory.

Many of us can sing along to popular songs on the radio and know the lyrics by heart. That is because we hear and/or sing the songs over and over again. Rehearsal is the key strategy in remembering information. If you don't rehearse material, it will never make it into memory. Repeating the information, summarizing it, associating it with other memories, and above all thinking about it when you first come across it will ensure that rehearsal will be effective in pushing the material into memory. If you scored high on musical intelligence, try developing a rap or a rhyme to help you remember course material.

Mnemonics

This odd word (pronounced in an equally odd fashion, with the "m" silent— "neh MON ix") describes formal techniques used to make material more readily remembered. **Mnemonics** are the tricks of the trade that professional memory experts use and will probably appeal most to people with an auditory/verbal learning style and a high score on linguistic intelligence.

Among the most common mnemonics are **acronyms**. You're already well acquainted with acronyms—words or phrases formed by the first letters of a series of terms. For instance, although you may not have known it, the word "laser" is actually an acronym for "light amplification by stimulated emissions of radiation," and "radar" is an acronym for "radio detection and ranging." If you took music lessons, you may know that FACE spells out the names of the notes that appear in the spaces on the treble clef of the music staff (F, A, C, and E, starting at the bottom of the staff).

The benefit of acronyms is that they help us to recall a complete list of items. P.O.W.E.R. stands for—well, by this point in the book, you probably remember.

Another type of mnemonic is an **acrostic**—a sentence in which the first letters of the words correspond to something that needs to be recalled. After learning to use the acronym FACE to remember the notes on the spaces of the music staff, many beginning musicians learn that the names of the lines on the staff form the acrostic "Every Good Boy Deserves Fudge." The benefits—as well as the drawbacks—of acrostics are similar to those of acronyms. (You can explore acronyms and acrostics in **Try It! 5** "Do-It-Yourself Acronyms and Acrostics.")

Although mnemonics are helpful, keep in mind that they have a number of significant shortcomings. First, they don't focus on the meaning

Rehearsal
The process of practising and learning material to transfer it into memory

Mnemonics
Formal techniques used to make material more readily remembered

Acronyms
Words or phrases formed by the first letters of a series of terms

Acrostic
A sentence in which the first letters of the words correspond to material that is to be remembered

5 | TRY IT! ⬛POWER⬛

Do-It-Yourself Acronyms and Acrostics

In the first part of this Try It!, work individually to create an acronym and an acrostic.

1. Figure out an acronym to remind you of the names of the five Great Lakes, using the first letters of their names (Erie, Huron, Michigan, Ontario, Superior).

2. The eight multiple intelligences you learned about in Chapter 1 are the following: naturalist, interpersonal, intrapersonal, musical, bodily kinesthetic, logical-mathematical, spatial, and linguistic. Here is an acrostic to help you remember them: **N**umerous **I**dealistic **I**nventors **M**ake **B**itter **L**emons **M**ellow, **S**weet, and **L**uscious. Now, devise your own acrostic to help you remember the learning styles: read/write, visual/graphic, auditory/verbal, and tactile/kinesthetic. Then create another to help you remember the eight striving styles: leader, socializer, performer, adventurer, artist, intellectual, visionary, and stabilizer.

After you've tried to create the acronym and the acrostic, discuss your answers with your classmates:

1. How successful were you in devising effective acronyms and acrostics?

2. Do some of your classmates' creations seem more effective than others? Why?

3. Is the act of creating them an important component of helping to remember what they represent, or would having them created by someone else be as helpful in recalling them?

For your information, a common acronym for the Great Lakes is **HOMES** *(Huron, Ontario, Michigan, Erie, Superior).*

To Try It online, go to the McGraw-Hill online resource.

of the items being remembered. Because information that is learned in terms of its surface characteristics, such as first letters that form a word, is less likely to be retained than information that is learned in terms of its meaning, mnemonic devices are an imperfect route to memorization.

There's another problem with mnemonics: Sometimes it takes as much effort to create a mnemonic device as it would to memorize the material in the first place. And because the mnemonic itself has no meaning, it can be forgotten.

Despite their drawbacks, mnemonics can be useful. They are particularly helpful when the material being memorized includes a list of items or a series of steps.

Involve Multiple Senses

No matter what your learning style, the more senses you can involve when you're trying to learn new material, the better you'll be able to remember.

Here's why: Every time we encounter new information, all of our senses are potentially at work. For instance, if we witness a car crash, we receive sensory input from the sight of the two cars hitting each other, the sound of the impact, and perhaps the smell of burning rubber. Each piece of sensory information is stored in a separate location in the brain, and yet all the pieces are linked in extraordinarily intricate ways.

What this means is that when we seek to remember the details of the crash, recalling a memory of one of the sensory experiences—such as what we heard—can trigger recall of the other types of memories. For example, thinking about the *sound* the two cars made when they hit can bring back memories of the way the scene looked.

When you learn something, use your body. Don't sit passively at your desk. Instead, move around. Stand up; sit down. Touch the page. Trace figures with your fingers. Talk to yourself. Think out loud. It may seem strange, but doing this increases the number of ways in which the information is stored.

Visualize

Visualization
A memory technique by which images are formed to help recall material

Visualization is a technique by which images are formed to ensure that material is recalled. For instance, memory requires three basic steps: initially recording information; storing that information; and, ultimately, retrieving the stored information. As you read the three steps, you probably saw them as logical and straightforward processes. But how do you remember them?

You might visualize a computer, with its keyboard, flash drive and monitor (see **Figure 3.4**). The keyboard represents the initial recording of information. The flash drive represents the storage of information, and the monitor represents the display of information that has been retrieved from memory. If you can put these images in your mind, it will help you to remember the three basic memory steps later.

Overlearn

Think back to when you were learning your basic multiplication facts ($1 \times 1 = 1$, $2 \times 2 = 4$, and so forth). Let's suppose you had put each multiplication problem on a flash card, and you decided to go through your entire set of cards, trying to get every problem right.

The first time you went through the set of cards and answered all the problems correctly, would you feel as if you'd memorized them perfectly and believe that you'd never again make an error? You shouldn't. You would need several instances of perfect performance to be sure you had learned the multiplication facts completely.

Overlearning
Studying and rehearsing material past the point of initial mastery to the point at which recall becomes automatic

Lasting learning doesn't come until you have overlearned the material. **Overlearning** consists of studying and rehearsing material past the point of initial mastery. Through overlearning, recall becomes automatic. Rather than searching for a fact, going through mental contortions until perhaps the information surfaces, overlearning permits us to recall the information without even thinking about it.

To put the principle of overlearning to work, don't stop studying at the point when you can say to yourself, "Well, I'll probably pass this test." You may be right, but that's all you'll do—pass. Instead, spend extra time learning the material until it becomes as familiar as an old pair of jeans.

figure 3.4 | Visualizing Memory

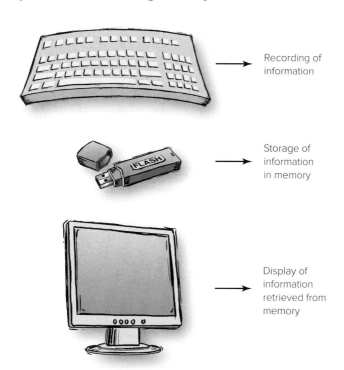

Recording of information

Storage of information in memory

Display of information retrieved from memory

LO 3.3 **E Evaluate** Evaluating What You Have Read

Evaluation is a crucial step in reading. You need to be able to answer the seemingly simple question, "What does all this mean?"

But there's another aspect to evaluation. You need to evaluate, truthfully and honestly, your own level of understanding. This process of evaluation will help you retain what you have read. What do you know as a result of your reading? Evaluation, then, consists of the following steps:

> **Identify the main ideas and themes and their value to you personally.** Try to determine the take-home message of the material you've read. For example, the take-home message of a chapter on accounting ethics might be: "Honest accounting practices benefit the long-term health of any business."

   Sometimes the main ideas and themes are spelled out, and at other times you will have to deduce them for yourself. Evaluating the main ideas and themes in terms of how they relate to you personally will help you understand and remember them more easily.

> **Prioritize the ideas.** Of all the information that is presented, which is the most crucial to the main message and which is the least crucial? List the main topics covered and try to rank them in order of importance.

> **Think critically about the arguments presented in the reading.** Do they seem to make sense? Are the author's assertions reasonable? Are there any flaws in the arguments? Would authors with a different point of view dispute what is being said? How would they build their own arguments?

> **Explain the material to someone else.** There is no better way to know if you understand the material than trying to explain it to someone else. Try explaining the material to a classmate who missed the assignment. In the absence of another person, you can use your smart phone or laptop to record yourself explaining the material and then play it back.

Talking out loud does two things. First, it helps you identify weak spots in your understanding and recall; talking to yourself will help you nail down concepts that are still not clear in your own mind. Second, and equally important, because you are transforming the written word into the spoken word, you are thinking about the information in another way, which will help you remember it better.

> **Use in-text and online review questions and tests.** Many textbook chapters end with a quiz or a set of review questions about the material or make these available on a companion website. Don't ignore them! Such questions indicate what the writer of the book thought was important for you to learn, and they can also provide an excellent opportunity to evaluate your memory.

> **Team up with a friend or use a study group.** When it comes to evaluating your understanding of a reading, two heads (or more!) are often better than one, particularly if you scored high on interpersonal intelligence back in Chapter 1. Working with a classmate or study group—especially with different preferred learning styles from your own—can help you test the limits of your understanding and memory of material and assess areas in which you need work.

> **Be honest with yourself.** Most of us are able to read with our minds on cruise control. But the net result is not much different from not reading the passage at all. If you have drifted off while you've been reading, go back and reread the passage.

☑ Rethink Getting It the Second Time

You're human, so—like the rest of us—when you finish a reading assignment you'd probably like nothing more than to heave a sigh of relief and put the book away.

As an experienced P.O.W.E.R. learner, by now you know that there's a key last step you should take that will assist you in cementing what you've learned in your memory: rethinking what you've read. If you do it within 24 hours of first reading the assignment, it can save you hours of work later. This review process also happens to be the third "R" in SQ3R: Going back to something you've read and reviewing it, along with any notes you've taken, is one of the most effective ways of remembering what you have read.

Yeah, right, you're probably thinking. *Like I have time for that.* The goal, though, is not a literal rereading. It isn't necessary to reread word for word. You already know what's important and what's not important, so you can skim some of the less important material. But it is wise to review the more difficult and important material carefully, making sure that you fully understand what is being discussed and that you'll remember the key details.

Career CONNECTIONS

The Job of Reading

Memos. Annual reports. Instructions. Continuing education assignments. Professional journals.

Each of these items illustrates the importance of developing critical reading skills for on-the-job success. Virtually every job requires reading expertise, and for some professions, reading is a central component. Polishing your reading skills will pay big dividends in the world of work. The better you are at absorbing and remembering written information, the better you'll be at your job.

For instance, in many corporations, vital information is transmitted through the written word, via emails, hard-copy memos, technical reports, or Web-based material. The job of repairing broken appliances or automobiles requires reading numerous service manuals to master the complex computer diagnostic systems that are now standard equipment. Nurses and others in the health-care field must read journals and reports to keep up with the newest medical technologies.

Furthermore, because not all supervisors are effective writers, you'll sometimes need to read between the lines and draw inferences and conclusions about what you need to do. You should also keep in mind that there are significant cultural differences in the way people write and the type of language they use. Being sensitive to the cultural background of colleagues will permit you to interpret and understand what you are reading more accurately.

In short, reading is a skill that's required in virtually every profession. Developing the habit of reading critically while you are in college or university will pave the way for future career success.

What's most critical, though, is that you think deeply about the material, considering the take-home message of what you've read. You need to be sure that your understanding is complete and that you're able to answer any questions that you had earlier about the material. Rethinking should be the central activity as you reread the passage and your notes.

The benefits of rethinking the material can't be overstated. Rethinking transfers material from your short-term memory to your long-term memory. It solidifies information so that it will be remembered far better over the long haul.

Time to Reflect: What **Did I Learn?**

1. Think about times when you read for pleasure compared with times when you read material for a class. How do the ways you read the two types of material differ?

2. Do you prefer reading traditional textbooks or e-texts? What are the reasons for your preference?

3. Based on what you learned about reading and remembering in this chapter, what do you plan to do differently to help you remember what you read in the future? Be specific.

Did You Know?

Canadians read more than than their American counterparts. Eighty-four percent of Canadians read at least one book in 2014, compared to 72 percent of Americans. For 18- to 29-year-olds, 88 percent of Canadians read at least one book, versus 80 percent of Americans in the the same age group. Of that group of young Canadians, 77 percent had read a printed book, 47 percent had read an e-book, and 23 percent had read an audiobook.[13]

Looking Back

What are the essential elements of successful reading?

> The most important aspect of reading is comprehension, not speed. Finishing a reading assignment quickly is far less important than understanding it fully.

> One problem people have with reading is a limited attention span. However, attention span can be increased with self-awareness and practice.

How can I improve my concentration and read more effectively?

> Reading should be approached with a clear sense of purpose and goals, which will vary from assignment to assignment. Examining the frontmatter of a book and creating advance organizers are useful strategies.

> As your read, identify and focus on the key material you will need to remember later. Don't try to memorize everything you read.

> Maintain focus by breaking down the reading into small chunks, taking breaks as needed, dealing with distractions, and writing while reading.

What are some techniques I can use to remember large amounts of information?

> Many techniques are available to improve your memory. Rehearsal is a primary one, as is the use of mnemonics such as acronyms and acrostics. Engaging with the material is another.

> Visualization and using multiple senses are also excellent techniques to help you learn new material.

> Overlearning is a basic principle of remembering.

How can I best retain what I have read?

> Understanding of reading assignments can be cemented in memory by identifying the main ideas, prioritizing them, thinking critically about the arguments, using in-text questions and tests, and explaining the writer's ideas to someone else.

> Quickly rereading assignments and the notes you took as you read can greatly help solidify your memory of the material.

RESOURCES

ON CAMPUS

If you are experiencing unusual difficulties in reading or remembering material, you may have a learning disability, as discussed in Chapter 10. If you suspect this is the case, take action. Many colleges and universities have an office that deals specifically with learning disabilities. You can also talk to someone at your college or university counselling centre; they will arrange for you to be tested, and this process can determine whether you have a problem.

Once again, don't forget that your instructors can be a great source of information!

IN PRINT

The seventh edition of Janet Elder and Joe Cortina's book *Opening Doors: Understanding College Reading* (McGraw-Hill, 2013) provides a complete set of guidelines for reading textbooks and other kinds of writing that you will encounter during college or university. Another useful volume is the eleventh edition of *Breaking Through: College Reading* (Pearson, 2015) by Brenda D. Smith and LeeAnn Morris.

For a fascinating look into memory and its impact on our lives, read *Moonwalking with Einstein* by Joshua Foer (Penguin Press, 2012). Foer takes us into the world of competitive memorizers and describes his unlikely journey into the finals of the U.S. Memory Championships.

You'll also want to check out Dr. Eric R. Braverman's *Younger Brain, Sharper Mind: A 6-Step Plan for Preserving and Improving Memory and Attention at Any Age from America's Brain Doctor* (Rodale Books, Reprinted 2013).

ON THE WEB

The following websites provide an opportunity to extend your learning about the material in this chapter:

> Check out this excellent three-minute video on how to help remember what you read. It is an interview with Dr. Cynthia R. Green, psychologist and author of *Total Memory Workout: Eight Easy Steps to Maximum Memory Fitness* (**howdini.com/howdini-video-6635124.html**).

> *Increasing Textbook Reading Comprehension by Using SQ3R* is the title of this site offered by Virginia Tech University (**ucc.vt.edu/academic_support_students/online_study_skills_workshops/SQ3R_improving_reading_comprehension/index.html**). Offered here is a clear and detailed outline on how to use the SQ3R reading method, as well as links to other reading comprehension aids, such as critical reading, proofreading, and selective reading.

> Need a mnemonic? Have one you'd like to share? Then just go to **mnemonic-device.com**, a site devoted entirely to mnemonics. This fun and educational site covers a variety of subjects, from arithmetic to weather.

> *Mind Tools* is a website worth visiting. It offers a number of free online articles on a wide range of topics, including reading strategies (**mindtools.com/rdstratg.html**), techniques for improving memory (**mindtools.com/memory.html**), and the SQ3R approach to reading (**mindtools.com/pages/article/newISS_02.htm**).

THERE'S AN APP FOR THAT

> Probably the best known memory app is Lumosity, available for either Android or iOS.

> For Android, check out memory apps Memory Trainer and Brain Workout.

> For iOS devices, FitBrains Trainer is a popular memory app.

TAKING IT TO THE WEB

1 Go to a newspaper's website, such as that of The *Globe and Mail* (**theglobeandmail.com**) or the *Calgary Herald* (**calgaryherald.com/**), and read one of the current editorials, which you can find in the Opinions section. Highlight key points of the editorial. Look up unfamiliar words in the dictionary. Make notes on what you've read. Review your notes. Then, with a classmate, recount the main points made in the editorial.

2 Practise the rehearsal technique for storing information in memory. Go to **canadaspremiers.ca/en/about** to find the names of five Canadian premiers. Repeat the names several times. Now explore another, unrelated site on the Web. After a few minutes, write down the names of the five premiers from memory. How did you do?

THE CASE OF . . .
The Five-Pound Reading Packet

The instructor dropped the thick packet of course readings on Anjana Fernandes's desk. It landed with a loud thunk.

"We'll be reading this packet over the next four weeks," the instructor announced.

But staring at the packet, all Anjana could think was, "I don't think I could even lift that, let alone read it in just a month!"

Sure, Anjana was interested in the topics of the readings. They all dealt with the history of computer programming, and Anjana was in university to get her degree in that field. She told herself a lot of the information in the readings would probably be very useful, both in university and throughout her programming career.

But all Anjana could focus on as she stared at the packet were nagging questions: How could she possibly read all of it in four weeks? How would she remember all that material for tests or on the job? And perhaps most urgently of all, how would she even get the massive packet home?

1. How would you advise Anjana to prepare for her course reading?

2. How would you suggest Anjana organize her time so she can finish the readings in the allotted four weeks?

3. How might Anjana stay focused on her reading? How might she most effectively use writing as a way to accomplish her task?

4. What techniques might Anjana use to memorize long lists or other key material from her reading?

5. In what ways can Anjana use rethinking techniques to improve her understanding of the readings in the packet?

CHAPTER 4
Taking Notes

Learning Outcomes

By the time you finish this chapter, you will be able to

LO 4.1 Identify the characteristics of effective notes.

LO 4.2 Demonstrate the various methods of note-taking: outlining, the Cornell method, concept mapping, and using a Microsoft PowerPoint handout.

LO 4.3 Demonstrate how to take study notes, which are created to review material.

As he took a seat in the front row of his marketing class in his second term of college, Matt Ortiz realized that something fundamental had changed.

For the whole first term, Matt had sat in the back of the room during classes, just as he'd done in high school. He figured that just showing up to class was all that mattered. What difference did it make where he sat? And what difference would it make if he occasionally sent text messages on his cellphone?

But then he had received mostly Cs in his first-term courses.

In a note-taking workshop Matt enrolled in after the term ended, he learned the importance of active listening and taking good notes in class. He also learned that one way to become more engaged in class is to sit close to the instructor.

Trying out the strategies he was taught in the workshop, Matt found—a bit to his surprise—that they helped. By the end of the term, he'd pulled his grades way up.

Looking Ahead

Matt Ortiz's move from the back to the front of the classroom is both a source and a symbol of his academic success. Matt's ability to take good notes is also likely to pay future dividends, because note-taking skills not only help produce academic success in college or university but also contribute to career success.

In this chapter, we discuss effective strategies for taking notes during class lectures, during other kinds of oral presentations, and from written sources such as textbooks. There's a lot more to good note-taking than you probably think—and a lot less if you view note-taking as "getting everything down on paper." As we explore the ins and outs of note-taking, we'll pause along the way to discuss the tools of the note-taking trade, how to be an active learner, and how to think your way to good notes.

LO 4.1 Taking Notes in Class

Why take notes in class? Because the simple act of taking notes—of engaging with the material—can help your recall.

There's no need to go to extremes. You know the type: the student who desperately tries to write down everything the instructor says. No spoken word goes unwritten. And you think to yourself, "If only I took such thorough notes—I'd do much better in my classes."

Contrary to what many students think, good note-taking does not mean writing down every word an instructor utters. With note-taking, less is often more. We'll see why as we consider the basic steps in P.O.W.E.R. note-taking.

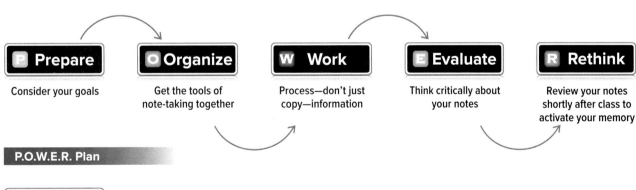

P Prepare	**O** Organize	**W** Work	**E** Evaluate	**R** Rethink
Consider your goals	Get the tools of note-taking together	Process—don't just copy—information	Think critically about your notes	Review your notes shortly after class to activate your memory

P.O.W.E.R. Plan

P Prepare Consider Your Goals

As with other academic activities, preparation is a critical component of note-taking. The following steps will prepare you for action:

> **Identify the instructor's goals for the course.** On the first day of class, most instructors talk about their objectives, what they hope you'll

get out of the class, and what you'll know when it's over. Most instructors restate the information on the class syllabus or course outline, the written document that explains the learning outcomes for the course, the learning objectives for each class, and the reading and assignments for the term. For example, they may say that they want you to "develop an appreciation for the ways that statistics is used in everyday life." The information you get during that first session and through the syllabus is critical. If the instructor's goals aren't stated explicitly, you should consider discussing them with the instructor after class.

> **Identify your own goals for the course.** In addition to those "external" goals, you should have your own goals. What is it you want to learn from the course? What kind of grade do you want, and what are you prepared to do to obtain it? How will the information from the course help you enhance your knowledge, improve your career prospects, and achieve your dreams?

> **Complete assignments before coming to class.** Always go to class prepared. Complete all of your reading and other assignments beforehand. Instructors assume that their students have done what they've assigned, and their lectures are based on that assumption. It's virtually impossible to get the gist of a lecture if you haven't completed the reading or the assignments. Good note-taking requires being prepared to listen to the material.

> **Be willing to make suggestions to the instructor that can help enhance your note-taking.** For example, if you have a visual/graphic learning style, you may want to suggest that the instructor put an agenda or outline of the main topics on the board or screen at the beginning of class, to help you follow how the information being presented that day is connected. You may also want to ask the instructor if they would be willing to post their slides ahead of time on the course website or learning management system (LMS). Students with an auditory/verbal learning style may want to ask for permission to record the lecture, or they may want to find out if a podcast is available.

> **Accept the instructor, whatever their teaching style.** Not every instructor teaches in the same way. Accept the fact that, just as students have different learning styles, instructors may approach teaching in different ways. Ultimately, it's your responsibility to adapt to an instructor's teaching style. When an instructor's teaching style does not fit well with your learning style, you must not use this as an excuse to do poorly or to give up. You cannot afford to let this get in the way of your education or interfere with your goals. If you need extra help or clarification, don't be afraid to approach the instructor and ask for it. If need be, investigate whether your college or university offers tutoring, which is often provided at no cost to you.

> **Perform a pre-class warm-up.** No, this doesn't mean doing stretches just before each class. As you head to class or settle into your seat, skim your notes from the previous lecture, looking over what the instructor said and where that lecture left off. You should also briefly review the main headings or summary section of the readings you've been assigned.

The warm-up doesn't have to be long. The goal is simply to refresh yourself, to get yourself into the right frame of mind for the class.

> **Choose a seat that will promote good note-taking.** You should certainly choose a seat that permits you to see and hear clearly, but

there's more to your choice than that. Picking the right seat in a classroom can make a big difference.

Where is the best place to sit? Usually it's front and centre. Instructors make more eye contact with the people near them, and they often believe that the best, most-engaged students sit closest.

Furthermore, sitting in the back of the class may make you feel disengaged and out of touch with what is happening at the front of the room. In turn, this lack of engagement may make it easier for your mind to wander.

Sometimes distracting seats have less to do with location and more to do with the person sitting next to you. Don't be afraid to put some physical distance between yourself and a distracting neighbour.

© Image Source

⊙ Organize Get the Tools of Note-Taking Together

If You Prefer to Go "Old School"

Do you have a favourite pen? A preferred type of notebook?

Most of us have distinct tastes in the type of tools we use for various tasks: a favourite screwdriver, a preferred style of mouse, a brand of running shoes we find most comfortable. You should determine your preferred classroom "tools," too. Taking your favourite kind of notebook and pen to class can give you the confidence and focus you need to take effective notes.

There are several things to consider as you prepare for class:

> **Choose the appropriate writing tool.** Generally, using a pen is better than using a pencil. Ink is less likely to smudge, and what you produce with ink is usually brighter and clearer—and therefore easier to use when studying. On the other hand, for math and accounting classes, where you may be copying down or even working through formulas in class, a pencil might be better, because it's easier to erase if you make a mistake when copying detailed, complex information.

> Sometimes you may want to use a combination of pen and pencil. And in some cases you might use several different pen colours, or highlighting markers. One colour might signify important information that the instructor mentions will be on the test. Another colour might be reserved for definitions or material that is copied from the board. And a third might be used for general notes on the lecture.

> **Choose a notebook that assists in note-taking.** Loose-leaf notebooks are particularly good for taking notes because they permit you to go back later and change the order of the pages or add additional material in the appropriate spot. But whatever kind of notebook you use, use only one side of the page for writing—keep one side free of notes. There may be times when you're studying when you'll want to

When you review your notes, do so with an eye to improving them. If any information is not entirely clear, change the wording in your notes, adding to or amending what's there. If certain words are hard to read, fix them. It won't be any easier to read them the night before a test; chances are you'll have even more trouble.

If, on rethinking the material, you don't understand something, ask your instructor or a friend to clarify it. And when you receive an explanation, add it to your notes so you won't forget it. (You might want to use a different-coloured pen for additions to your notes, so you'll know they came later.)

> **Think critically about the material in your notes.** As you review the information, think about the material from a critical point of view. Go beyond the facts and pieces of information, integrating and evaluating the material.

In addition, as you rethink your notes, don't think of them only in terms of a single lecture or a single class. Take a longer view. Ask yourself how they fit into the broader themes of the class and the goals that you and the instructor have for the term. How will the information be useful to you? Why did the instructor emphasize a particular point?

To practise the techniques we've been discussing, complete **Try It! 4** "Practise Your Note-Taking Skills."

---

4 | TRY IT! POWER

Practise Your Note-Taking Skills

Practise your note-taking skills, using any techniques you find helpful, in one of the classes you are enrolled in this term. Analyze your notes to answer these questions:

1. Which specific techniques did I use in taking notes?

2. Which of the note-taking techniques detailed in this chapter was I unable to use, and why?

3. Could I take the notes I made in class and redo them, using one of the techniques in this chapter, such as creating a concept map?

After you have taken notes, use the techniques discussed in this chapter to evaluate and rethink them. Creating a concept map on a separate sheet of paper may be particularly helpful.

To Try It online, go to the McGraw-Hill online resource.

LO 4.3 Creating Study Notes

Weighing as much as 2.5 kilograms, bulky and awkward, and filled with more information than you think anyone could ever need to know, it's the meat and potatoes of post-secondary work: your course textbook. You might feel intimidated by its size; you might be annoyed at its cost; you might think you'll never be able to read it, let alone understand, learn, and recall the material in it. How will you manage?

The answer involves taking **study notes**, notes taken for the purpose of reviewing material. They are the kinds of notes that you take now to study from later.

Here are some suggestions for creating study notes:

Study notes
Notes taken for the purpose of reviewing material

> **Integrate your text notes into your study notes.** Start by annotating the pages, using the techniques that work best for you: highlighting, underlining, circling, and/or making marginal notes. Keep in mind that writing on the text, by itself, is not sufficient to promote learning; it's what you do *next* that counts.
>
> Specifically, after you've finished reading and annotating the material, create study notes. The study notes should summarize the key points, in outline form or in the form of concept maps. Either form of summary should supplement the annotations you've made on the printed page.
>
> Furthermore, any notes you take should stand on their own; that is, they should include enough information to be useful whether or not you have the book or article on hand.

> **Use flash cards.** If you feel confident that the annotations you've written in the book are sufficiently comprehensive, you might consider taking notes on flash cards. **Flash cards** are simply index cards that contain key pieces of information that you need to remember.
>
> Flash cards are particularly useful in subjects that present many small bits of information to remember, such as technical vocabulary words or scientific formulas. When you need to learn a new term, for instance, you can write the term on one side of a card and its definition on the other side.
>
> One of the greatest virtues of flash cards is their portability. Because they are small, they can fit into your pocket or handbag, and you can look at them at odd times when you have a spare moment.

Flash cards
Index cards that contain key pieces of information to be remembered

> **Create a separate glossary or definitions page.** Having all the definitions in one place can make studying easier.
> **Keep your notes organized by the chapter they refer to.** Put the date of the lecture on them. Add a reference in your notes to the textbook page they refer to, and vice versa, making it easier for you when it comes time to study and review for a quiz or test.

Career CONNECTIONS

Taking Notes on the Job: Meetings of the Minds

The principles of good note-taking discussed in this chapter are useful in the classroom, and they can also help you as you make your way in your career. For instance, you may need to take notes on lengthy memos or reports that detail company procedures you will need to master for your job.

Further, one of the most important settings in which you'll want to take effective notes is in meetings. Meetings take up a good part of many people's professional workdays, and being able to take effective notes can provide a significant career advantage.

Meetings are similar to class discussions. During a meeting, you will want to look for key topics and make note of the ideas that receive the most emphasis or enthusiastic response. Note these areas and keep them in mind as likely priorities.

During meetings, tasks are often assigned. You will want to note clearly what you are supposed to do and when you are supposed to do it, and keeping track of what others are doing will also be helpful, because you may need to get information from them or otherwise coordinate efforts. For instance, if you are assigned the task of managing the development of your company's website, you'll want to clarify in your notes which person has agreed to do which portion of the task.

Taking notes when others are speaking also shows that you are paying attention to what the speaker is saying. It's a kind of compliment that suggests you find what the speaker is saying to be so important that you will want to refer to it later.

Finally, note-taking plays another role: It can make seemingly interminable meetings appear to proceed faster by providing something for you to do that's more active than simply listening. In short, not only can note-taking provide you with a clear record of what occurred in a meeting, but it can also keep you engaged in what is going on.

Time to Reflect: What **Did I Learn?**

1.   Overall, how effective are your current note-taking techniques?

2.   Describe the way(s) in which you think your note-taking style is a reflection of your learning style.

3.   Based on what you learned about note-taking in this chapter, what do you plan to do differently in the future? Be specific.

Did You Know?

"The United States and Canada are the world's largest producers of paper and paper products.... In the last 20 years, the usage of paper products has increased from 92 million tons [1 ton = 2,000 pounds] to 208 million, which is a growth of 126%.... Americans still consume more paper per capita—upwards of 500 lbs. annually—than anyone else on earth."[4]

Looking Back

What is effective note-taking?

> The central feature of good note-taking is listening and distilling important information, rather than writing down everything that is said.

How can I take good notes in class?

> Prepare for taking notes by identifying the instructor's and your own goals for the course, completing all assignments before arriving in class, and warming up for class by reviewing the notes and assignments from the previous class.

> Before writing notes, listen to the instructor and carefully process the information that the instructor is attempting to deliver.

> One note-taking method is to take down notes as brief phrases rather than full sentences and, if possible, in outline form to reveal the structure of the lecture. Other methods include the Cornell method, concept mapping, and Microsoft PowerPoint handouts. Material written on the board should usually be copied word for word.

> Before leaving class, evaluate your notes, verifying that they are complete and easy to understand, while you can still recall what was said.

> As soon as possible after class, integrate your text and class notes to create a set of study notes that you can use for quizzes or tests.

RESOURCES

ON CAMPUS

If you are having difficulty taking class notes effectively, talk with your course instructor. Bring your notes with you soon after a class has ended, and let the instructor assess what you are doing correctly and what could stand improvement.

If your problems persist, and you have great difficulty translating the spoken word into notes, then there's a small possibility that you suffer from an auditory learning disability. Be tested by your campus learning disabilities office or counselling office to rule this out.

And, once again, don't forget that your instructors can be a great source of information!

IN PRINT

Check out Fiona McPherson's *Effective Notetaking,* 2nd edition (Wayz Press, 2013), which goes into depth on topics such as highlighting and summarizing text.

Described as "brilliant" by mind-mapping blogger Chuck Frey, Michael Rohde's *The Sketchnote Handbook: The Illustrated Guide* (Peachpit Press, 2012) is a visual/graphic learner's dream guide to note-taking through sketching.

ON THE WEB

The following websites provide an opportunity to extend your learning about the material in this chapter:

> Mount Royal University in Calgary provides some excellent note-taking tips on its website (**mtroyal.ca/AcademicSupport/ResourcesServices/ StudentLearningServices/StudyingWritingEffectively/notetaking.htm**).

> California Polytechnic State University offers a good overview of several note-taking systems: Cornell, outline, mapping, charting, and sentence methods (**sas.calpoly.edu/asc/ssl/notetakingsystems.html**).

THERE'S AN APP FOR THAT

> Xmind describes itself as the "most popular mind mapping software on the planet" and is available for both Android and iOS.

> Evernote is a robust multi-platform note-taking app that automatically processes, indexes, and allows you to organize and search text-based notes, photos of notes (e.g., notes on a whiteboard), webpages, and screenshots.

> Squid (formerly Papyrus) is an Android note-taking app that allow you to hand-write your notes with a stylus.

TAKING IT TO THE WEB

1 The best way to improve note-taking skills is to practise. One possible strategy is to go to the home page for Canoe.ca, a well-known Canadian website (**canoe.ca**). Click on one of the categories (e.g., Money, Lifewise, etc.), look for a story that sounds interesting, and take notes while reading it.

2 Taking notes during lectures is an important part of classroom learning, but keeping up with a speaker for an entire hour can be difficult. You can improve your note-taking skills for lectures by taking notes while listening to recorded speeches on the Internet. For example, go to the TED site (**ted.com/talks/steve_jobs_how_to_live_before_you_die.html**) and listen to Apple and Pixar co-founder, the late Steve Jobs, and his inspiring commencement speech to a Stanford graduating class. Take notes while listening to the speech. Afterward, go back and indicate the key points and terms. You can check your comprehension by comparing the speech to news articles reporting on it. (You can also check the articles for bias!)

3 Finally, there are some excellent videos on YouTube about the Cornell style of note-taking—Google it!

THE CASE OF . . .
Not Missing a Thing

Some people write down a few things in class. Others write down most things. Jennifer Beck wrote down *everything*.

The woman was virtually a human dictation machine. She spent her time in class in a whirlwind of note-taking, writing down in a clear, meticulous script seemingly every word her instructor uttered. By the end of a term, her notebooks were so lengthy that they approached the size of telephone books from a small city.

Yet despite her thorough notes, Jennifer was only a mediocre student. She was a hard worker and studied her many notes thoroughly before tests. But she never managed to get grades higher than a C+. It seemed unbelievable to her. She worked incredibly hard in class taking good notes. Why wasn't it paying off?

1. How do you think Jennifer defines "good note-taking"?

2. Why does Jennifer's method of note-taking produce such poor results? What is she missing?

3. If you asked Jennifer to summarize the instructor's main ideas after a class lecture, how successful do you think she would be? Why?

4. Do you think it would be easy or hard to study for a final exam using Jennifer's notes? Why?

5. Do you think Jennifer evaluates her notes during or after class? Do you think she ever rethinks them? What questions would you ask to help her perform these steps?

6. In general, what advice would you give Jennifer on note-taking?

CHAPTER 5
Taking Tests

Learning Outcomes

By the time you finish this chapter, you will be able to

LO 5.1   Employ various strategies to prepare for tests.

LO 5.2   Discuss effective strategies for writing tests.

LO 5.3   Analyze the strengths and weaknesses of your performance on a test.

Months of study and classes and reading and commuting to and from his college . . . and now it all came down to one exam.

That was the thought that ran through Rob Smythe's head as he sat down to take the final exam in his computer programming course. Rob knew the test would count for 65 percent of his final grade. If he passed, he would have enough credits to get the graphic design diploma he'd been working toward for years. If he failed—well, Rob tried not to think about that.

He'd taken tests before, but the stakes had never been so high for a single exam. Although he was fairly confident—he had studied hard—he couldn't altogether relax. He told himself that he had always done well on tests in the past; he wasn't going to fail now. But still, Rob couldn't help but feel as if his entire school career, maybe his entire future, was on the line.

Looking Ahead

Although most tests are not as critical as Rob's computer programming final, tests do play a significant role in everyone's academic life. Students typically experience more anxiety over tests than over anything else in their college or university careers. If you're returning to post-secondary education after a long break, or perhaps struggled with tests earlier in your academic career, you may find the prospect of taking a test especially intimidating.

But tests don't have to produce so much anxiety. There are strategies and techniques you can learn to reduce your fear of test-taking. In fact, learning how to take tests is, in some ways, as important as learning the content that they cover. Taking tests effectively involves mastering information, but it also requires mastering specific test-taking skills.

One of the most important goals of this chapter is to take the mystery out of the whole process of taking tests. To do that, you'll learn about the different types of tests and about strategies you can start using even before you take a test. You'll gain insight into how different kinds of tests work and how best to approach them. As well, you'll learn about the various types of test questions and strategies for responding most effectively to each type.

This chapter also explores two aspects of test-taking that may affect your performance: test anxiety and cramming. You will learn ways to deal with your anxiety and strategies to keep cramming to a minimum—but you will also learn how to make the most of cramming, if you do have to resort to it.

The chapter ends with suggestions for evaluating your performance toward the end of a test as well as after it's been graded, to learn how to improve your performance the next time around.

What Tests Measure

Tests may be the most unpopular part of college and university life. Students hate them because they produce fear, anxiety, and apprehension about being evaluated, and they focus on grades instead of learning for learning's sake. Instructors often don't like them very much either, because they produce fear, anxiety, and apprehension about being evaluated, and they focus on grades instead of learning for learning's sake. That's right: Students and instructors dislike tests for the very same reasons.

But tests are also valuable. A well-constructed test identifies what you know and what you still need to learn. Tests help you see how your performance compares with that of others. And knowing that you'll be tested on a body of material is likely to motivate you to learn the material more thoroughly.

However, there's another reason you might dislike tests: You may assume that tests have the power to define your worth as a person. If you do badly on a test, you may be tempted to believe that you've received some fundamental information about yourself from the instructor and the educational institution, information that says you're a failure in some significant way.

This is a dangerous—and wrong-headed—assumption. If you do badly on a test, it doesn't mean you're a bad person. Or stupid. Or that you don't belong in college or university. If you don't do well on a test, you're the same person you were before you took the test—no better, no worse. You just did badly on a test. Period.

In short, tests are not a measure of your value as an individual. They are only a measure of how well (and how much) you studied, and your test-taking skills.

Tests are tools; they are indirect and imperfect measures of what we know. Someone with a great deal of knowledge can do poorly on a test; tension or going too slowly can lead to unwelcome results in some cases. Another person may know considerably less and still do well on the test simply because they have learned some test-taking skills along the way.

How we do on a test depends on a number of considerations: the kind of test it is; the subject matter involved; our understanding of test-taking strategies; and, above all, how well we prepare for it. Let's turn, then, to the first step in test-taking: preparation. (The five steps are summarized in the P.O.W.E.R. Plan below.)

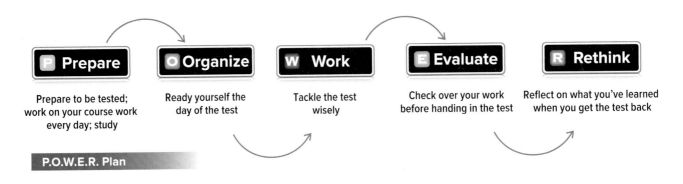

P Prepare	**O** Organize	**W** Work	**E** Evaluate	**R** Rethink
Prepare to be tested; work on your course work every day; study	Ready yourself the day of the test	Tackle the test wisely	Check over your work before handing in the test	Reflect on what you've learned when you get the test back

P.O.W.E.R. Plan

LO 5.1 **P** Prepare

Preparing to Be Tested

Preparation for tests requires a number of strategies. Many of the most important are listed below.

Course Work as Test Preparation

Many of the things you do during a course will help prepare you for a test. There is no surer way to get good grades on tests than to take these steps:

> **Read** assigned chapters before every class.

> **Attend** class faithfully and pay attention while you are there.

> **Review** your notes following each class.

> **Create** a set of study notes, as described in **Chapter 4.**

> **Complete** all assignments, and review the instructor's feedback when you receive the assignment back.

Preparing for tests is a long-term proposition. It's not a matter of giving your all the night before the test. Instead, it's a matter of giving your all to *every* aspect of the course, throughout the semester.

Know What to Prepare For

Determine as much as you can about the test before you begin to study for it. The more you know about a test beforehand, the more efficient your studying will be.

To find out about an upcoming test, ask these questions of your instructor:

> Is the test called a "test," an "exam," a "quiz," or something else? Is the assignment just an assignment, or is it a "term project"? As you can see in **Table 5.1,** the names imply different things. For simplicity's sake, we'll use the term "test" throughout this chapter; but you need to know that these distinctions exist, and they should affect the way you prepare.

> What material, that is, which chapters, will the test cover?

> How many questions will be on it and what will they be worth?

> Will there be a choice of which questions to answer?

> What is the format of the test (e.g., multiple choice, short answer, essay), and what percentage of the test marks will be allocated to each question type?

table 5.1	Quizzes, Tests, Exams, Assignments, Term Projects . . . What's in a Name?

Although they may vary from one instructor to another, the following definitions are most commonly used.

Quiz: A quiz is a brief assessment, usually covering a relatively small amount of material. Some quizzes cover as little as one class's worth of reading. Although a single quiz usually doesn't count for very much, instructors often add quiz scores together, and collectively they can become a significant part of your final course grade.

Test: A test is a more extensive, more heavily weighted assessment than a quiz, covering more material. A test may come every few weeks of the term, often after each third or quarter of the term has passed, but this varies with the instructor and the course.

Exam: An exam is the most substantial kind of assessment. In many courses, just one exam is given—a final exam at the end of the term. Sometimes there are two exams, one at the midpoint of the term (called, of course, a midterm) and the second at the end. Exams are usually weighted quite heavily because they are meant to assess your knowledge of all the course material covered up to that point. A comprehensive exam is usually an exam that covers all material in the course.

Assignment: An assignment usually is done individually outside class, has a relatively narrow focus, and is not worth more than 10 to 15 percent of your final grade. It may involve researching a specific topic or reading a particular article and providing your own perspective on it. Where possible, you should ask the instructor if a *marking rubric* is available for the assignment, so you can see how marks will be allocated and, as a result, how to allocate your time and effort.

Term project: A term project is completed, for the most part, outside class, may be done individually or in a group, and usually spans the full semester or term. It is usually broad in focus, and it can be worth a significant portion of your final grade, depending on the course. Analyzing the state of an entire industry and the major competitors within it is an example of a term project. Again, you should ask your instructor if a marking rubric is available so you can see how marks will be allocated and where you should put most of your effort.

> What tools will I need to bring? Is it open book? Can I bring a dictionary? Do I need a calculator? Do I need both a pen and a pencil?

> How much time is it expected to take? A full class period? Only part of a period?

> Will sample questions be provided? Will you provide a review before the test?

> Are tests from previous terms available?

> How much does the test contribute to my final course grade?

While an instructor is highly unlikely to tell you what will be on a test, if you can think like an instructor, you may be able to figure it out yourself. Look for clues in the course outline, in the content of assignments, and in the way the instructor introduces or summarizes certain topics. If the instructor says things like "this is very important" or "you need to pay special attention to the concept I am about to introduce," they will probably test on this material. Put an asterisk beside it so it will stand out when you are ready to study for the test.

Test Preparation Strategies

Match Study Methods to Question Types

Test questions come in different types (see **Table 5.2**), and each requires a somewhat different style of preparation.

> **Essay questions.** Essay questions focus on the big picture—ways the various pieces of information being tested fit together. You'll need to know not just a series of facts, but also the connections among these facts, and you will have to be able to discuss these ideas in an organized and logical way. A good study tactic is to play instructor: After carefully reviewing your notes and other course materials, think of likely exam questions. Then, without looking at your notes or your readings, answer each potential essay question, either aloud or by writing out the major points an answer should include. After you've

table 5.2	Types of Test Questions
Essay	Requires a fairly extended, on-the-spot composition about some topic. Examples are questions that call on you to describe a person, process, or event, or those that ask you to compare or contrast two separate sets of material.
Multiple choice	Contains a question or statement, followed by a number of possible answers (usually four or five). You must choose the best response from the choices offered.
True–false	Presents statements about a topic that are either accurate or inaccurate. You are to indicate whether each statement is accurate (true) or inaccurate (false).
Matching	Presents two lists of related information, arranged in column form. Typically, you are asked to pair up the items that go together (e.g., a scientific term and its definition).
Definition	Requires you to provide the meaning of a word.
Short answer	Requires brief responses (usually a few sentences at most) in a kind of mini-essay.
Fill-in	Requires you to add one or more missing words to a sentence or series of sentences.

answered the questions, check yourself by looking at your notes and the course readings once again.

> **Short-answer and fill-in questions.** Short-answer and fill-in questions are similar to essays in that they require you to recall key pieces of information rather than finding the information on the page in front of you. However, short-answer and fill-in questions—unlike essay questions—typically don't demand that you integrate or compare different types of information. Consequently, the focus of your study should be on the recall of specific, detailed information, such as the steps in a process, or the the parts of whole.

> **True–false and matching questions.** While the focus of review for essay questions should be on major issues and controversies, studying for true–false and matching questions requires more attention to the details.

What is good about these kinds of questions is that they put the material right there on the page for you to react to—for example, "Jacques Cartier arrived on New Brunswick's Bay of Chaleur in 1534. True or False?" In these types of questions, you are not asked to remember the names and dates yourself (as in the case of the essay or short-answer question). Nevertheless, to do well on these tests, you must put your memory into high gear and master a great many facts. Matching questions can be made tricky if your instructor decides to put more options than there are items to match, for example, 8 items to match, but 10 choices to match them to.

> **Multiple-choice questions.** Many tests will include a multiple-choice component that is scored using a machine that reads a card that must be filled out using a pencil. Alternatively, the test itself—and the multiple choice questions within it—may be done online. Multiple-choice questions usually offer the test-taker a choice of four or five answers, and for someone whose first language is English, the assumption is that each question will take about one minute to complete. A test with 50 multiple choice questions should therefore take you less than an hour to complete. Often, textbook websites offer practice tests that use questions that are very similar, if not identical, to the test bank used by your instructor to create the test. It is to your advantage to complete as many of these practice tests as you can. It will give you a good idea of the type of question that could be asked, and the types of answer options to expect.

Use Index Cards

It's a particularly good idea to write down important facts on index cards. The advantages of these cards are that they're portable and available all the time, and the act of creating them helps drive the material into your memory. Furthermore, you can shuffle them and test yourself repeatedly until you've mastered the material.

Another helpful strategy is to write the name of a particular concept or theory on one side of a note card and then write an example of it on the other side. Studying the cards will ensure that you fully understand the concepts and theories and can generalize them to different situations.

Test Yourself

Once you feel you've mastered the material, test yourself on it. There are several ways to do this. Textbooks are often accompanied by websites that offer automatically scored practice tests and quizzes. (*P.O.W.E.R. Learning* does: Visit the McGraw-Hill online resource.)

You can also create a test for yourself, in writing, making its form as close as possible to what you expect the actual test to be. For instance, if your instructor has told you the classroom test will be primarily made up of short-answer questions, your test should reflect that.

You might also construct a test and administer it to a classmate or a member of your study group. In turn, you could take a test that someone else has constructed. Constructing and taking practice tests is an excellent way of studying the material and cementing it into memory.

To be sure you're fully prepared for your next test, complete **Try It! 1** "Complete a Test Preparation Checklist."

1 | TRY IT! POWER

Complete a Test Preparation Checklist

It takes more than simply learning the material to prepare for a test. You also need a strategy that will help you understand what it is you are studying for. To do that, you need to learn as much as you can about the test. The more you know about the kind of test it is and what it will cover, the better you'll be able to target your studying, and the less anxious you will feel when you first see the test.

To focus your studying, complete the following test preparation checklist before your next test. When it comes to items like the test format or what will be covered, don't be afraid to ask your instructor for input.

TEST PREPARATION CHECKLIST

- ☐ I know whether it's a quiz, a test, or an exam.
- ☐ I know what kinds of questions will be on the test.
- ☐ I understand what material will be covered.
- ☐ I know how many questions will be on the test.
- ☐ I know how long I will have to complete the test.
- ☐ I know how the test will be graded, and how the grade contributes to my final course grade.
- ☐ I obtained sample questions and/or previous tests, if available.
- ☐ I formed or participated in a study group.
- ☐ I used different and appropriate preparation strategies for different types of questions.
- ☐ I read and studied my class notes.
- ☐ I composed some questions of the kind that will be on the exam.
- ☐ I answered essay questions aloud.
- ☐ I actively memorized facts and details.
- ☐ I made and used index cards.
- ☐ I created and used a test like the real test.

After completing the checklist, ask yourself these questions:

1. How can I use this checklist to study more effectively for tests?
2. How might completing the checklist change the way I study for tests?
3. What new strategies might I follow to prepare for tests more effectively in the future?

To Try It online, go to the McGraw-Hill online resource.

Form a Study Group

Study groups are small, informal groups of students who work together to learn course material and study for a test. A study by Stanger-Hall, Lang, Maas, and Reiness found that "Study group participation was correlated with reduced failing grades and course dropout rates in both semesters, and participants scored better on the final exam and earned higher course grades than nonparticipants."[1] Forming such a group can be an excellent way to prepare for any kind of test. Some study groups are formed for particular tests, whereas others meet consistently throughout the term.

Study groups can be extremely powerful tools because they help accomplish several things:

Study groups, made up of a few students who study together for a test, can help organize material, provide new perspectives, and motivate members to do their best. Do you think you would function well in a study group? Why or why not?

© PeopleImages/Getty Images

> They help members organize and structure the material to approach their studying systematically and logically.

> They allow students to share different perspectives on the material.

> They make it more likely that students will not overlook any potentially important information.

> They force members to rethink the course material, explaining it in words that other group members will understand.

There are some potential drawbacks to keep in mind. Study groups don't always work well for students with learning styles that favour working independently. In addition, "problem" members—those who don't pull their weight—may cause difficulties for the group. In general, though, the advantages of study groups far outweigh their disadvantages. To set up your own study group, see **Try It! 2** "Form a Study Group."

Study groups

Small, informal groups of students whose purpose is to help members work together and study for a test

---

2 | TRY IT! POWER

WORKING IN A GROUP

Form a Study Group

The next time you have to prepare for a test, form a study group with three to five classmates. They may have a variety of study habits and skills, but all must be willing to take the group seriously.

The first time you meet, compare notes about what is likely to be on the test, and brainstorm to come up with possible test questions. If the instructor hasn't given you detailed information about the test (i.e., number and types of questions, weighting, etc.), one of you should be delegated to ask for it. Plan to meet once more closer to the test date to discuss answers to the questions you've come up with, share any new insights, and quiz each other on the material.

After you've taken the test and gotten your results, meet again. Find out if members felt the group was effective.

1. Did the members feel more confident about the test?
2. Do you all think you did better than you would have without the group?
3. What worked? What didn't?
4. What could you do differently next time?

To Try It online, go to the McGraw-Hill online resource.

Use On-Campus Resources

Many colleges and universities have a learning centre, tutorial centre, or other office that can help you cope with test anxiety and show you how to approach studying for a test. Don't wait until after you do badly on a test to visit your campus learning or tutorial centre. A visit before your first test is a good use of your time, even if you feel it's not essential. Just knowing what resources are available can boost your confidence.

Deal with Test Anxiety

What does the anticipation of a test do to you? Do you feel shaky? Frantic, like there's not enough time to get it all done? Is there a knot in your stomach? Do you grit your teeth?

Test anxiety

A temporary condition characterized by fears and concerns about test-taking

Test anxiety is a temporary condition characterized by fears and concerns about test-taking. Almost everyone experiences it to some degree, although for some people it's more of a problem than it is for others. The real danger with test anxiety is that it can become so overwhelming that it can hurt test performance.

You'll never eliminate test anxiety completely, nor do you want to. A little bit of nervousness can energize you, making you more attentive and vigilant. Like other competitive events, testing can motivate you to do your best. You might think of moderate test anxiety as a desire to perform at your peak—a useful quality at test time.

On the other hand, for some, anxiety can spiral into the kind of paralyzing fear that makes their minds go blank. There are several ways to keep this from happening to you:

> **Prepare thoroughly.** The more you prepare, the less test anxiety you'll feel. Good preparation can give you a sense of control and mastery, and it will prevent test anxiety from overwhelming you.

> **Take a realistic view of the test.** Remember that your future success does not hinge on your performance on any single test or exam. Think of the big picture: Put the particular test in context, and remind yourself of all the hurdles you've passed so far.

> **Eat right and get enough sleep.** Good mental preparation can't occur without your body being well prepared.

> **Learn relaxation techniques.** You can learn to reduce or even eliminate the jittery physical symptoms of test anxiety by using relaxation techniques. The basic process is straightforward: Breathe evenly, gently inhaling and exhaling. Focus your mind on a pleasant, relaxing scene such as a beautiful forest or a peaceful farm, or on a restful sound such as the sound of ocean waves breaking on the beach.

> **Visualize success.** Think of an image of your instructor handing back your test marked with a big fat "A." Or imagine your instructor congratulating you on your fine performance the day after the test. Positive visualizations that highlight your potential success can help replace images of failure that may fuel test anxiety.

> **See a counsellor.** If you are still having difficulty coping with anxiety after using the techniques recommended in this chapter, you may wish to book an appointment with a counsellor. Your college or university campus most likely has a learning resource centre or a counselling centre. Talking through your anxiety may help, and the counsellor can offer help specific to your needs.

3 | TRY IT! [POWER]

Measure Your Test-Taking Style

Do you feel anxious at the very thought of a test, or are you cool and calm in the face of testing situations? Get a sense of your test-taking style by checking off every statement below that applies to you.

☐ 1. The closer a test date approaches, the more nervous I get.

☐ 2. I am sometimes unable to sleep on the night before a test.

☐ 3. I have "frozen up" during a test, finding myself unable to think or respond.

☐ 4. I can feel my hands shaking as I pick up my pencil to begin a test.

☐ 5. The minute I read a tough test question, all the facts I ever knew about the subject abandon me and I can't get them back no matter how hard I try.

☐ 6. I have become physically ill before or during a test.

☐ 7. Nervousness prevents me from studying immediately before a test.

☐ 8. I often dream about an upcoming test.

☐ 9. Even if I successfully answer a number of questions, my anxiety stays with me throughout the test.

☐ 10. I'm reluctant to turn in my test paper for fear that I can do better if I continue to work on it.

If you checked off more than four statements, you have experienced fairly serious test anxiety. If you checked off more than six statements, your anxiety is probably interfering with your test performance. In particular, statements 3, 5, 6, 7, and 10 may indicate serious test anxiety.

If, based on your responses to this questionnaire and your previous experience, your level of test anxiety is high, what are some of the steps described in this chapter that might be helpful to you?

To Try It online, go to the McGraw-Hill online resource.

To assess your own test-taking style and the degree of anxiety around tests that you experience, see **Try It! 3** "Measure Your Test-Taking Style."

For more on dealing with test anxiety, particularly where math is concerned, see the **Course Connections** feature on the next page.

When Anxiety Leads to Cramming

You know, of course, that **cramming**—hurried, last-minute studying—is not the way to go. You know that you're likely to forget the material the moment the test is over because long-term retention is nearly impossible without thoughtful study. But …

> … it's been one of those weeks where everything went wrong
> … the instructor sprang a quiz on you at the last minute
> … you forgot about the test until the night before it was scheduled.

Whatever the reason, there may be times when you can't study properly. What do you do if you have to cram for an exam?

Don't spend a lot of time on what you're unable to do. Beating yourself up about your failings as a student will only hinder your efforts. Instead, admit you're human and imperfect like everyone else. Then spend a few minutes developing a plan about what you can accomplish in the limited time you've got.

Cramming
Hurried, last-minute studying

Course CONNECTIONS

Special Techniques for Dealing with Math Anxiety

For many students, the greatest test anxiety comes when they're taking a test involving math. Math seems to bring out the worst fears in some people, perhaps because it's seen as a discipline in which answers are either totally right or totally wrong, or perhaps because they've felt they've "hit the wall" and they'll never be able to understand a new concept, no matter how hard they try.

Such feelings about math can be devastating, because they can prevent you from doing well even if you know the material. If you suffer from math anxiety, keep these things in mind:

- Math is like any other subject: The greatest component of success is the effort you put in, not whether you have a "math gene" that makes you naturally good at math. It's not true that you are either born "good at math" or not, or that there's some "secret" about math that some people know and others don't.
- It's also not true that there's only one way to solve a math problem. Sometimes there are a variety of routes to coming up with a solution. And keep in mind that the solution to math problems often calls for creativity, not just sheer logic.
- It's a false stereotype that women are not as good at math as men, but it's a stereotype that many women accept, and it causes even the top achievers to report more anxiety. Don't fall prey to this narrow thinking. It could result in you ignoring opportunities in the well-paying and fulfilling STEM-related (science, technology, engineering, and math) careers.

Use these special strategies to deal with math problems on exams:

BEFORE TESTS:

1. Math is cumulative, building on prior concepts and knowledge. Make sure you review math fundamentals before moving on to more advanced topics.
2. Ask questions in class. Don't be afraid that you'll ask the wrong question in the wrong way. Instructors want you to understand their subject.
3. Make use of review sessions and other study resources.
4. Practise, practise, practise. The more experience you have completing math problems under pressure, the better you'll do. Practise math problems using a timer to simulate an actual test.

DURING TESTS:

1. Analyze math problems carefully. What are the known quantities or constants, and what pieces of information are missing? What formula(s) or theorem(s) apply?
2. Consider drawing a diagram, a graph, or a probability tree.
3. Break down calculations into their component parts.
4. Check your math carefully.
5. Be neat and logical in your presentation, and show every step as you solve problems. Your instructor may give you partial credit if you lay out every step you're going through. In addition, instructors may require you to show your work.

The first thing to do is choose what you *really* need to study. You won't be able to learn everything, so you have to make choices. Figure out the main focus of the course—a detailed course outline can help you with this—and concentrate on it.

Once you have a strategy, prepare a one-page summary sheet with hard-to-remember information. Just writing the material down will help you remember it, and you can refer to the summary sheet frequently over the limited time you do have to study.

Next, read through your class notes, concentrating on the material you've underlined and the key concepts and ideas that you've already noted. Forget about reading all the material in the books and articles you're being tested on. Instead, only read the passages that you've underlined and the notes you've taken on the readings. Finally, maximize your study time. Using your notes, index cards, and concept maps, go over the information. Read it. Say it aloud. Think about it and the way it relates to other information. In short, use all the techniques we've talked about for learning and recalling information.

When the exam is over, material that you have crammed into your head is destined to leave your mind as quickly as it entered. If you've crammed for a midterm, don't assume that the information will still be there when you study for the final. In the end, cramming often ends up taking more time for worse results than does studying with appropriate techniques. To ensure the material makes it into your long-term memory, consider going back through the material one more time.

Cramming can be exhausting, but it is on occasion necessary. With the family and personal responsibilities many students face, sometimes it can't be avoided. There are, however, strategies you can use to help you make the best use of limited time.

© Andersen Ross/Stockbyte/Getty Images

 **Organize** Reducing Anxiety on the Day of the Test

You've studied a lot, and you're happy with your level of mastery. Or perhaps you have the nagging feeling that there's something you haven't quite gotten to. Or maybe you know you haven't had enough time to study as much as you'd like, and you're expecting a disaster. Before going any further, reflect on your Striving Style™ and how it might affect your approach to test-taking. Then, examine the suggestions and recommendations provided below.

Taking Tests and Striving Styles™

Leaders	Enjoy being tested to demonstrate achievement. Tend to plan and prepare. Prone to over-studying. Organize and lead study groups.
Socializers	Try to do well to please teachers. Study groups lead to more socializing than study. Often unprepared, tending to cram and pull all-nighters.
Performers	Enjoy recognition for achieving top marks but have difficulty disciplining themselves to study. Study sporadically; have difficulty focusing. Will ask for makeup exams.
Adventurers	Dislike studying and exams. Organize study groups that turn into play. Cut corners to get good marks. Would rather show what they know than write about it.
Artists	Diligent around studying because they are afraid of failing. Anxious even when they know their stuff. Perfectionism causes them to underachieve due to pressure they create.
Intellectuals	Enjoy studying subjects they like and will wing it on subjects they don't. Can over-focus on one subject and have to cram for others. Don't enjoy study groups.
Visionaries	Do best on theoretical or interpretive tests. Have difficulty memorizing. Have to review excessively to retain facts. Don't trust they know enough.
Stabilizers	Structure and prepare in advance. Excel with factual subjects but have difficulty with theoretical or interpretive. Rarely guess. Feel it is their duty to perform well.

Whatever your frame of mind, it will help to organize your plan of attack on the day of the test. What's included on the test is out of your hands, but you can control what you bring to it. Here's how:

> **Bring the right tools to the test.** Have at least two pens with you. It's usually best to write in pen because, in general, writing tends to be easier to read in pen than in pencil. But you also might want to have pencils and a good eraser on hand. Sometimes instructors will use machine-scored tests that require the use of a pencil. Or there may be test questions that involve computations, and solving them may entail frequent reworking of calculations.

> **Bring a watch** to the test, even if there will be a clock on the wall of the classroom. You will want to be able to pace yourself properly during the test. Also, if you usually use a cellphone to determine the time, remember that many instructors will ask you to put it away during the test. If they do so, ask if the instructor can write the time on the board at half-hour intervals.

> **Bring your study notes and/or textbook, if allowed.** Sometimes instructors permit you to use notes and books during the test. If you haven't brought them with you, they're not going to be much help, so make sure you bring them if they're permitted. (Even for closed-book tests, having such material available when you arrive in the classroom allows you a few minutes of review before the test actually starts.) And don't be lulled into thinking an open-book test is going to be easy. Instructors who allow you to use your notes and books during a test may not give you much time to look things up, so you still need to study.

> **Resist the temptation to compare notes with your friends** about how much you've studied. Yes, you might end up feeling good because many of your classmates studied less than you did. But chances are you'll find others who seem to have spent significantly more time studying than you, and this will do little to encourage you.

> **Plan on panicking.** Although it sounds like the worst possible approach, permitting yourself the option of spending a minute feeling panicky will help you to recover from your initial fears.

> **Listen carefully to what an instructor says before the test is handed out.** The instructor may tell you about a question that is optional or worth bonus marks or inform you of a typographical error on the test. Whatever the instructor says just before the test, you can be sure it's information that you don't want to ignore.

LO 5.2 [**W Work**] # Test-Taking Strategies

Take a deep breath—literally.

There's no better way to start work on a test than by taking a deep breath, followed by several more. The deep breaths will help you overcome any initial panic and anxiety you are experiencing. It's OK to give yourself over for a moment to panic and anxiety, but, to work at your best, use the relaxation techniques that we spoke about earlier to displace those initial feelings. Tell yourself, "It's OK. I am going to do my best."

Read test instructions carefully. Even if instructors talk about what a test will be like beforehand, at the last minute they may make changes. Consequently, it's critical to read the instructions for the test carefully. In fact, you should skim through the entire exam before you begin. Look at the kinds of questions and pay attention to the way they will be scored. If the weighting of the marks for the various parts of the exam is not clear, ask your instructor to clarify it.

Knowing the weighting of the marks is critical, because it will help you to allocate your time. You don't want to spend 90 percent of your time on an essay that's worth only 10 percent of the marks, and you want to be sure to leave time at the end of the test to check your answers.

An initial read-through will also help you verify that you have every page of the exam and that each one is readable. It may also provide you with "intra-test knowledge"—sometimes terms defined or mentioned in one part of a test trigger memories that can help answer questions in another part of the test.

If there are any lists, formulas, or other key facts that you're concerned you may forget, jot them down now on the back of a test page or on a piece of scrap paper. You may want to refer to this material later during the test.

Once this background work is out of the way, you'll be ready to proceed to actually answering the questions. These principles will help you to do your best on the test:

> **Answer the easiest questions first.** By initially getting the questions out of the way that are easiest for you, you accomplish several important things. First, you'll be leaving yourself more time to think about the tougher questions. In addition, moving through a series of questions without a struggle will build your confidence. Finally, working through a number of questions will build up a base of marks that may be enough to earn you at least a minimally acceptable grade.

> **Write legibly and only on one side of the paper.** If an instructor can't read what you've written, you're not going to get credit for it, no matter how brilliant your answer. So be sure to keep your handwriting legible.

  It's a good idea to write your answers to essay questions on only one side of a page. This will allow you to go back later and add or revise information.

> **Master machine-scored tests.** Tests will sometimes be scored, in part, by computer. In such cases, you'll usually have to indicate your answers by filling in—with a pencil—circles or squares on a computer answer sheet.

  Be careful! A stray mark or smudge can cause the computer scanner to misread your answer sheet, producing errors in grading. Be sure to bring a good eraser in addition to a pencil; the biggest source of mistakes in machine grading is incomplete erasing. If you find yourself having to erase more than once, you should probably ask for a fresh answer sheet.

  It's best to write your answers not only on the answer card, but also on the test itself (if the test is not intended for reuse). That way you can go back and check your answers easily—a step you should take frequently. It's also a good idea to match up your answers on the test with the numbers on the answer sheet every five or so items. This will help you make

© Red Chopsticks/Getty Images

sure you haven't skipped a space or gotten off track in some other way. If you catch such problems early, they're easy to fix.

> **Prepare for online testing.** A variant of machine-scored testing is online testing. In such cases, you'll be completing a quiz, test, or exam on a computer in a lab, or on your own device inside or outside class. Special preparations are required *before* taking an online test to ensure that technical difficulties don't arise that prevent you from logging in or don't give you enough time to finish when you are in test mode. First, if you need a "lockdown browser" that prevents you from doing other things online while you are taking the test, be sure to download it in advance of the test. Second, if there is a practice test available, be sure to try it out to ensure you can access it. Third, ensure your device is fully charged, and bring your charger with you to the test room, just in case. If your device has difficulty keeping a charge, choose a seat that is close to a power outlet or bring a portable charger. Finally, be sure to have paper and pencil available, assuming your instructor permits it. Even though you use the computer to record your answers, you may want to outline an answer or do a calculation by hand.

Answer Specific Types of Test Questions Appropriately

Every type of question requires a particular approach. Use these strategies:

> **Essay questions.** Essay questions, with their emphasis on description and analysis, often present challenges because they are relatively unstructured. Unless you're careful, it's easy to wander off and begin to answer questions that were never asked. To prevent that problem, the first thing to do is read the question carefully. If your essay answer will be lengthy, you might want to write a short outline or a note using the Cornell note-taking method discussed in Chapter 4.

Pay attention to keywords that indicate what, specifically, the instructor is looking for in an answer. Certain action words are commonly used in essays, and you should understand them fully. For instance, knowing the distinction between "compare" and "contrast" can spell the difference between success and failure. **Table 5.3** defines common action words. Complete **Try It! 4** "Understand Action Verbs in Essay Questions" to see how being precise about addressing the action word can change your answer completely.

Use appropriate language in essays. Be brief and to the point in your essay. Avoid flowery introductory language. Compare the two sentences that follow:

"Management techniques have evolved to a point never before seen in the history of our country, or perhaps even our world."

"Many new management techniques have been developed in recent years."

The second sentence says the same thing much more effectively and economically.

> **Short-answer and fill-in questions.** Short-answer and fill-in questions require you to generate and supply specific information. Unlike essays, which are more free-form and may have several possible

table 5.3 Action Words for Essays

These words are commonly used in essay questions. Learning the distinctions among them will help you answer essay questions effectively.

Analyze: Examine and break into component parts.

Clarify: Explain with significant detail.

Compare: Describe and explain similarities.

Compare and contrast: Describe and explain similarities and differences.

Contrast: Describe and explain differences.

Critique: Judge and analyze, explaining what is wrong—and right—about a concept.

Define: Provide the meaning.

Discuss: Explain, review, and consider.

Enumerate: Provide a list of ideas, concepts, reasons, items, etc.

Evaluate: Provide pros and cons of something; provide an opinion and justify it.

Explain: Give reasons why or how; clarify, justify, and illustrate.

Illustrate: Provide examples; show instances.

Interpret: Explain the meaning of something.

Justify: Explain why a concept can be supported, typically by using examples and other types of support.

Outline: Provide an overarching framework or explanation—usually in narrative form—of a concept, idea, event, or phenomenon.

Prove: Using evidence and arguments, convince the reader of a particular point.

Relate: Show how things fit together; provide analogies.

Review: Describe or summarize, often with an evaluation.

State: Assert or explain.

Summarize: Provide a condensed, precise list or narrative.

Trace: Track or sketch out how events or circumstances have evolved; provide a history or timeline.

answers, short-answer and fill-in questions are usually quite specific, requiring only one answer.

Use both the instructions for the questions and the questions themselves to determine the level of specificity that is needed in an answer. Try not to provide too much or too little information. Usually, brevity is best. Be guided by the mark allocation when deciding how much information to include.

> **Multiple-choice questions.** If you've ever looked at a multiple-choice question and said to yourself, "But every choice seems right," you understand what can be tricky about this type of question. However, there are some simple strategies that can help you deal with multiple-choice questions.

4 | TRY IT! POWER

Understand Action Verbs in Essay Questions

Part A: An article in the Economist suggests that Donald Trump's indifference to climate change has not changed China's view. The article can be found at **www.economist.com/news/china/21721227-once-foot-dragger-it-now -wants-lead-trumps-indifference-climate-change-has-not-changed**.

Obtain and read the article, and then answer the following three questions about China's initiatives with regard to climate change. As you respond to each, pay special attention to the different action verbs that introduce each question.

1. **Summarize** China's climate change initiatives.

2. **Analyze** China's climate change initiatives.

3. **Discuss** China's climate change initiatives.

Part B:

1. How do your answers differ for each of the questions?
2. Which of the questions provoked the lengthiest response?
3. Which of the questions could you answer best?

To Try It online, go to the McGraw-Hill online resource.

First, read the question carefully. Note any specific instructions. In most cases, only one answer will be correct; but some questions will you ask you to select multiple items.

Then, before you look at the possible answers, try to answer the question in your head. This can help you avoid confusion over inappropriate choices.

Next, carefully read through every possible answer. Even if you come to one that you think is right, read them all—there may be a subsequent answer that is better.

Look for absolutes like "every," "always," "only," "none," and "never." Choices that contain such absolute words are rarely correct. For example, an answer choice that says, "There has never been a woman prime minister in Canada" is incorrect due to the presence of the word "never." On the other hand, less-absolute words, such as "generally," "usually," "often," "rarely," "seldom," and "typically" may indicate a correct response.

Be especially on guard for the word "not," which negates the sentence ("The one key concept that is not embodied in the Canadian Privacy Principles ..."). It's easy to gloss over the "not," and if you have the misfortune of doing so, it will be nearly impossible to answer the item correctly.

If you're having trouble understanding a question, underline key words or phrases, or try to break the question into different short sections. Sometimes it is helpful to work backward, *Jeopardy*-style, and look at the possible answers first to see if you can find one that is clearly accurate or clearly inaccurate.

Use an **educated guessing** strategy—which is very different from wild or random guessing. Unless you are penalized for wrong answers (a scoring rule by which wrong answers are deducted from the points you have earned on other questions, rather than merely not counting at all toward your score), it always pays to guess.

The first step in educated guessing is to eliminate any obviously false answers. The next step is to examine the remaining choices closely. Does one response choice include an absolute or qualifying adjective that makes it unlikely, for example, "the probability of a leadership review *always* increases when a Canadian prime minister is facing political difficulties"? Does one choice include a subtle factual error? For example, the answer to a multiple-choice question asking why Columbus took his journey to the new world that says "The French monarchy was interested in expanding its colonial holdings" is wrong because it was not the French monarchy, but the Spanish monarchy, that funded Columbus's journey.

> **True–false questions.** Although most of the principles we've already discussed apply equally well to true–false questions, a few additional tricks of the trade may help you with this type of question.

> Begin a set of true–false questions by answering the ones you're sure you know. But don't rush; it's important to read every part of a true–false question, because key words such as "never," "always," and "sometimes" often determine the appropriate response.

> If you don't have a clue about whether a statement is true or false, here's a last-resort principle: Choose "true." In general, more statements on a true–false test are likely to be true than false.

> **Matching questions.** Matching questions typically present you with two columns of related information, which you must link, item by item. For example, a list of terms or concepts may be presented in one column, along with a list of corresponding definitions or explanations in the second column. The best strategy is to reduce the size of both columns by matching the items you're most confident about first; this will leave a short list in each column, and the final matching may become apparent.

Educated guessing
The practice of eliminating obviously false multiple-choice answers and selecting the most likely answer from the remaining choices

About Academic Honesty

It's tempting: A glance at a classmate's test may provide the one piece of information that you just can't remember. But you owe it to yourself not to do it. Copying from a classmate's paper is no different from reaching over and stealing that classmate's cellphone. It is a violation of **academic honesty**, one of the foundations of civility in the classroom, as well as in society. Unless the work you turn in under your own name is your work, you are guilty of academic dishonesty.

A violation of academic honesty can take many forms. It may involve **plagiarism**—taking credit for someone else's words, thoughts, or ideas. Academic dishonesty may also include using a calculator when it's not allowed, discussing the answer to a question, copying an unauthorized

Academic honesty
Completing and turning in only one's own work under one's own name

Plagiarism
Taking credit for someone else's words, thoughts, or ideas

computer file, taking an exam for another person, or stealing an exam. It can take the form of ripping a page out of a book in the library, or lying to an instructor about the reason for a late paper. It includes using your textbook or conferring with a friend when taking a closed-book exam in an online distance-learning course.

You may feel that "everyone does it," so cheating is not so bad. Wrong! Everyone doesn't do it, just as most people don't embezzle from their companies or steal from others. Although you may know of a few cases of exceptionally dishonest classmates, most of your classmates try to be honest—you just don't notice their honesty.

Whatever form it takes, academic dishonesty is just plain wrong. It makes the grading system unfair, it reduces the meaning of your grade, and it lowers the level of civility in the classroom. It certainly hinders academic and personal growth. It can't help but rob the cheater of self-respect. Don't do it!

Finally, academic dishonesty violates the regulations of every college and university (rules you should familiarize yourself with), and instructors know it is their obligation to uphold standards of academic honesty. Violations of honesty policies will lead to any number of potentially

Career CONNECTIONS

Tests for a Lifetime

If you think the last tests you'll ever have to take are the final exams just before you graduate, you're probably wrong.

Increasing numbers of professions require initial licensing exams, and some even require periodic exams to remain in good standing within the profession. For example, in Canada, people who wish to become dental hygienists must pass a licensing exam in the province in which they wish to practise. And even experienced hygienists are expected to remain current with the latest tools and techniques by participating in professional development activities throughout their careers.

In short, good test-taking skills won't just bring you success in college or university. They're something that may benefit you for a lifetime as you pursue your career.

devastating scenarios: failing the exam on which the cheating has taken place, failing the entire course, being brought before a disciplinary board, having a description of the incident permanently placed on your grade transcript, being placed on academic probation, or even being thrown out of school. A single instance of cheating can permanently prevent you from embarking on the career of your choice. Cheating is simply not worth it.

E Evaluate | Check Your Work

The last few minutes of a test may feel like the final moments of a marathon. You need to focus your energy and push yourself even harder. It can be make-or-break time.

Save some time at the end of a test so you can check your work. You should have been keeping track of your time all along, so plan on stopping a few minutes before the end of the test period to review what you've done. It's an important step, and it can make the difference between a terrific grade and a mediocre one. You are a rare person if you can work for an uninterrupted period of time on a test and commit absolutely no errors—even if you know the material backward and forward. Consequently, checking what you've done is crucial.

Start evaluating your test by looking for obvious mistakes. Make sure that you've answered every question. If there is a separate answer sheet, check to see that all of your answers have been recorded on the answer sheet and are in the right spot.

If the test included essay and short-answer questions, proofread your responses. Check for obvious errors—misspellings, missing words, and repetition. Make sure that you've responded to every part of each question and that each essay, as a whole, makes sense.

Check over your responses to multiple-choice, true–false, and matching questions. If there are some items that you haven't yet answered because you couldn't remember the necessary information, now is the time to take a stab at them. As we discussed earlier, it usually pays to guess, even randomly if you must. On most tests, no answer and a wrong answer are worth the same amount—nothing!

What about items that you initially guessed at? Unless you have a good reason to change your original answer—such as a new insight or a sudden recollection of some key information—your first guess is likely your best guess.

Know When to Stop

After evaluating and checking your answers, there may still be some time left. What to do? If you're satisfied with your responses, it's simply time to tell yourself, "Let it go."

Permit yourself the luxury of knowing that you've done your best, and hand the test in to your instructor. You don't have to review your work over and over just because there is time remaining and some of your classmates are still working on their tests. In fact, such behaviour is often counterproductive, because you might start overinterpreting and reading things into questions that really aren't there.

On the other hand, what if you've run out of time? It's a nightmarish feeling: The clock is ticking relentlessly, and it's clear that you don't have enough time to finish the test. What should you do?

Stop working! Although this advice may sound foolish, in fact the best thing you can do is take a minute to calm yourself. Take some deep breaths to replace the feelings of panic that are likely welling up inside you. Collect your thoughts, and plan a strategy for the last moments of the test.

If there are essays that remain undone, consider how you'd answer them if you had more time. Then write an outline of each answer. If you don't have time even for that, write a few key words. Writing anything is better than handing in a blank page, and you may get at least some credit for your response. The key principle here: Something is better than nothing, and even one mark is worth more than zero marks.

The same principle holds for other types of questions. Even wild guesses are almost always better than not responding at all to an item. So rather than telling yourself you've certainly failed and giving up, do as much as you can in the remaining moments of the exam.

LO 5.3 R Rethink Post-test Analysis

Your instructor is about to hand the graded exams back. All sorts of thoughts run through your head: How did I do? Did I do as well as my classmates? Will I be happy with my results? Will the results show how much I studied? Will I be embarrassed by my grade?

The first thing you should do when you get your test back is ensure the instructor has added up your mark correctly; instructors are human, and they sometimes make mistakes. It is always worth checking to be sure you have received all the marks you are due. You may also want to ask your instructor about the class average on the test, so you can determine how well you did relative to the rest of the class.

Most of us focus on the evaluative aspects of tests. We look at the grade we've received on a test as an end in itself. It's a natural reaction.

But there's another way to look at test results: They can help guide us toward future success. By looking at what we've learned (and haven't learned) about a given subject, we'll be in a better position to know what to focus on when we take future exams. Furthermore, by examining the kinds of mistakes we make, we can improve our test-taking skills.

When you get your test back, you have the opportunity to reflect on what you've learned and to consider your performance. Begin by actively listening to what your instructor says as they hand back the test. You may learn about things that were generally misunderstood by the class. You may also pick up some important clues about what questions will be on future tests.

Then examine your own mistakes. Did you misunderstand or misapply some principle? Was there a certain aspect of the material that you missed? Were there particular kinds of information that you didn't realize you needed to know? Or did you lose some points because of your test-taking skills? Did you make careless errors, such as forgetting to fill in a question or misreading the directions? Was your handwriting so sloppy that your instructor had trouble reading it?

Once you have a good idea of what material you didn't fully understand or remember, get the correct answers to the items you missed—from your instructor, your classmates, or your textbook. If it's a math test, rework problems you've missed. Finally, summarize—in writing—the material you had trouble with. This will help you study for future exams that cover the same material.

Finally, if you're dissatisfied with your performance, talk to your instructor—not to complain, but to seek help. Instructors should be able to point out problems in your test that you can address readily so you can do better in the future. Demonstrate to your instructor that you want to do better and are willing to put in the work to get there. The worst thing to do is crumple up the test and quickly leave the class in embarrassment. Remember, you're not the first person to get a bad grade, and the power to improve your test-taking performance lies within you. (Now, take a deep breath and complete **Try It! 5** "Take a Test on Test-Taking.")

5 | TRY IT! POWER

Take a Test on Test-Taking

Part A: Take the following test on test-taking skills, which illustrates every question type discussed in this chapter.

Before taking the test, think of the test-taking strategies we've discussed in the chapter and try to employ as many of them as possible.

MULTIPLE-CHOICE SECTION

Choose one of the possible responses following each question.

1. Tests are useful tools for which of the following purposes?
   a. Determining people's likely level of future career success.
   b. Indicating strengths and gaps in people's knowledge.
   c. Defining people's fundamental abilities and potentials.
   d. Evaluating people's individual worth and contributions.

2. One of the main advantages of study groups is that
   a. Every individual must contribute equally to the group.
   b. Group members can help each other during the test.
   c. Each member has to memorize only a fraction of the material.
   d. They allow each member to share different perspectives on the material.
3. Which of the following is a good way to deal with test anxiety?
   a. Visualizing success on the test.
   b. Drinking coffee or other stimulants.
   c. Telling yourself to stop worrying.
   d. Focusing on the importance of the test.

MATCHING SECTION

_____1.	Essay question	A.	A question in which the student supplies brief missing information to complete a statement.
_____2.	Multiple-choice question	B.	Hurried, last-minute studying.
_____3.	Matching question	C.	Deduction of points for incorrect responses.
_____4.	Fill-in question	D.	A question requiring a lengthy response in the student's own words.
_____5.	Guessing penalty	E.	A question in which the student must link information in two columns.
_____6.	Cramming	F.	Representing someone else's work as one's own.
_____7.	Plagiarism	G.	A question that requires selection from several response options.

(*continued*)

FILL-IN SECTION (continued)

1. Fear of testing that can interfere with test performance is called_____.
2. The primary source of error on machine-scored tests is incomplete_____.

TRUE–FALSE SECTION

1. The best way to prepare for an essay test is to review detailed factual information about the topic.
   T_____ F_____

2. True–false questions require students to determine whether given statements are accurate or inaccurate.
   T_____ F_____

3. You should never permit yourself to feel panicky during a test.
   T_____ F_____

4. A good evaluation strategy toward the end of a test is to redo as many questions as time permits.
   T_____ F_____

5. In a multiple-choice question, the words "always" and "never" usually signal the correct response.
   T_____ F_____

6. If you run out of time at the end of a test, it is best to write brief notes and ideas down in response to essay questions rather than leave them completely blank.
   T_____ F_____

SHORT-ANSWER SECTION

1. What are five things you should find out about a test before you take it?
2. What is academic honesty?

ESSAY SECTION

1. Discuss the advantages of using a study group to prepare for an examination.
2. Why is academic honesty important?

(Answers can be found at the end of the chapter.)

PART B:

After you have completed the test, consider these questions:

1. Did you learn anything from taking the test that you might not have learned if you hadn't been tested?
2. How effective were the test-taking strategies you employed?
3. Were any types of strategies easier for you to employ than others?
4. Were any types of questions easier for you to answer than others?

 THINK-PAIR-SHARE

Exchange your essay responses with a classmate, and critique the essays. How do the responses of your partner compare with your own?

To Try It online, go to the McGraw-Hill online resource.

Time to Reflect: What **Did I Learn?**

1. Generally speaking, how does being tested make you feel?

2. What factors seem to contribute to your success or failure on a particular test or exam? Which of these factors are under your control?

3. What strategies do you plan to use in the future to improve your performance on tests?

Did You Know?

An organization called the American Test Anxieties Association (**amtaa.org**) "joins test anxiety pioneers and researchers with school counsellors and educators, to share concerns and find practical solutions" to the problem of test anxiety. Those of you who experience test anxiety will be relieved to know that you are not alone. According to the AMTAA, "about 16–20% of students have high test anxiety … another 18% are troubled by moderately-high test anxiety."[2]

Looking Back

What kinds of tests will I encounter in college and university?

> There are several types of tests, including brief, informal quizzes; tests, which are more substantial; and exams, which are even more significant and tend to be administered at the midpoint and end of a course.

> Although tests are an unpopular fact of college and university life, they can provide useful information about your level of knowledge and understanding about a subject.

What can I do to prepare for a test?

> Good test preparation begins with doing the course assignments, attending class regularly, and paying attention in class. It also helps to find out as much as possible about a test beforehand and to form a study group to review material.

> If cramming becomes necessary, focus on summarizing factual information broadly, identifying key concepts and ideas, and rehearsing information orally.

> If you are preparing for an online test, ensure that you have downloaded the "lockdown browser" (if required) and that your device is fully charged.

What can I do during the test to maximize my test results?

> When you first receive the test, you should skim it to see what kinds of questions are asked, figure out how the different questions and sections will be weighted, and jot down complex factual information you might need for the test.

> Answer the easiest questions first, write legibly, use only one side of each sheet of paper, mark answer sheets carefully, and record answers in the test book as well as on the answer sheet.

What are the best strategies for answering specific kinds of test questions?

> For essay questions, you should work to understand each question and each of its parts, interpret action words correctly, write concisely, organize the essay logically, and include examples.

> The best strategy for short-answer and fill-in questions is to be very sure what is being asked. Keep answers complete but brief.

> For multiple-choice items, read the question very carefully and then read all response choices. Educated guessing based on eliminating incorrect response choices is usually a reasonable strategy.

> For true–false and matching questions, answer all the items that you are sure of quickly and then go back to the remaining items.

What can I learn from taking the test?

> Analyzing the graded test will help you see weaknesses in your understanding of the material tested. You can study these weak areas further before you take your next test or exam on that material.

> You may see places in the test where you have misread questions or misallocated your time. Recognizing these tendencies in yourself can help you to be more test-wise in the future.

RESOURCES

ON CAMPUS

Colleges and universities provide a variety of resources for students having difficulties with test-taking. Some offer general workshops reviewing test-taking strategies. As well, if you are planning to take a specific standardized test, you may be able to sign up for a course offered through your college or university (or through such commercial organizations as Princeton Review and Kaplan).

If you are experiencing difficulties in a specific course, you may be able to find a tutor to help you. Some institutions have tutoring centres or campus learning centres that can provide one-on-one assistance. It's also important to speak to your instructor, who has likely encountered many students with similar problems and may have some useful test-taking strategies.

If you find that you are experiencing significant test anxiety when taking a test or in the days leading up to it, talk to one of the professionals at your campus counselling centre or health centre. They can help you learn relaxation techniques and can provide counselling to help make your anxiety manageable.

And, once again, don't forget that you can always ask your instructors for help!

IN PRINT

If you have difficulty with test anxiety, you'll want to check out *Insider's Guide to Beating Test Anxiety* (Bedford, 2010).

Blythe Grossberg's *Test Success: Test-Taking and Study Strategies for All Students, Including Those with ADD and LD* (Specialty Press, 2009) is an excellent guidebook for first-year college and university students. It covers learning styles and how they influence your test-taking strategies; how to study for pop quizzes, essay tests, and multiple choice tests; and strategies for students with attention deficit disorders or learning disabilities.

Test-Taking Power Strategies (LearningExpress, 2007), provides a variety of techniques to help you improve your performance on any kind of test.

ON THE WEB

The following websites provide an opportunity to extend your learning about the material in this chapter:

> "The Multiple-Choice Exam," an online handout from the University of Victoria's Learning Skills Program (**coun.uvic.ca/learning/exams/multiple-choice.html**), offers some valuable suggestions on how to approach multiple-choice exams. Several types of multiple-choice questions are described, and strategies for answering them are explained. There are also helpful hints about what to look for in the wording of both the questions and the answer choices.

> "Coping with Exams and Exam Anxiety" (**coun.uvic.ca/personal/stress-anxiety .html**) offers several suggestions that you might find helpful in managing and reducing your level of stress and anxiety. The techniques may help you deal with test-related anxiety as well as academic anxiety in general. Not all of the techniques work for everyone. Try them and adopt the ones that work best for you.

THERE'S AN APP FOR THAT

> For a list of some of the best anxiety reduction apps out there, visit **healthline. com/health/anxiety/top-iphone-android-apps#1.**

TAKING IT TO THE WEB

1 Seeing exams from other classes can help you get an idea of the kinds of questions that are often asked on exams. Use an Internet search engine to locate examples of exams from other colleges and universities. One strategy is to use the Google search engine at **google.ca** and type "examples of exams" (including the quotation marks) at the search prompt. Look at several exams. How many of the questions on these exams were true–false? How many were multiple choice? How many were essays?

2 Practise answering essay questions by comparing and contrasting the information different Web pages offer about the same topic. For example, go to Yahoo! (**ca.yahoo.com**) and enter the phrase "essay exams" (using quotation marks). Read the strategies for essay exams offered at two different websites. Then write a paragraph describing the information both sites had in common, and another paragraph describing the information that was unique to each site.

ANSWERS TO ITEMS IN TRY IT! 5

Multiple-choice: 1b, 2d, 3a
Matching: 1D, 2G, 3E, 4A, 5C, 6B, 7F
Fill-in: test anxiety, erasing
True–False: 1F, 2T, 3F, 4F, 5F, 6T

Short answer:

1. Possible answers include what type of test it is, what it will cover, how many questions will be on it, how much time it will take, what kinds of questions will be on it, how it will be graded, whether sample questions will be provided, and whether tests from prior terms are available.

2. Academic honesty is completing and turning in only one's own work under one's own name.

Essay:

1. Strong essays should include a brief definition of a study group, followed by a discussion of the advantages of using study groups (including such things as helping to organize and structure material, providing different perspectives, and rethinking material). A mention of the disadvantages of study groups would also be reasonable.

2. After starting with a brief definition of academic honesty, the bulk of the answer should concentrate on why academic honesty is important and the consequences of academic dishonesty.

THE CASE OF . . .
That Sinking Feeling

This is going to be easy, Janelle Ross said to herself as she sat down to take her test, a midterm exam covering the basics of restaurant management. She had spent a few hours the previous night and an hour right before class studying key terms and concepts. She felt she knew the material. She felt ready.

Janelle was surprised to see, though, that the exam had two parts: a multiple-choice section and an essay section. Janelle hadn't really thought about what she might say in an essay. But she figured working on the multiple-choice questions might help give her some ideas.

The first two multiple-choice questions Janelle answered easily, but she got stuck on the third one.

She went back and forth over two possible answers and finally decided just to leave that question blank. The pattern was the same for the rest of the multiple-choice questions: A few questions Janelle would answer easily, and then she'd get stuck on a hard one.

Finally, Janelle finished the multiple-choice questions and came to the essay. Only then did she notice the instructions that indicated the essay was worth 50 marks, and the multiple-choice questions 25 marks. Then Janelle got another shock: She had only 10 minutes left to write her essay! Her mind froze—and Janelle had the horrible feeling that she didn't have enough time to complete the test. Even though she had studied, Janelle now felt certain she would fail.

1. What mistakes did Janelle make in her test preparation that probably harmed her performance?

2. What mistakes did Janelle make during the test that hurt her?

3. What was right about Janelle's initial approach to the test?

4. What should Janelle have done differently in calculating the amount of time to devote to each portion of the test? Why?

5. What specific strategies would have helped Janelle with the multiple-choice questions? What strategies could she have used on the essay?

6. If you were in Janelle's shoes, what would you do with only 10 minutes left in the test?

CHAPTER 6
Leveraging Technology and Developing Information Competency

Learning Outcomes

By the time you finish this chapter, you will be able to

LO 6.1   Identify technologies that contribute to your efficiency and effectiveness in your academic and everyday life.

LO 6.2   Determine whether taking a distance learning course is the right choice for you and for your learning style.

LO 6.3   Discuss the principles of effective online communication and the protection of online privacy.

LO 6.4   Demonstrate information competency by identifying techniques and technologies that help you locate and evaluate information and organize the information that you find.

LO 6.5   Identify the different types of plagiarism, and explain how plagiarism can be avoided through proper citation methods and the use of citation software.

Throughout high school, Melissa Khan had always been a serious student. She did her readings before class, wrote summaries of what she'd learned after each class, and studied hard for tests and exams. Her efforts had resulted in excellent marks, and her goal was to maintain this type of performance now that she was in college. But the one thing Melissa hadn't counted on was how much of her grade would depend on group work. It was one thing to count on herself, but a totally different thing to have to depend on others to get their work done on time and to the same level of quality she expected from herself.

So when Melissa's business analysis instructor announced on the first day of class that the course involved two major group projects worth 40 percent of the overall course grade, Melissa was far from enthusiastic. And when the instructor went on to say that the teams would be self-managed, and that everyone on the team would get the same mark, Melissa became downright nervous.

But then, the instructor went one step further. He indicated that all documents relating to the project would be worked on in a collaborative space on the Internet (or "in the cloud"). The instructor did an in-class demonstration of the technology, showing how it would allow members of a group to use the same workspace, track who made changes or additions to a document, and send emails notifying members when changes were made. The technology had its own chat function, as well as tools like calendars and project plans to keep everyone on track. No more wondering if Person A and Person B had done their work and would deliver it on time—it was there for everyone else in the group to see.

Melissa quickly realized that group work would become much more manageable if she used collaboration technology in all of her classes that involved group work, and she went away from the demo feeling much more comfortable with the prospect of working on group projects.

Looking Ahead

Like every other aspect of society, education is changing, as technologies— MOOCs (Massive Open Online Courses), cloud computing, social media, blogs, tablets, smartphone apps, social bookmarking, and so forth—become more and more a part of how we learn and how we live our lives. Today, business people regularly hold meetings and instructors teach courses without being in the same room as their co-workers or students.

Technology is making a profound difference in how we are taught, how we study and carry out our work, and how we communicate with others. It is changing the way we access the vast quantities of information published each year— tens of thousands of books, journals, and other print materials, and literally billions of Web pages. But successfully wading through all that information to find the "nuggets" requires skills that weren't necessary in the past.

In this chapter, we discuss how technological advances increase your opportunities to achieve success in college and university and on the job. First, we'll examine some general tools that can help you use technology more effectively. Then, we'll talk about some of the technologies that are specific to your role as a student, including course management systems, e-texts, distance/online learning, and MOOCs. Finally, we'll consider how you can use technology to develop information competency—how to locate and assess sources, how to reference them properly, and how to avoid plagiarism—essential skills in a world where we are drowning in data but have difficulty finding information that is both relevant and credible.

You and Technology

It is a great tool that can help you achieve success in your classes. It can save you hours of time on your job, whether you work in a cubicle or in a garage. At the same time, it can be extremely frustrating, annoying, and maddening, and it can eat up hours of your time.

"It," of course, is technology. Today, it's as much a necessity to use technology as it was for you to learn to write using pen and paper earlier in your schooling. No one facing the job market in the 21st century will want to leave college or university without a strong working knowledge of a variety of technologies and what they can do for you.

Perhaps you are a mature student who is not yet at ease with technology. If so, relax. No one is born with technology expertise. With practice, however, using a broad range of technologies can become second nature.

Use Technology to Get Organized and Stay Organized

There are many technologies that can make your life easier, so many that most of us aren't even aware that some of them exist. In this and other chapters, we introduce you to a number of tools and applications. Some you may be interested in adopting; others you may not. Some will work on your computer system, tablet, or smartphone; others may not. But all are worthy of exploration. A small investment of time spent leveraging some of these tools can add up to a huge increase in your personal efficiency, so it is worth taking a look at a few of them.

Your browser, which is your entry to the Internet, is a tool that can be modified to better suit your needs. Whether you use Apple Safari, Google Chrome, Internet Explorer, or Mozilla Firefox, one feature worth looking at is the ability to open several pages (or tabs) at once as your home page, or include a set of shortcuts to favourite sites in a toolbar. For example, when you open your browser, you could have immediate access to your course management system (e.g., Blackboard or D2L), your college or university's email system, your Facebook home page, the front page of your favourite newspaper, and the local forecast from The Weather Network, each with its own tab, each ready to jump into, as you sip your morning coffee.

The advent of cloud computing is making it easier for most of us to stay organized, whether we are sitting home at our computer or thousands of kilometres away, vacationing on a sandy beach. In the not-too-distant past, your programs, documents, email, bookmarks, and calendar were probably housed on a specific desktop computer and were reachable only when you were sitting in front of that computer. These days, all of this information can be housed "in the cloud"—that is, on the Internet—and is available to you anywhere, any time, as long as you have a device to reach it, such as a laptop, a tablet, or a smartphone, and access to the Internet.

If you are always on the move and "anywhere, any-time" access is key to your being able to organize your life, then cloud computing is the answer. For document sharing or transfer, you'll want to investigate **Google Docs** or **Dropbox**. Your to-do lists can be stored on sites like **Remember the Milk** and **toodledo.com**. For online access to notes you've created, whether they are based on text, images, audio, or even entire Web pages, try **Evernote**. For access to your bookmarks online, and the ability to share them with others, look to social bookmarking applications like **Delicious**. Cloud computing also extends to sites where you can share your photos (e.g., **Instagram**, **Flickr**, **Google Photos**); your presentations (e.g., **Slideshare**); and every single thought going through your head at any moment, as long as you can express it in 140 characters or less (**Twitter**)! And, finally, don't forget about backup storage on the cloud. One of your authors recently found herself working for months to rename 19,000 files that had to be restored after her hard drive failed. You don't want that to happen to you!

So now you have the tools you need to get organized. Next comes the most important step of all: *staying* organized. For many of us, this is the hardest part. To keep on top of it, we recommend that you do the following:

1. Set time aside at the end of each semester to purge unnecessary files, folders, and emails; to clean up your virtual desktop; and to archive the previous semester's work.

2. To ensure that your operating system and main software are always up to date, consider signing up for automatic upgrades, which you can program to run while you are sleeping. Frequent upgrades are especially important for your operating system and security software, as the former is prone to attack by hackers, and the latter protects you from them.

3. For the rest of your software, consider setting aside one day every year—preferably *before* the academic year begins—to make all of the necessary upgrades. Often, deeply discounted student rates are available on software in your campus bookstore, so you'll want to check there first. Let's face it—you don't want to find yourself trying to read an important file sent to you by a fellow student in the middle of the night, only to find you can't because you have the previous version of the software!

4. Virtually all computer applications will continue to evolve as more and more people take advantage of them. As such, it is probably worthwhile to allocate time during the year to catch up on the many developments that have occurred. You will probably find many new applications that you didn't even know existed—some of which could make your life a lot easier!

A final note of caution: There are many, many "free" applications on the Internet, like the ones just mentioned, but as with most things in life, there really is no such thing as a free lunch. The price to be paid for some of these free applications can include having to watch advertising before the application loads; allowing a cookie or small tracking device to be put on your computer; providing some of your demographic information; or allowing the information you provide, such as your status updates, to be harvested and used to deliver targeted advertising to you (this is how Facebook works). Be aware that you are usually giving something up, often your time or your privacy, to get something "free." Before taking advantage of a free application, ensure you *know* what you are giving up in return.

Use Technology to Get the Most out of Your Courses

Technology now plays a big role in your life, whether you are proficient with its use or not. Computers run your car's engine, make your smartphone work, allow you to listen to your music on a device that is smaller than a credit card, and make sure the bus you're waiting for runs on time. Technology has revolutionized academic life as well, both inside and outside the classroom. Here are some of the ways technology can be used to support your course work:

> **Course or learning management systems.** Whether it resides on Blackboard or Desire2Learn or another course management system, most college and university courses now have a site associated with them. The site is likely to contain basic information about the course, such as a copy of the syllabus or course outline, and information on how to contact your instructor. It may also be used to provide important last-minute updates, such as class cancellations or changes in a paper's due date.

> The course site will often play a central role as a repository for presentation slides, assignments, online quizzes, discussion threads, and your grades to date. If your instructor elects to post slides before class, consider printing them out using the print option in PowerPoint that allows you to create handouts. Select the "three to a page" option, which will provide you with room for notes, and bring the handouts to class. You will then be able to concentrate on the examples the instructor is using, rather than trying to capture the content of each slide. (For tips on making the best use of instructors' presentation slides, see the **Course Connections** box.)

> In some courses, you can electronically deposit papers and essays into a "digital drop box" on the class website. Later, your instructor can read them online, post comments on your submissions, and return them to you on the website. You may collaborate on group projects and hold virtual discussions on the site. You may even be required to take your major tests and final exams on the course site.

> **Publisher-based online learning centres and companion websites.** Many publishers offer websites that are tied to the textbooks they publish. The website typically includes chapter summaries, interactive reviews, flash cards, and practice tests. These resources, which are usually described in the preface to the textbook, can be extremely valuable study tools. (You'll find the companion website for this text on the McGraw-Hill online resource.)

> **E-books.** Textbook publishers have responded to those who prefer to read the material on a tablet or e-reader by creating e-book versions of their texts. In addition to making your backpack significantly lighter, e-books have many other useful features: They are searchable, allowing you to find specific text, highlight that text, and then create a side note and save it as a useful study tool. While the jury is still out on how much you will enjoy reading your textbooks on a screen, there is no question that the lower cost of an e-book, when compared to a traditional paper-based textbook, is very appealing to cash-strapped students.

> **Podcasts.** In some classes, instructors produce an audio or a video recording, called a **podcast**, of lectures or other instructional material relevant to the class. You can either access podcasts on the Web or download them to a mobile device (such as an iPod or your smartphone) that permits you to listen to and view them outside of class whenever you want. For podcasts of the best lectures, on any topic, delivered by some of the most dynamic professors in the world, check out iTunes U (**apple.com/apps/itunes-u/**).

Podcast
An audio or video recording that can be accessed on the Internet and viewed on a computer or downloaded to a mobile device

> **Plagiarism detection technology.** Plagiarism do's and don'ts are covered later in this chapter, but technologies are available that can help you ensure that you have done everything you can to avoid plagiarizing. The best known is TurnItIn (**turnitin.com**), a detection service to which many colleges and universities subscribe. Submitting your essays, projects, or reports to a service like **turnitin.com** *before* you submit them to your professor allows you to see an "originality report," which can point out where you may have forgotten quotation marks, in-text citations, or references and give you a chance to correct what you've overlooked.

> **Blogs and vlogs.** Some instructors maintain blogs or vlogs of their own. A **blog** is a Web-based public diary in which a writer offers ideas, thoughts, short essays, and commentary; a **vlog** is a video-based version of a blog. If your instructor has a blog or vlog and tells you to take a look at it, get in the habit of checking it routinely. It will contain information relevant to the course, and it may also reveal personal insights that can help you get to know your instructor better.

Blog
A Web-based public diary in which a writer provides written commentary, ideas, thoughts, and short essays

Vlog
A video-based version of a blog

Course CONNECTIONS

Getting the Most out of Instructors' Slide Presentations

Traditional "chalk-and-talk" lectures are a thing of the past in many classes. Instead, increasing numbers of instructors are using presentation programs such as PowerPoint or PREZI to project material in their classes.

This technology calls for fresh strategies for taking notes and absorbing the information. Here are some tips:

- **Listening is more important than seeing.** The information that your instructor projects on screen, while important, is ultimately less critical than what they are saying. Pay primary attention to the spoken word and secondary attention to the screen.

- **Don't copy everything that is on every slide.** Instructors can present far more information on their slides than they would if they were writing on a blackboard. Often there is so much information that it's impossible to copy it all down. Don't even try. Instead, concentrate on taking down the key points.

- **Remember that key points on slides are . . . key points.** The key points (typically indicated by bullets) often relate to central concepts. Use these points to help organize your studying for tests, and don't be surprised if test questions directly address the bulleted items on slides.

- **Check to see if the presentation slides are available online.** Some instructors make their class presentations available to their students, either before or after class time. If they do this before class, print the slides out and bring them to class. Then you can make notes on your copy, clarifying important points. If they are not available until after a class is over, you can still make good use of them when it comes time to study the material for tests.

- **Remember that presentation slides are not the same as good notes for a class.** If you miss a class, don't assume that getting a copy of the slides is sufficient. Studying the notes of a classmate who is a good note-taker will be far more beneficial than studying only the slides.

LO 6.2 Using Technology to Learn at a Distance

Do you find that your schedule changes so much from one day to the next that it's hard to fit in a course that meets at a regularly scheduled time? Interested in an unusual course topic that your own college or university doesn't offer? Want to take a class during the summer, but your college or university doesn't have a summer program?

Distance or online learning
A form of education in which students participate via the Web or other kinds of technology

The solution to your problem may be to enroll in a **distance or online learning** course. Distance learning is a form of education in which students participate via the Web or other kinds of technology. In the United States in the autumn of 2014, 5.8 million students were enrolled in at least one online course, up 3.9 percent over the previous year.[1]

The key feature of distance learning courses is the nature of interaction between instructor and students. Rather than meeting in a traditional classroom, where you, the instructor, and the other students are physically present, distance learning classes are most often virtual. Although some schools use Webcasts of lectures with virtual discussion rooms, most students in distance learning courses will never sit through a lecture or participate in a real-time conversation with students in the class. They may never know what their instructor or classmates look like or hear their voices.

If you take a distance learning course, you may read lecture notes posted on the Web, search and browse websites, write papers, post replies to discussion topics on a message board, and take online quizzes and exams. You will see your instructor's and classmates' responses through comments they post on the Web. You may be expected to read a textbook entirely on your own.

Blended (or hybrid) courses
Courses in which instruction is a combination of traditional face-to-face classroom interaction and a significant amount of online learning

You may already be familiar with the kinds of technologies used in distance learning courses, because many traditional, face-to-face courses already contain elements of distance learning. In **blended (or hybrid) courses**, instruction is a combination of traditional face-to-face classroom interaction and a significant amount of online learning. Students in blended courses generally spend more time working alone or in collaboration with others online than in traditional classes.

Distance learning is not for everyone. It is important to determine if this type of course suits your preferred style of course-taking. Complete **Try It! 1** "Assess Your Course-Taking Style" to see whether you are suited to learning at a distance.

Distance learning classes have both advantages and disadvantages. On the plus side, distance learning courses offer the following:

> **You can take a Web-based distance learning course anywhere that you have access to the Web.** You can take a higher education class no matter where you live. You can be at home, at the office, or on a beach and still participate.

> **Distance learning classes are more flexible than traditional classes.** You can participate in a course any time of the day or night. You set your own schedule. This is particularly helpful for those with time-consuming family obligations such as child care.

> **Distance learning classes are self-paced.** You may be able to spread out your work over the course of a week, or you may do the work in a concentrated manner in one day.

1 | TRY IT!

Assess Your Course-Taking Style

Your preferred course-taking style—how you participate in classes, work with your classmates, interact with your teachers, and complete your assignments—may make you more or less suitable for distance learning. Read the following statements and indicate whether you agree or disagree with them to see if you have what it takes to be a distance learner.

	Agree	Disagree
1. I need the stimulation of other students to learn well.		
2. I need to see my instructor's face, expressions, and body language to interpret what is being said.		
3. I participate a lot in class discussions.		
4. I prefer to hear information presented orally rather than reading it in a book or article.		
5. I'm not very good at keeping up with reading assignments.		
6. I'm basically pretty easily distracted.		
7. I'm not very well organized.		
8. Keeping track of time and holding to schedules is *not* a strength of mine.		
9. I need a lot of hand-holding while I work on long assignments.		
10. I need a close social network to share my feelings, ideas, and complaints with.		
11. I'm not very good at writing.		
12. Basically, I'm not very patient.		

The more you agree with these statements, the less your course-taking style is suited to distance learning. Interpret your style according to this informal scale:

Disagreed with 10–12 statements = Excellent candidate for distance learning

Disagreed with 7–9 statements = Good candidate for distance learning

Agreed with 7–9 statements = Probably better taking classes on campus

Agreed with 10–12 statements = Avoid distance learning

To Try It online, go to the McGraw-Hill online resource.

> **You may have more contact with your instructor than you do with a traditional class.** Even though you may not have face-to-face contact, you may have greater access to your instructor than in traditional classes, via email and the Web. You can leave messages for your instructor any time of night or day; most instructors of distance learning classes respond in a timely way.

> **Shy students may find it easier to "speak up" in a distance learning class.** You can think through your responses to make sure you are communicating just what you wish to say. You don't have to worry about speaking in front of other people. For many people, distance learning is liberating.

> **You can become a better writer.** Because distance learning usually involves more writing than traditional courses, you receive more practice writing—and more feedback about it—than in traditional classes.

On the other hand, distance learning has disadvantages that you should keep in mind:

> **You are dependent on technology.** If you lose access to a computer and the Web, you won't be able to participate in the class until the problem is fixed.

> **You won't have direct, face-to-face contact with your instructor or other students.** Distance learning can be isolating, and students sometimes feel alone and lost in cyberspace.

> **You probably won't get immediate feedback.** In a distance learning class, it may be hours, or sometimes days, before you receive feedback on what you have posted to a message board, depending on how well the pace of other students matches your own.

> **Distance learning classes require significant discipline, personal responsibility, and time management skills.** You won't have a set time to attend class as you do in traditional courses. Instead, you must carve out the time yourself. Although instructors provide a schedule of when things are due, you have to work out the timing to get them done.

Consequently, many students believe that distance learning courses are more difficult than traditional classes. You must be focused and committed to keeping up with the course. You need to be prepared to work hard on your own for a substantial number of hours each week.

Despite these potential challenges to distance learning courses, they are becoming increasingly popular. More and more colleges and universities are offering them. Many companies encourage employees with crowded schedules to take distance learning as a way of providing continuing education.

If you are considering taking a distance learning course, follow these steps, which are summarized in the P.O.W.E.R. Plan here.

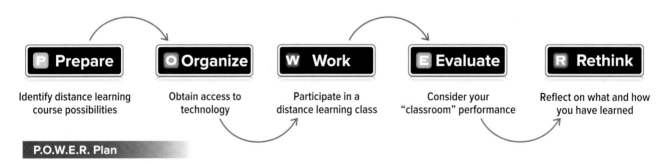

P **Prepare** — Identify distance learning course possibilities

O **Organize** — Obtain access to technology

W **Work** — Participate in a distance learning class

E **Evaluate** — Consider your "classroom" performance

R **Rethink** — Reflect on what and how you have learned

P.O.W.E.R. Plan

P Prepare Identify Distance Learning Course Possibilities

How do you find a distance learning course? In some cases, your own college or university may offer courses on the Web and list them in your course catalogue. In other cases, you'll have to find courses on your own.

The best place to look is on the Web itself. By searching the Web, you can find distance learning courses ranging from agronomy to zoology. Don't be deterred by the physical location of the institution that offers the course. It doesn't matter where the college or university is located, because for most distance learning classes, you'll never have to go to the campus itself.

One of the more interesting developments in recent years is the emergence of **MOOCs**, or Massive Online Open Courses. These are courses offered on a global scale, often by professors who are leaders in their field, and by colleges and universities that are renowned for a particular field of study—for example, behavioural economist and bestselling author Dan Ariely offers "A Beginner's Guide to Irrational Behavior," and Berklee College of Music offers "Introduction to Guitar." People register for MOOCs with different purposes in mind, and, while many may register, often only a small percentage of these actually obtain a statement of accomplishment or course credit (see **Figure 6.1**).

MOOCs
Massive Online Open Courses

Before you sign up for a potential course that you would like to count toward your degree, make sure that your own college or university will give you credit for it. Check with your adviser and registrar's office to be certain.

You should also find out what the requirements or prerequisites of a course are before you sign up for it. Check the syllabus carefully and see how it meshes with your schedule. If it is a summer course and you are going to be away from your computer for a week, you may not be able to make up the work you miss.

Finally, try to talk with someone who has taken the course before. Was the instructor responsive, providing feedback rapidly? If necessary, could you speak with the instructor by phone? Was the course load reasonable? (**Try It! 2** "Get Some Distance on the Problem" will help you work through the process.)

figure 6.1 | Behaviour of MOOC[2] Registrants

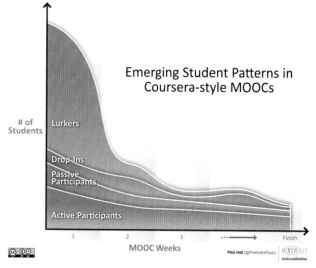

Only a small percentage of registrants actually make it to the MOOC finish line.

Emerging Student Patterns in Coursera-style MOOCs by Phil Hill, e-Literate, work released under a Creative Commons Attribution, no Derivatives license.

⊙ Organize Obtain Access to Technology

Although you don't need to be a computer expert, you will need chat, email, discussion thread, and basic Web research skills to take a distance learning course. If you don't have sufficient technological expertise, beef up your computer skills by taking a computer course or workshop *before* you sign up for the distance learning course.

You'll also need access to a computer connected to the Internet. It doesn't have to be your own computer, but you will certainly need regular and convenient access. Make sure you have access to a sufficiently fast network if you are planning to take a course over the Internet; a very slow connection is frustrating. It is also a good idea to make all your arrangements for computer access *before* the start of a course. Depending on where you live, it can take up to a week to set up Internet service on a home computer if you don't have it already.

2 | TRY IT! [POWER]

CLASS DISCUSSION

Get Some Distance on the Problem

Working by yourself initially, see if you can find distance learning courses that might be of interest to you. Start by checking your school's course catalogue to see what is offered there. If you're already comfortable online, you might also try the following:

- Athabasca University offers all of its courses online. Visit **athabascau.ca**.
- Mount Saint Vincent University in Halifax offers many of its courses online. Visit **msvu.ca/en/home /programsdepartments/distancelearning/default.aspx**.
- Coursera (**coursera.org**), Udacity (**udacity.com**), and Udemy (**www.udemy.com/**) are three popular MOOCs that offer a wide range of courses.

Try to find five courses you would be interested in, and list them below. After you have completed your list, share it with others in a group, and discuss these questions.

1. How diverse were the courses you found?

2. Were particular subject areas better represented than others?

3. Why do you think this might be?

To Try It online, go to the McGraw-Hill online resource.

 ## Participate in a Distance Learning Class

Successfully participating in a distance learning course involves several skills that are distinct from those needed for traditional classes. To get the most out of a distance learning course, you'll need to do the following:

> **Manage your time carefully.** You won't have the luxury of a regular schedule of class lectures, so you'll have to manage your time carefully. No one will remind you that you need to sit down at a computer and work. You will need self-discipline to be successful in a distance learning course.

- **Check in frequently.** Instructors may make crucial changes in the course requirements. Make sure to check for any changes in due dates or class expectations.
- **Find a cyber-buddy.** At the start of the semester, try to make contact with at least one other student in the class. You can share study strategies, form a study team, and share notes. Connecting with another student can help you avoid feelings of isolation that may interfere with your success.
- **Make copies of everything.** Don't assume everything will go well in cyberspace. Make a printed copy of everything you submit, or have a backup stored on another computer or in the cloud.
- **Have a technology backup plan.** Computers crash, your connection to the Internet may go down, or an emailed assignment may be mysteriously delayed or sent back to you. Don't wait until the last minute to work on and submit assignments, and have a plan in place if your primary computer is unavailable.

E Evaluate Consider Your "Classroom" Performance

As with any class, you'll be receiving feedback from your instructor. But unlike many courses, in which almost all the feedback comes from the instructor, much of the feedback in a distance learning course may come from your fellow students. Consider what you can learn from their comments, while keeping in mind that they are, like you, students themselves.

At the same time you'll be receiving feedback, you will likely be providing feedback to your classmates. Consider the nature of feedback you provide, and be sure that you use the basic principles of classroom civility. (See **Section 6.3**, "Using Netiquette as You Connect with Others.")

R Rethink Reflect on What and How You Learned

Distance learning is not for everyone. If your preferred learning style involves extensive, face-to-face interaction with others, you may find a distance learning experience less than satisfying. On the other hand, if you are at ease with computers and enjoy working on your own, you may find distance learning highly effective.

As you reflect on your distance learning experience, go beyond the technology and think about the learning outcomes. Ask yourself whether you learned as much as you would have in a traditional class. You should also consider ways that the experience could have been more effective for you. And think about whether you were so absorbed by the technology that you lost sight of the real goal of the course: learning new material.

Distance learning is playing an increasingly important role in higher education. Furthermore, because it offers an efficient way of educating people in far-flung locations, it is a natural means of promoting lifelong learning experiences. In short, the first distance learning class you take will likely not be your last.

LO 6.3 Using Netiquette as You Connect with Others

Netiquette

Guidelines for demonstrating civility and respect in an online environment

While we've come a long way since the introduction of email to connect with others over the Internet, many of us still have a lot to learn about connecting and collaborating with others through the use of technology. Let's start with good manners. The rules of basic etiquette, or **netiquette** as it is called on the Internet, may not seem that important to you in your role as a student, but they are essential to your success when communicating with others online, while enrolled in distance learning, and also once you enter the work world.

Show Civility on the Web

Although email and text communication is usually less formal than a letter, it is essential to maintain civility and demonstrate good manners when you communicate electronically. Here are some rules you should follow:

> **Consider having an email address for social purposes and another to communicate with potential employers.** You do *not* want to have an email address at the top of your resumé that says sexy@hotmail.com.

> **Don't write anything in an email or text message, or attach anything, such as a photo, that you would regret seeing on the front page of the newspaper.** Yes, emails and texts are usually private, but the private message you write can easily be forwarded by the recipient to another person or even scores of other people. Worse yet, it's fairly easy to hit "reply all" when you mean simply to "reply": in this case, you might think that you are responding to an individual, when in fact the email will go to everyone who received the original message.

> **Consider carefully the tone you convey.** It is harder in email and texts to express the personality and subtlety that your voice, your handwriting, or even your stationery can add to other forms of communication. This means that attempts at humour—and especially sarcasm—can backfire. If you're using humour, consider adding **emoticons** to clarify the intent of your message—although you will want to refrain from using emoticons in formal correspondence.

Emoticons

Symbols used in email messages and other online communication that provide information on the emotion that the writer is trying to convey

> **Never write anything in an email or text, or on a social networking site, that you wouldn't say in person.** If you wouldn't say something in a face-to-face conversation, don't say it electronically.

> **Don't use all capital letters.** Using all caps MAKES IT LOOK AS IF YOU'RE SHOUTING.

> **Never send an email or text when you are angry.** No matter how annoyed you are about something someone has written in a message, don't respond in kind. Wait until you've cooled down. Take a deep breath, and wait for your anger to pass. You can always save an email as a "draft" and revisit it later on.

> **Be professional when writing to instructors and on-the-job supervisors.** *Before* emailing an instructor, ensure that you have taken whatever alternative steps you could to find out the

information you need. For example, if you missed a class and want to find out what happened, check first with your fellow students or on the course management system for a set of notes. If your instructor is the only person who can answer your question, then by all means, email them. Ensure you use an informative subject line that includes the name of the relevant course in the subject line and the nature and urgency of your request—for example, "Urgent—MKTG742—link to Porter analysis is not working." Address the recipient of the email politely, and always end with a thank you and your full name.

> **Manage your expectations when it comes to getting a reply from your instructor.** In many cases, instructors get dozens, and sometimes hundreds, of emails and texts from their students every week. In many offices, supervisors receive just as many messages. While instructors do their best, expecting a reply on a weekend or within a few hours of sending your message is simply not reasonable.

Use Email Effectively

Texting may be the most popular way of keeping in touch with friends and family, but email is still the most widely used tool for communicating with professors or in a business setting. Even if you consider yourself a savvy email user, you can still do several things to improve the effectiveness of the messages you send. Keep the following suggestions in mind when writing formal email messages:

> **Use an informative subject line.** Don't say "IMPORTANT" or "meeting" or "question." Those subject lines don't help recipients sort out your message from the dozens of others that may be clogging their inboxes. Instead, something like "Reminder: supervisor applications due 5:00 p.m. 13/10" is considerably more useful. In addition, *always* use a subject line: Some recipients routinely delete messages without a subject line, fearing they contain viruses. If your message is really short, you may want to use *only* the subject line to communicate it!

> **Make sure the recipient knows who you are.** If you are writing someone you know only casually, jog their memory with a bit of information about yourself. If you don't know the recipient at all, identify yourself early in the message ("I am a college/university student who is interested in an internship . . .").

> **Keep messages short and focused.** Email messages are most effective when they are short and direct. If at all possible, keep your message short enough to fit on a smartphone screen. If you do need to include a good deal of material, number each point or set points off by bullets so recipients will know they should read down.

> **Try to include only one major topic per email.** It's often better to write separate emails rather than including a hodgepodge of unrelated points in an email. This is especially true if you want a response to each of the different points.

> **Put requests near the beginning of the email.** If you want the recipient to do something in response to your message, respectfully put the request at the very beginning of your message. Be explicit, while being polite.

- **Keep attachments to a minimum.** If possible, include all relevant information in the body of your email. Large attachments clog people's email accounts and may be slow to download. In addition, recipients who don't know you personally may fear your attachment contains a virus and will not open it.

- **Avoid abbreviations and emoticons in formal emails.** When writing informal emails to friends, abbreviations such as AFAIK ("as far as I know"), BTW ("by the way"), CYA ("see ya"), OIC ("oh, I see"), and WTG ("way to go") are fine. So are emoticons, which signal the emotion that you are trying to convey. However, they should be avoided in formal emails. Recipients may not be familiar with them, and they may make your email seem overly casual.

Use **Try It! 3** "Use Email Netiquette" to consider email netiquette more closely.

In-Person Netiquette

There are standards for appropriate use of technology. An instructor doesn't want you to answer a call while he or she is speaking; neither does your boss.

Follow these guidelines to ensure you don't offend anyone with your use of technology:

- **Turn off your cellphone in formal settings.** If you're in a meeting or a class, keep your phone off (or in vibrate or (preferably) mute mode). Phones ringing at random times are distracting and annoying.

- **Don't send text messages or make calls while someone else is speaking to you.** You should be paying attention to what co-workers, classmates, or instructors are saying, rather than what's going on in the rest of the world. This goes for times when you are with friends as well. Texting one friend while you are with another friend is disrespectful and demeaning to the person you are with, unless, of course, you are all making plans together.

- **If you use your laptop to take notes in class, stay on task.** No matter how tempting it is to check your email messages, IM with a friend, or check out Instagram, don't do it. When in class, use your device to take notes, and nothing else.

- **Never use your cellphone to text answers to problems in class.** Cheating is cheating, whether done using high-tech or low-tech methods. Don't do it.

Protecting Your Privacy Online

Ever tried Googling yourself? Of course you have. The more interesting question is . . . what did you find? If your privacy settings are wide open on social media sites like Facebook, you can rest assured that you and your friends are not the only people who know about your ill-advised experimentation with tequila shots! Way back in 2007, a study by ExecuNet, a recruiting firm, revealed that 83 percent of people in charge of hiring looked online for information about potential candidates, and 43 percent eliminated candidates as a result of what they found. You should not be at

3 | TRY IT! POWER

Use Email Netiquette

Read the email below, written by a student to his instructor, and respond to the questions that follow.

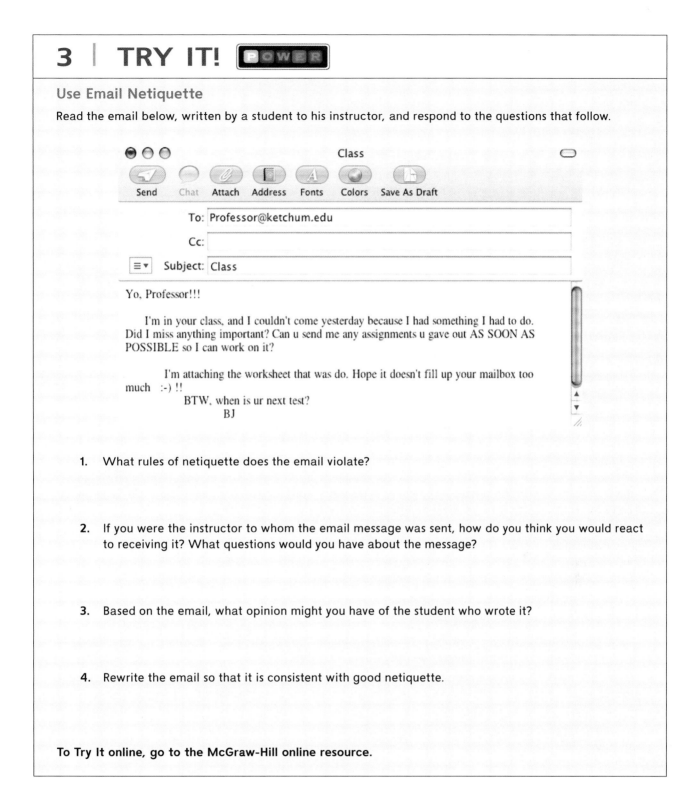

Class

Send   Chat   Attach   Address   Fonts   Colors   Save As Draft

To: Professor@ketchum.edu

Cc:

Subject: Class

Yo, Professor!!!

I'm in your class, and I couldn't come yesterday because I had something I had to do. Did I miss anything important? Can u send me any assignments u gave out AS SOON AS POSSIBLE so I can work on it?

I'm attaching the worksheet that was do. Hope it doesn't fill up your mailbox too much   :-) !!

BTW, when is ur next test?
BJ

1. What rules of netiquette does the email violate?

2. If you were the instructor to whom the email message was sent, how do you think you would react to receiving it? What questions would you have about the message?

3. Based on the email, what opinion might you have of the student who wrote it?

4. Rewrite the email so that it is consistent with good netiquette.

To Try It online, go to the McGraw-Hill online resource.

all surprised if, today, every single recruiter out there uses this technique to eliminate unsuitable candidates. You don't want to be one of them.

The Office of the Privacy Commissioner of Canada suggests[3] that you consider the following before posting information or images on social networking sites:

> Find out how the privacy settings offered can limit access to your personal information.

table 6.1　Top 10 Tips to Protect Your Inbox, Computer, and Mobile Device[4]

Protect your e-mail address from being harvested: Spam starts with a practice called "address harvesting," where computer programs indiscriminately collect email addresses that are sold to spammers. And so, your first line of defence is protecting your email address. Here are some ways to do this:

- **If posting your email address to a website, do not use the "@" or "." symbols.** Instead, use a format such as "jane **at** myDomain **dot** com." This can help prevent "spambot" software, often used to seek out and extract email addresses online, from recognizing it.

- **Use a primary email address for your trusted contacts and consider creating additional addresses for use in online activities,** such as filling out forms or joining communities. These addresses can be easily changed if they are harvested and you start receiving spam.

Protect your inbox from being a launchpad for spyware and other types of malware: While address harvesting leads to spam, spam may spread spyware, which can transmit your personal information to unauthorized parties. In some cases, your key strokes can be monitored, revealing sensitive information like account passwords. To help avoid this:

- First and foremost, **don't open e-mails** from an unfamiliar person or organization. Deleting mail from unknown senders can avoid a host of future problems.

- But, if you do, **don't reply to spam** as that can confirm your address as being active and cause you to receive more spam. For the same reason, never click on a "remove" or "unsubscribe" link in a suspicious spam message. You may be unwittingly "subscribing" to receiving even more spam.

- And **don't click on links or attachments** in an e-mail if the message is suspicious. They may be harbouring malware, which, if unleashed from your inbox, can jeopardize your privacy or compromise your device.

- Malware can even come from the accounts of your friends or other known sources if their computers have been hijacked. So, **if you are in doubt about an attachment,** don't reply to the email itself and before opening it **check with the sender** by phone or in person. In other words, if an email from a trusted source seems out of character, it may indeed be from an altogether different character.

- **Report unsolicited e-mail containing suspicious attachments** or content to the Spam Reporting Centre at **www.fightspam.gc.ca.** By analyzing accumulated reports and identifying trends gathered by the Centre, the Office of the Privacy Commissioner of Canada is working with its enforcement partners to identify address harvesters and sources of spyware for investigation.

Protect your device or computer: Think of these next steps as a sort of insurance policy for your device in the event your first two lines of defence fail:

- Install security software from a reliable company on your computer. Security software should include features like anti-spam, anti-virus, anti-malware, and a firewall.

- Ensure your operating system and other software suites, including security software, are set to automatically update. If you're not sure how, use your "Help" function and search for "Automatic Updates."

- Don't acquire security software in response to unexpected calls, messages, or pop-ups. This type of marketing is commonly used for malicious purposes. Instead, only download security software from websites you know and trust. Free software might sound appealing but can hide malware. In the same vein, apps for your mobile device should only be downloaded from reputable marketplaces.

© Office of the Privacy Commissioner of Canada

> Adjust your privacy settings so that information about your family and children is shared only with those you know well.

> Don't include too much personal information that could make you vulnerable to identity fraud.

> Think carefully before posting information—would you want your employer or potential employer to see those compromising photos?

- Review your information regularly—what may have seemed like a good idea at the time may not seem like such a good idea months or years later. But remember that while there are often tools to delete or hide information, data posted online can persist in different places, and permanent removal can be difficult if not impossible.
- Get people's consent before you upload their pictures or personal information.
- Use strong passwords and logins to prevent your account from being hacked.

Devices such as smartphones and tablets are now part of everyday life for most Canadian students. The Office of the Privacy Commissioner of Canada has developed a number of fact sheets to help protect your privacy, both online and on devices such as smartphones, tablets, and laptops. **Table 6.1** outlines the Office's tips for protecting information on personal devices.

LO 6.4 Developing Information Competency

Learning *how* to learn in the 21st century is about understanding where and how to locate the information and expertise you need, how to evaluate the credibility of an information source, and how to credit sources that you use. In other words, learners today need to develop **information competency**. To view a short but fascinating video that summarizes how all of these skills come together under the umbrella term "connectivism," visit YouTube and find a video created by Wendy Drexler called "Networked Student."

Information competency
The ability to determine what information is necessary, and then to locate, evaluate, credit, and effectively use that information

Locate Information in the Library

Students are often mystified by the notion that anyone would want to make the effort of going to a library database to find information, when the Web is at their fingertips. Why bother? **Table 6.2** will help you understand why the library is the hands-down winner in this battle.

No matter how imposing or humble their physical appearance, whether they contain only a few hundred volumes or hundreds of thousands, libraries are a good place to focus your efforts as you seek out and gather information. Although every library is different, all share two key elements: the material they hold—whether paper-based or electronic—and trained librarians and tools available to help you locate the material you need.

What Can Be Found in a Library's Basic Collection?

Libraries obviously contain books—some of which are now available in the form of e-books—but they typically have a lot more than that, including some or all of the following:

- **Paper-based periodicals.** While recent issues of journals, newspapers, and magazines may be found in paper form, older issues are usually available through **online databases**.

Online database
An electronic, organized body of information on a related topic, or dealing with related media

table 6.2　The Web versus Library Databases—A Comparison

	The Web (e.g., Google, Wikipedia, DotDash (formerly About.com))	Library Databases (e.g., Lexis-Nexis)
Authority	Varies at best. Difficult to verify. Cannot limit to professional, scholarly literature. Information on the Web is seldom regulated, which means authority is often in doubt.	Easy to determine. Most databases have scholarly/peer-reviewed filters or contain only scholarly literature. Authority and trustworthiness are virtually guaranteed.
Number of Hits	Thousands, sometimes millions, of hits, much of the same information repackaged or duplicated. Duplicates are not filtered out.	Dozens to hundreds of hits (sometimes thousands but not hundreds of thousands)—a more manageable number, and duplicates can be filtered out.
Relevance	Lack of subject focus resulting in numerous irrelevant hits—or "junk"—to wade through. Much Web information is opinionated and biased. Unless you are using a subject-specific search engine, expect "everything including the kitchen sink" in the results. Quantity ≠ Quality.	Focus by subject (business, art, Canadian history) and/or format (journals, books, book reviews), often meaning more relevant information and less time wasted dealing with junk. Information comes from legitimate, quality-controlled sources.
Search Features	Varies by search engine, but often limited. Can limit by document type (.doc, .pdf) or language, but limiting by publication date, format (article, book, etc.), scholarly/peer-reviewed, and more is unavailable.	Numerous advanced search features determined by database subject focus, e.g., limiting by publication type, date, language, document format, scholarly/peer-reviewed status. The list of features is as long as the number of databases available.
Access to Published Information	Web information often lives and dies on the Web and can come from anyone with Internet access. Information seldom comes from legitimate published sources: magazines, academic journals, books, etc. When it does, the user usually has to pay to access it.	Databases dealing only with published information, that is, information that originally appeared in print: magazine and journal articles, books, etc. More stable than the Web. Through the library's paid access, all of this information is available to you, the user, for free.

© University of Maryland

> **Online databases.** A significant proportion of your college or university's library holdings are actually not in the library itself; instead, they can be found online. Most university and college libraries subscribe to a wide variety of online databases that are accessible to enrolled students anywhere, any time, without the students ever having to set foot in the library.

> An online database usually includes a searchable listing of periodical articles by title, author, subject, and keyword. These databases contain advanced search options that allow you to perform these functions:

> • Search in particular kinds of publications, e.g., academic journals versus newspapers or trade magazines.

> • Specify date ranges or page ranges, e.g., only articles published after 2010 that are at least three pages in length.

- Choose to obtain a short summary (called an *abstract*) of the contents of available articles, or to see only articles that appear with "full text," i.e., the entire contents of the article, including images.

> **Government documents.** Census records, laws, and tax codes are some of the millions of government documents that are stored in libraries.

Searching for materials in the library stacks can be frustrating if the materials you need are not on the shelves. Don't forget to ask your librarian whether what you are looking for can be found in an online database instead.

Locate Information on the Web

The Web is vast—sometimes frustratingly so. Add to that the fact that anyone can put information on it, and therein lies both the biggest asset and the greatest disadvantage of using the Web as an information source. Because minimal computer skill is the only expertise a person needs to set up a Web page, there may be as much misinformation on the Web as there is information, so keep the usual consumer rule in mind: Buyer beware. Unless the website was established and is maintained by a reliable organization, the information it contains may not be accurate.

A search engine is your gateway into the Web, with Google far and away the most well known. Other commonly used search engines are Bing, Yahoo!, and Ask.com. There's no single search engine that works best, although Google Scholar, with its focus on peer-reviewed publications, is particularly appropriate for work done in colleges and universities. Most people develop their own preferences based on their experience. The best advice: Try out several of them and see which works best for you. To get started, work through **Try It! 4** "Work the Web: Information, Please!"

Evaluate the Credibility of a Website

While you can be pretty much assured of the credibility of what you find in a library's online database, the same cannot be said for what you find on the Web. Indeed, the cruise line Royal Caribbean International was chastised[5] some years ago for allegedly creating a group of sanctioned contributors to travel discussion boards. Today, most people check reviews before they make decisions about travel, but, clearly, you can't always believe what you read. You must carefully assess the content of every website you choose to reference in your academic work. Yale University, working from a tool developed by the University of Maryland and the University of Dallas, developed five criteria for evaluating websites.[6] (These criteria are applicable to any medium.) To determine whether a site's contents can be trusted, it is best that you carefully evaluate the site. Ask yourself the following questions to determine whether a site (or other media source) contains sound information:

1. **Audience.** To whom is the site directed—children, adults, students; a certain ethnicity, gender, or political affiliation? Is it understandable by the layperson, or is it highly technical, requiring specialized knowledge?

4 | TRY IT! POWER

Work the Web: Information, Please!

Part A: Try to find the answer to the first question below on Yahoo! (**ca.yahoo.com**), Google (**google.ca**), and Dogpile (**dogpile.com**). Then use whichever search engine you prefer to find answers to the remaining questions.

1. What was Bill 101, and where and when was it passed?

2. Who is Jason Reitman?

3. Actor Kiefer Sutherland's grandfather was famous in his own right. What was his name, and what is he known for?

4. Is the birth rate in Canada higher or lower than that in Brazil?

5. What is the Paris Agreement?

Part B:
1. How easy was it for you to find the answers to the questions?
2. Which search engine(s) did you prefer, and why?

To Try It online, go to the McGraw-Hill online resource.

"First, they do an online search."

2. **Authority.** Is the author of the site listed? Can you determine their expertise? Is contact information given—phone number, address, email? With what organization are they associated?

3. **Bias.** Does the language, tone, or treatment of its subject give the site a particular slant or bias? Is the site objective? Is it designed to sway opinion? (Note that the organizational affiliation can often indicate bias.)

4. **Currency.** Is the site up to date? Do the links work? Are dates given for when the site was created and last updated? Is the topic current?

5. **Scope.** Is the site an in-depth study of the topic going several pages deep, or is it a superficial, single-page look at the subject? Are statistics and sources that are referenced properly cited? Does the site offer unique information not found anywhere else—including print sources?

Find the Information You Need Efficiently and Effectively

Whether you are searching an online library database or the Web, the process is very similar and is based on your ability to use key words appropriately to find what you are looking for. Use too few key words, and your search will turn up too many documents, many of which will not be directly relevant to your topic. On the other hand, use too many key words or use quotation marks around them, and you may find nothing at all.

Once you have narrowed your search appropriately, using the list of sites generated by the search is simple. Click or tap on the site address of the relevant document, and the site will appear on your screen. You can then take notes on the material, in the same way you'd take notes on material in a book.

How can you limit your search in the first place, so that you find sites that are more directly relevant to your research topic? The following tips can help you to get the most from a search:[7]

> **Phrase your search as a question** before you type anything into your computer.

> **Identify the important words in that question.** Then think of words that are related to the important words. Write all of these words down.

> **Type these keywords into a search engine** like Google.

You can do several things to limit the number of results returned, thus making your search more efficient and effective. Most search engines (including those for online databases) have advanced search features (see **Figure 6.2**) that allow you to use some or all of the following:

> **Quotation marks** to denote a phrase—words that should appear together, in a specific order (e.g., "animal rights").

> **Plus signs** before terms that must appear in all results returned (+"animal rights" +experimentation).

> **Hyphens (minus signs)** before terms you do not want to appear in results (+"animal rights" +experimentation -fur).

> **An asterisk** to denote that the word can have more than one ending (auto* can be automobile or automotive) or to be a placeholder for an unknown term (e.g., Trudeau voted * on the bill).

> **Boolean operators**—words like AND, OR, NOT, and NEAR (e.g., "animal rights" AND experimentation NOT fur).

Another approach to consider, particularly when you are working on a specific report or assignment, is to have the information come to you, rather than you going to the Web to retrieve the information. Sound intriguing? Well, it's really not hard to do. For instance, let's say that you are doing a group report on the auto industry, and you've been assigned to work on Toyota.

figure 6.2 | Using Advanced Search in Google

Advanced search functionality is also available on many search engines. Google allows you to specify language, date, region, and so forth.

Through Google Alerts, you can specify that any article on the Web or in a blog that mentions Toyota be emailed to you on a regular basis—as it happens, daily, or weekly, for example. The email will contain a short description of each article and a link to it that can be accessed immediately. It's a simple way to stay on top of the latest information about a particular topic.

Evaluate the Information You Find

In most instances, you'll find more information than you need. Try using more keywords to home in on what you need. Once you've found what you're looking for and have determined that the website you're looking at is reliable, you will have to evaluate the information you have found there. Here are some important questions you must address before you can feel confident about what you've found:

> **How authoritative is the information?** It is absolutely essential to consider the source of the material. Approach every piece of information with a critical eye, trying to determine what the author's biases might be. The best approach is to use multiple sources of information. If one source diverges radically from the others, you may reasonably question the reliability of that source.

Another approach is to consider the publisher of the material or its sponsoring institution. For instance, sites established by well-known publishers and organizations are more likely to contain accurate information than those created by unknown (and often anonymous) authors. Remember, the Web is completely unregulated: *Anyone* can put *anything* on the Web. The best example of this is Wikipedia, a widely used online encyclopedia created by people just like you. *Anyone* can contribute to Wikipedia—from a six-year-old to your grandmother. You do *not* have to be an established authority on a subject to contribute. For this very reason, Wikipedia should *never* be used as a source for academic work.

> **How current is the information?** No matter what the subject, information is changing rapidly. Consider whether what you've found is the most recent and up-to-date material. Compare older sources to newer ones to identify changes in how the topic is considered.

> **How well are claims documented?** Are there references and citations to support the information? Are specific studies identified?

On balance, when doing scholarly research (i.e., for college or university requirements), you should lean far more heavily toward library databases, as this is where references and citations get the respect they deserve.

Analyze the Information You Find

Perhaps the most common illusion under which students operate when it comes to Internet research is that once they have found the information they need, then their work is done. Far from it. Nicholas Carr, author of

"On the Internet, nobody knows you're a dog."

The Shallows, wrote a compelling cover story in *The Atlantic* called "Is Google Making Us Stupid?"[8] where he argues that easy access to information in the age of Google is compromising our ability to read and think more deeply. Your instructors will expect more than a few quotes from a few sources. They will expect you not only to read the information you find, but also to analyze it and go deeper, adding your own thoughts and testing out your own theories. They will expect you to summarize what you've found, look for patterns in the findings, and come to your own conclusions. They will expect you to challenge what you've found or integrate your findings in a compelling way. Keep this in mind: finding the information is only the first step.

Wondering how your Striving Style™ and your research skills are related? See the table below.

Research Skills and Striving Styles™

Leaders	Focused, organized and thorough. Eager to get what they need and do it efficiently. Skim through to get main points that support their argument. Quickly categorize what is useful and what isn't. Weed out facts, discarding theory or conjecture.
Socializers	Prefer doing research with others, sharing their enthusiasm for what they are finding. Enjoy reading and gathering information when researching topics of a personal nature. Challenging to do factual research and can lose their motivation easily.
Performers	Once they get started, enjoy doing research and the process of learning new things. Sometimes don't know when to stop. Can go off on tangents, gathering research outside the scope of the project. Analyze their research and easily connect patterns.
Adventurers	Do not enjoy research and do the bare minimum necessary. No intrinsic instant gratification in researching. Will procrastinate or distract themselves and then rush to finish. Need to research with others to keep themselves focused.
Artists	Immerse themselves in doing research and do it wholeheartedly. Gather a wealth of information with great depth and breadth. Can become overwhelmed, not knowing when they have done enough. Difficulty organizing research materials.
Intellectuals	Love research and will lose themselves in the process. Don't always know when to stop. Dig deeply into subjects and find obscure references others don't. Easily see which facts support their argument and which don't. Are meticulous about their research.
Visionaries	Enjoy research and the process of organizing and systematizing information. Mind takes leaps in understanding; only need to read small amounts to understand. Can be impatient with detail and dry facts. Try to make the research fit their theory.
Stabilizers	Thorough, methodical, and detailed. Do not stray from what is being asked for. Choose reliable sources for research and discount less credible or acceptable sources. May become overwhelmed with the information and data they have compiled.

And, Finally, Recognize That Even Technology Has Its Limitations

Author Tom Clancy once said: "It was one thing to use computers as a tool, quite another to let them do your thinking for you."[9] It is important to keep in mind that while technology can facilitate many tasks and can be a source of endless entertainment and information, it is not a replacement for deep thinking, or for animated discussions with your classmates, or for respectfully confronting someone about their behaviour. Nor is it a replacement for communicating and interacting with the people in your life that you really care about. As powerful as it can be, even technology has its limitations!

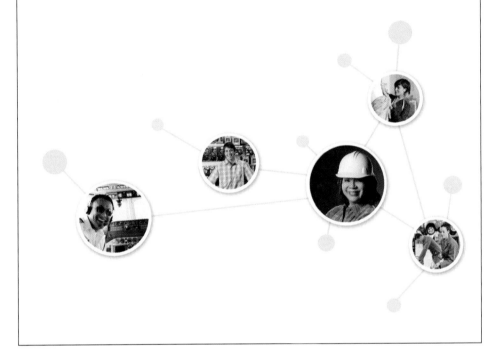
LO 6.5 Plagiarism: What It Is and How to Avoid It

Not so long ago, aspiring scholars would find that one of their most difficult tasks came not *during* the research process but, rather, at the *end* of the process, when they found themselves having to pull together the many sources used in their work to ensure they avoided plagiarism. Depending on the nature of their research, they might use the Modern Language Association (MLA) or American Psychological Association (APA) standard of citing sources, making careful note of the type of source being cited, what needed to be italicized or underlined, and the order in which to place each part of the reference. They had to capture all their in-text citations, and then they would find themselves collecting all of their sources in a bibliography at the end of their research document. To call this a major effort is an understatement, and if a researcher was collaborating with other authors who had their own list of references, this last step was a nightmare. For many students, the temptation to "lift" the information, without bothering to cite the source, became increasingly hard to resist: It was simply too much effort to do it right.

But times have changed.

The recent introduction of user-friendly citation or reference management software has made it much, much easier to be an ethical researcher. Products like **Zotero**, **EndNote**, **NoodleTools**, and **RefWorks** help you collect, manage, cite, and share your research sources and avoid plagiarism by making it easy to practise proper citation methods. Much of this citation software is either free online or available free of charge through your school's library. To see a table comparing the functions of Zotero and Endnote, visit **libguides.mit.edu/references**.

So what exactly is plagiarism? As noted in Chapter 5, in simplest terms, plagiarism is taking credit for someone else's words, thoughts, or ideas. According to the website **plagiarism.org**, *all* of the following are considered plagiarism:

> turning in someone else's work as your own

> copying words or ideas from someone else without giving credit

> failing to put a quotation in quotation marks

> giving incorrect information about the source of a quotation

> changing words but copying the sentence structure of a source without giving credit

> copying so many words or ideas from a source that it makes up the majority of your work, whether you give credit or not

Virtually every college and university today has a plagiarism policy. Increasingly, institutions are turning to plagiarism detection programs like the one found at **turnitin.com** to identify students who contravene their policy. The penalties for plagiarism can range from getting a zero on an assignment or on the course to being expelled.

If you are working in a group, the penalty incurred could affect more than just you. If your name is on the title page, you are responsible for the content, even if it is someone else who plagiarized. Always be on the lookout—and upload your report to a plagiarism detection site and do a self-check so you can catch plagiarism before your instructor does!

Resist the temptation to simply cut and paste the material into a new document once you've found the information you're looking for. It's too easy to succumb to plagiarism if you simply copy material. Instead, take notes on the material using the critical thinking and note-taking skills you've been developing throughout this course. If you must quote a source directly, use proper citation methods: Put quotation marks around the quotation, insert an in-text citation, and ensure that you have the full reference in your bibliography or works cited list. It is not worth taking the chance—especially when there are so many tools available that make citing easy. Visit **plagiarism.org** for more details on how to detect and prevent plagiarism.

Time to Reflect: What **Did I Learn?**

1. In an average day, how much time do you spend using technology (e.g., smartphone, laptop, tablet)?

2. Thinking about both the positive and the negative, in what way does technology affect your relationships with others?

3. Which technological device could you live without? Which device could you *not* live without? Why?

Did You Know?

In 1876, Alexander Graham Bell was the first to acquire a patent for the telephone. We've come a long way since then. As of 2016, 75 percent of Canadians owned a smartphone capable of accessing the Internet,[10] and as of July 2016, according to Internet Live Stats, there were 32,120,519 "Internet users"[11] in Canada, representing 88.5 percent of our population. This places Canada in 21st place on a per capita basis among all countries in the world.[12]

Looking Back

How is technology used in education?
> Course websites (including instructor's presentation slides), textbook websites, e-books, podcasts, blogs, and vlogs are among the major educational uses of technology.

How can I use technology to become a better student?
> You can organize your materials and your work using technology.
> You can use technology as a support to your in-class learning or to take courses at a distance.
> You can use technology to connect with your fellow students.
> You can use technology to network with your peers and to maintain contact with your industry and potential employers.

What is distance learning?
> Distance learning is a form of education that does not require the physical presence of a student in a classroom. It is usually conducted over the Web.
> Distance learning requires some adjustments for students, but it is becoming an increasingly popular choice as people try to balance their lives and as their competency with technology increases.

What is netiquette, and why does it matter?
> Netiquette is the guidelines for interacting politely on email and other electronic devices.
> Your manners on electronic devices, like your manners in person, contribute to people's overall impression of you. If you behave inappropriately in cyberspace, you will present an image of yourself that could undermine your effectiveness in groups, interfere with your friendships, and even affect job and career prospects.

How can I develop information competency?
> There are two main sources of information today: libraries and the Web.
> Information in libraries is available in print form and in electronic form.

> Library resources can be found by using the library catalogue, which may be digital or print based.

> Your library likely subscribes to several online databases, which are an excellent source of information.

> The Web is another major source of information, although it needs to be used with some caution.

What do I need to keep in mind as I use the Web to gather information?

> Using the Web effectively to find information can be tricky. It has many dead ends, false trails, and distractions, and the accuracy of the information presented as fact can be difficult to assess.

> You must carefully evaluate information on the Web by considering how reliable the source is, how current the information is, and how well the source's claims are documented.

How can I avoid plagiarism?

> The only way to avoid plagiarism is to cite your sources, both in the context of your report (called in-text citations) and in a bibliography at the end.

RESOURCES

ON CAMPUS

If you are having difficulty getting into your college or university's password-protected site or using its learning management system, the first place to turn is your college's computer centre or help desk. Most campuses have consultants who can help you with the technical aspects of computer use.

If you've forgotten your laptop at home and need access to a computer on campus, most colleges and universities have computer labs or will lend out computers through their library. Typically, computer labs provide computers with standard software, as well as access to printers. It's important to check lab hours, as they are usually not open 24/7. In addition, you may have to wait in line for a computer, so it is a good idea to bring some other work to the lab so you have something to do while waiting.

The librarians at your college or university library are the people you should turn to first if you need help locating information. In recent years, librarians—most of whom hold advanced degrees—have undergone a significant change in what they do. Most are equally at home using traditional print material and searching electronic information storehouses. Some colleges and universities have librarians that are available through a chat function—a good thing if you are working on something that is due tomorrow!

And, once again, don't forget that your instructors can be a great source of information.

IN PRINT

For a guide to going beyond Google when searching the Internet, take a look at Randolph Hock's *The Extreme Searcher's Internet Handbook: A Guide for the Serious Searcher*, 4th edition (Information Today, Inc., 2013).

A classic that will help you with library research is the 4th edition of *The Oxford Guide to Library Research: How to Find Reliable Information Online and Offline* by Thomas Mann (Oxford University Press, 2015).

The Savvy Student's Guide to Online Learning, by Kristen Sosulski and Ted Bongiovanni (Routledge, 2013), is a quick read that will show you how to become an effective online learner.

For a compelling book on how technology has affected our relationships, look for MIT Professor Sherry Turkle's *Alone Together: Why We Expect More from Technology and Less from Our Relationships* (Basic Books, 2011) or *Reclaiming Conversation: The Power of Talk in a Digital Age* (Penguin Books, 2015). If you'd rather watch her speak, check out her TED Talk "Connected but Alone?" at **ted.com/talks/ sherry_turkle_alone_together?language=en**.

ON THE WEB

The following websites provide an opportunity to extend your learning about the material in this chapter:

> The WWW Virtual Library (**vlib.org/**) is one of the oldest catalogues on the Web, providing useful links to thousands of subjects.

> Questia (**questia.com**) is the world's largest online library of books, with over 83,000 full-text books; 10 million articles; an entire reference set complete with a dictionary, an encyclopedia, and a thesaurus; and citation and bibliography tools.

> For a shot of "YouTube for the brain," spend a few minutes on **ted.com**. The site, which has as its tag line "ideas worth spreading," contains videos of some of the most compelling people in the world speaking on every topic imaginable. A good place to start is with *Wired* magazine's Chris Anderson on the concept of technology's "long tail," or, on a lighter note, Canadian writer Malcolm Gladwell's talk on why there are so many versions of spaghetti sauce available.

> Having difficulty grasping a concept dealing with math, science, humanities, finance, or economics? You'll want to check out the excellent resources at **khanacademy.org**.

THERE'S AN APP FOR THAT

Because it is a regulated industry with few competitors, telecommunications providers in Canada charge some of the highest wireless rates in the developed world. Where a basic wireless package in Canada averages $41.08, that same package in Germany would cost only $17.15.[13]

Tracking usage is key to keeping your telecommunications costs under control. An app that can help you do that is called **My Data Manager**, and it is available for both iOS and Android. The app tracks specific cycles (daily, monthly) for your mobile, WiFi, and roaming usage; allows you to set custom alarms that notify you when you are getting close to your data limit; and helps you avoid overage charges.

TAKING IT TO THE WEB

1 In Canada, the Personal Information Protection and Electronic Documents Act (PIPEDA) outlines 10 privacy principles that businesses must adhere to if they collect customer information. Find these 10 principles, and, as you read through them, ask yourself if they are sufficient to protect your private information.

2 Increasingly, smartphone and tablet apps are targeting the specific needs of students. Some address grammar and spelling; others address study skills or time management. To see for yourself what's currently available, Google "best apps for students" or "top apps for students" and see what you can find.

THE CASE OF . . .
The Empty Page

It had already been a long day for Naomi Erikson.

She'd worked two hours of overtime at her job supervising a call centre. She'd driven home and immediately sat down at her computer to start work on a paper for her marketing class the next day. It was already 11:00 P.M. by the time she finished her research on the Web. Then she began writing, opening a new file in her word-processing program.

Naomi worked hard, drinking coffee to help her concentrate on the paper—and to keep her eyes open. When she was about three-quarters of the way done, her computer screen suddenly froze. Naomi pushed every button she could think of, but finally had to switch her computer off and then switch it back on. She opened the file for her paper . . . and saw an empty page.

To her horror, Naomi realized that her paper had been lost. She looked at the clock—it was almost 3:00 A.M. Did she really need to start her paper all over again?

1. How well did Naomi use her time to work on her paper? What advice would you give her about the preparation stage of working on a paper?

2. Clearly, Naomi should have saved her work frequently while she was working. What else should she have done while working on her paper to help her recover from such a catastrophe?

3. Do you think Naomi's instructor would be sensitive to her problem? Do you think they would be willing to give her an extension? What could Naomi do to make her case that she had nearly finished the paper?

4. What should Naomi do next to begin reconstructing her paper and recovering as much of her work as possible?

Right: © HeroImages/Corbis/Glow Images
© HeroImages/Getty Images;

CHAPTER 7
Writing and Presenting

Learning Outcomes

By the time you finish this chapter, you will be able to

LO 7.1 Describe the type of writing done at the post-secondary level.

LO 7.2 Explain the process involved in preparing and writing a report or case analysis.

LO 7.3 Discuss the process involved in creating and delivering effective presentations.

Mack Tran was terrified. It was only the third week of classes and it was gradually sinking in that he was not going to be able to avoid making presentations in class; in fact, it was looking like presentations were going to account for an important part of his mark in several courses. He had always been a good student, turning in well-thought-out written reports, but when it came to having to explain his findings to others in his class—well, let's just say it was not his strong suit. But now, with his college marks depending on it, he knew he had no choice. Mack was going to have to find some help.

Mack confided his fears to a classmate, who, as it turned out, was a member of Toastmasters, an organization that has helped hundreds of thousands of people get over their fear of speaking in public. After some gentle prodding, Mack agreed to accompany his friend to the next Toastmasters meeting, where he observed that the participants learn by doing—giving impromptu speeches on specific topics and delivering prepared speeches to an audience that provides useful feedback in a supportive environment.

In just over a year, Mack worked his way through Toastmasters' *Competent Communication* manual, a series of self-paced speaking assignments that teach the foundations of public speaking. Feeling far more confident about his ability to speak in public, Mack now looked forward to the opportunity to practise his newfound skills through the remainder of his college career and beyond.

Looking Ahead

As Mack discovered, communication is the foundation of education. Being able to speak and write clearly and communicate your ideas with conviction orally and in writing are skills that will go a long way toward getting you through college or university, regardless of your major. But the need for good communication skills doesn't end when you graduate. Whether it's writing a resumé, interviewing for a job, pitching an idea to your co-workers, or coming up with a unique way to propose to your partner, learning how to get your ideas across to others is an investment that offers a lifetime payout.

In the first two sections of this chapter, you'll learn the "how to" of good writing: how to generate ideas and come up with a main thesis, how to structure your report in a logical fashion, how to make a compelling argument for your point of view, how to cite supporting evidence, and how to produce a conclusion that ties the whole report together. In the last section of the chapter, the focus will be on transforming your thoughts and ideas into vivid and memorable presentations. You'll get tips for creating effective presentations, suggestions on how to reduce the anxiety associated with public speaking, and ways to make your presentations come alive with visuals.

LO 7.1 Writing at the Post-secondary Level

With the arrival of texting and email, where abbreviations like LOL, BTW, and TTFN are ubiquitous, and with the increasing reliance on simple Microsoft PowerPoint slides to communicate increasingly complex ideas, writing in the traditional sense is starting to look downright quaint. You'll soon find out, however, that it has *not* gone out of style in post-secondary educational institutions, where it remains the main method of communicating thoughts and ideas.

Some General Guidelines

You may be called upon to use many different types of writing in college or university, and these will depend on your area of study. English majors may be asked to analyze a poem, art majors might be asked to describe a famous painting, chemistry students may be asked to write a lab report, and business students may be asked to complete a case analysis to recommend a specific course of action. There are also different ways that the various Striving Styles™ approach the task of writing papers.

Writing Papers and Striving Styles™

Leaders	Disciplined and organized, will provide objective, fact-based content. Present logical arguments and are confident in their position. Tend to overstate and assume authoritative position. Don't allow their ideas and facts to be influenced by feelings. Ensure papers only contain what is asked for and information is presented in a practical and efficient fashion.
Socializers	Natural communicators who express themselves easily. Impatient to finish and with details, they will omit facts, filling them in with fiction and imagination. Personal and conversational, they argue from their values with conviction and personal anecdotes. Jump to conclusions and may not test their theory. Need engagement, feedback, and encouragement to do their best work.
Performers	Enjoy the process of generating ideas and following different streams of creativity. Can have difficultly reining in their focus. Writing style is a blend of the personal and the rational. Tend to infuse their writing with enthusiasm and energy. See what their paper will look like once completed and can find the writing process dull in comparison to coming up with the ideas.
Adventurers	Organize material logically and efficiently. Like to discuss their ideas with others before starting. Don't work from an outline; instead, collect facts and eliminate what doesn't work. Don't enjoy planning and will wait until the deadline looms to energize them. Persuasive in their writing style and argue their point well, backing it up with enough facts to get alignment.
Artists	Creative, imaginative, and descriptive writers. Writing is a natural form of self-expression. Prefer writing from the personal perspective rather than the factual or the technical. Can see different sides to an argument and may have difficulty deciding what side to argue. Need quiet and solitude to do their best work. May fear they will not meet expectations and deliver far more than what is expected of them.
Intellectuals	Have an unquenchable appetite for information and prefer research to writing. Seek facts and enjoy subjects that can be proven. Gather information, sort and classify, and write what they believe is relevant, whether asked for or not. Can be terse and impersonal in their writing style. Have difficulty writing if they think the topic is irrelevant.
Visionaries	Enjoy exploring, analyzing, and problem solving. Conceptualize their paper first, envisioning both the problem and the solution. Need time to see what it will look like and to write without distraction. Ideas are well developed and organized. First develop the framework and then flush out the body. Original and innovative, their unique ideas are sometimes difficult for others to grasp.
Stabilizers	Follow instructions to the letter and need clear, detailed expectations to do their best work. Do their research, complete a first draft, and then finalize their work. Disciplined, thorough, and efficient. Deliver what is expected of them on time. Need a quiet environment without interruptions to do their best work. Won't include personal or descriptive content unless explicitly asked.

While there are different types of writing and approaches to writing, there are still some general guidelines to keep in mind when you are asked to write at the college or university level. First, you need to write with a specific **thesis** or "angle" in mind. Writing an essay on "Aboriginals in Canada" is far too broad a topic for the post-secondary level; instead, try writing a critique of "the policy of 'aggressive assimilation' of Aboriginal children in residential schools in Canada in the 19th century." In the next section, we introduce mind mapping, an excellent way to uncover an appropriate thesis or angle for your essays. Second, you need to produce **arguments** (facts or evidence that support your thesis). This means you need to keep track of your research sources, as academic writing requires

Thesis
A closely related set of ideas that suggest an angle or way of approaching a topic

Arguments
Facts, research findings, or other evidence used to support a thesis

that you cite sources and produce a comprehensive bibliography of these sources. And, finally, outlining a logical progression of your ideas and the evidence supporting them, and doing so *before* you actually begin to write, is essential to high-quality writing.

LO 7.2 The Process of Writing

Writing is *not* a one-step process. In fact, the writing process follows the five steps in the P.O.W.E.R. Learning framework. Procrastinators, take note: This means that sitting down and attempting to write a complete essay in one sitting is unlikely to produce a good outcome. To write a good report, you need to take the time to proceed through each of the steps in sequence. Before you begin, consider drawing up a "workback" schedule, a technique you learned back in Chapter 2: Work your way back from the report due date, give specific deadlines for each step in the writing process, and record these deadlines on your work calendar. This approach will ensure that you don't find yourself trying to wing it the day before the report is due.

| **P** Prepare | **O** Organize | **W** Work | **E** Evaluate | **R** Rethink |
| Figure out what to write about; do the necessary research | Identify major themes, find an angle, and outline the flow | Write the initial draft | Rest, reread, revise; rewrite, if necessary | Reflect on instructor feedback |

P.O.W.E.R. Plan

The longer you wait to start writing an essay or report, the harder it will be to produce a good result.

© Ron Leishman/Clipart Of

Mind mapping

A visual technique that involves writing a central idea in the middle of a sheet of paper and then drawing "branches"—i.e., subtopics or themes that stem from the central idea. These subtopics can then be used to form a new thesis

P Prepare Explore Your Topic

How do you prepare to start writing? The first thing you need to do is figure out what to write about. Instructors at the post-secondary level will often assign a broad topic, and it will be up to you to determine what angle or perspective you want to bring to that topic. To get started, you'll want to use some of the research techniques you learned about in Chapter 6 to find articles about the topic that interests you most. Then, do some reading to get a sense of what others have already written on the issue. This part of the process can take almost as much time as the writing itself, so be sure to include it in your workback schedule! Next, you'll want to engage in a free-form exercise such as brainstorming or **mind mapping** to identify existing approaches and come up with new angles and unique approaches to the topic.

Mind mapping allows you to explore your associations with a main idea or theme and to uncover subtopics or supporting ideas that you can use in your report (see **Figure 7.1**). Mind mapping can also be used to identify tasks in a project, components of a new website, and so forth. While a mind map is usually created by linking a central idea on a piece of paper to other ideas, you can also

© www.goconqr.com

---

1 | TRY IT! POWER

Create a Mind Map

One way to generate ideas and angles for a report is to create a mind map.

Try making your own mind map for a topic assigned by one of your instructors. Follow the example in Figure 7.1.

To Try It online, go to the McGraw-Hill online resource.

---

create a mind map by using sticky notes on a table or wall. The sticky note approach works well if you are generating ideas in a group. This approach can save you organizational time, as it allows you to go back and put your ideas into a logical order simply, thereby creating a framework for your report writing or presentation planning. (See **Try It! 1** "Create a Mind Map.")

Organize Create an Outline

The second step in the writing process is getting organized to write. At this point, you've

You can create a writing framework or outline by using sticky notes and moving them around until you get a logical flow.
© Fuse/Getty Images

- **Use pictures instead of words** where possible. There is a good reason for the expression "a picture is worth a thousand words." You can use the free clipart images that come with Microsoft Word or you can obtain royalty-free images on the Internet on sites like **freedigitalphotos.net**. If you are presenting data, use pie charts, bar charts, and graphs that summarize your findings rather than showing the raw data.

- **Add variety.** Switch it up a bit. Feel free to go from a slide with bullet points over to a website and back, or from a bullet point to a visual and back. Your audience will appreciate the break from words, words, and more words.

- **Plan for questions.** Decide ahead of time whether you want the audience to hold its questions until the end. If so, ensure you have a "Questions?" slide to wrap up your talk—and make sure you've left enough time to field questions.

- **Prepare a handout** of your presentation slides by printing them out three to a page. Be sure to put your detailed contact information somewhere in the handout, and print more than enough copies for the number of people you are expecting in the audience.

Dressing the Part

Whether you are speaking in front of your instructor and fellow students, or at a convention of the best minds in the world, your clothing should be inwardly comfortable and outwardly presentable. This is *not* the time to wear your flashiest clothes, or your torn hoodie and grubby running shoes. Your clothing choices should convey a crispness and professionalism that conveys the message "I am the expert," while at the same time allowing you to move freely across a stage or into an audience. Think about what you'll wear several days before you make your presentation. This will give you time to ensure that the clothing you've selected is clean and in good repair, and that your shoes are shined and ready to go. The extra care you take with dress and grooming on presentation day will be noticed—and first impressions being what they are, it could even have an impact on your grade.

You're On!

The day of your presentation has arrived. You've done all the recommended preparation, your slides and visuals have been created, your USB stick is in your pocket, and you are raring to go. Not so fast. There are still a few things to do *before* the presentation actually begins.

Never, ever stand in front of a projector.

© Pavel L Photo and Video/Shutterstock

Owning Your Environment

Always be sure to arrive early for your presentation, and check out the room in which it will take place. Examine the room carefully. Is there a podium or lectern? Where is the projector? Do you need to move anything around? Own your environment by ensuring that it is optimized for the type of presentation you plan to deliver. Now, check and double-check that the technology is working. There is nothing more distressing than having to troubleshoot a projector or a laptop while your audience waits for the presentation to start. Bring up the programs and content you plan to use, and then minimize them or bring up your title slide. If you are planning to use videos from YouTube or the Internet, make sure they have time to buffer before the presentation starts. In a nutshell, make sure everything is ready ahead of time.

Beginning Confidently

Your opening statement is an important one. It needs to engage your audience and pique their interest for what is to come in the remainder of the presentation. The traditional recommendation of opening with an elaborate entrance or some sort of joke is *not* the way to go unless you are a stand-up comedian. Canned humour generally sounds contrived and rarely achieves the objective of leaving the audience wanting more. Instead, consider starting with a visual, an anecdote, or a pointed question that introduces one of your main themes. You want your audience to sit up and take notice of what you have to say. A good opening statement can pave the way.

Next, always have an agenda slide. It introduces your audience to the structure and flow of the presentation, so your audience knows where you are headed and how you plan to get there. The agenda slide, because it is relatively straightforward, and something you should be able to present without having to think too much about it, gives you a moment to get physically comfortable in front of the audience. It will also give you an opportunity to size up the audience.

Switching It Up

To keep your audience interested, you need to make a conscious effort to vary your tone of voice and move around the room. Do not stand perfectly still, glued to a podium. Your slides, while benefiting from a consistent background look and feel, should also be varied: Switch up traditional bullet point slides with video, audio, charts, and website links. Using a variety of techniques to make your points will appeal to the varied learning styles of your audience and keep them engaged.

Always encourage your audience to ask questions.
Copyright 2007, Mike Watson Images Limited/Glow Images

Involving Your Audience

You'll need to determine ahead of time whether you want members of your audience to ask questions as you go along, or whether you prefer that they wait until the question period at the end of your presentation. Let them know your preference early in the presentation, but always, always make time for questions. People may not remember half of what you said in your presentation but they *will* remember how you answered their question—and you just never know who might be in your audience asking the question. Finally, if you *don't* know the answer, the simple reply is "I'm sorry, I don't know the answer to that, but I will find out for you." Then get their contact information, and make sure you follow up as promised.

Finishing Memorably

How you end your presentation is just as important as how you begin it. There are many different ways to end a presentation. A common one is to reiterate your main themes one last time and invite your audience to ponder some take-away questions. Another is to use a cartoon, quotation, or other visual that sums up what you've presented. Another is to thank those who invited you to present and offer to stay after the presentation should anyone have further questions. You'll need to decide what makes sense for you, given the topic and purpose of your presentation. See the **Course Connections** feature for some do's and dont's for presentations.

Using Handouts Effectively

If you want your audience to stay focused on what you're saying during the presentation, don't give them a handout of your slides in advance. Indicate at the beginning of your presentation that a handout is available and will be distributed at the end of the presentation. Always make a few extras, and in your contact information, be sure to include your email address so audience members can request additional electronic copies if they are interested.

Course CONNECTIONS

The 10 Do's and Don'ts of Making Effective Presentations

1. DO remember that YOU are the expert—the person who knows the most about the presentation—so speak with confidence.
2. DO use a font size that can be seen from the back of the room.
3. DO involve your audience by inviting their comments and questions.
4. DO provide a means for your audience to provide anonymous feedback.
5. DO prepare handouts for everyone in the audience, but DON'T hand them out until after the presentation.
6. DON'T bore your audience by speaking in a monotone voice and standing perfectly still. Vary your tone and volume, and feel free to gesture and move around as you speak.
7. DON'T try too hard by attempting elaborate or contrived presentation openers.
8. DON'T show a slide that has more than three bullet points on it.
9. DON'T stand in front of the projector when you are showing slides.
10. DON'T rely exclusively on Microsoft PowerPoint bullet slides. Use photos, quotations, illustrations, graphs, and other visuals to make your presentation come alive.

"Well, Ladies and Gentlemen, I'm sure my little talk has made you all think."

© RGJ -Richard Jolley/www.CartoonStock.com

After the Presentation

While you might assume your message got through to the members of your audience, you will never know for sure unless you invite them to provide feedback. If you are given the opportunity to obtain feedback from your audience, be ready with a quick survey that can be handed out along with the copy of your slides. Check out **Try It! 4** "Get Feedback on Your Presentation" for a sample survey. Once you've received feedback—and it should be provided *anonymously*—take it to heart and use it to make improvements in future presentations.

---

4 | TRY IT!

Get Feedback on Your Presentation

The very best way to improve your presentation skills is to practise, practise, practise. It's a good idea to get feedback from your audience after each presentation. Most people don't like to make critical comments out loud, and they would probably be more honest if their comments were anonymous. To get their honest feedback, consider making copies of the short survey shown below, and have your audience members hand it in anonymously after you've made your presentation.

Feedback on My Presentation

1. What is the one thing that stood out for you in this presentation, i.e., the one idea or fact that you will take away from it?
2. What is the one thing that could have been done differently to make this presentation more effective for you?
3. What is the one thing that could have been done differently to make this presentation more effective for everyone in the audience?

To Try It online, go to the McGraw-Hill online resource.

A Final Word

Communication is the lifeblood of the 21st century. You cannot have an impact on the world around you if you keep your thoughts and ideas to yourself. You may choose to start a blog; upload a video to YouTube; or communicate with friends and family by text message, Twitter, or email, or you may write a traditional report or make a formal presentation. You can begin by creating a presentation out of the material you've learned in this chapter. See **Try It! 5** "Create a Presentation out of the Material in This Chapter" for instructions on how to go about this. Use the methods that best suit your learning style and Striving Style™, and examine the suggestions and recommendations in the table below.

Career CONNECTIONS

Presenting Yourself in a Job Interview

It is one thing to create and deliver a presentation that you've had the luxury of practising over and over; it is quite another to find yourself having to present your own skills and abilities during a job interview. Since you don't have any control over the questions that will be asked, interviews are never predictable. You might face an interviewer who starts with an open-ended question like "Tell me about yourself," or you might find yourself in a highly structured group interview, where several individuals ask you questions in turn. The interviewer may decide to approach the interview using behaviour-based questions like "Tell me about a time when ...." This lack of predictability—and the high stakes—are what make job interviews so fraught with anxiety.

But in spite of their unpredictability, you can take concrete steps to prepare more thoroughly for job interviews. Aside from doing research on the company and having a well-constructed resumé and cover letter that are tailored to the job in question, you should also consider preparing your own "tip sheet"—a few pages where you've summarized your main skills and abilities and listed at least one concrete example that illustrates each. It is also worthwhile to get a friend or parent to ask you typical interview questions and provide feedback on your responses. For 10 tough interview questions and 10 great answers to them, visit **collegegrad.com/jobsearch/mastering-the-interview/ ten-tough-interview-questions-and-ten-great-answers**.

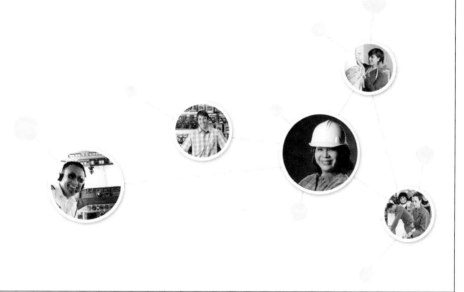

5 | TRY IT! POWER

Create a Presentation out of the Material in This Chapter

In this chapter, you've been provided with numerous suggestions on how to improve both your writing and presentation skills. Now it's time to apply what you've learned by developing and delivering a presentation on the topic of either (1) writing or (2) presenting. Summarize the main points, and follow the guidelines for creating compelling slides.

To Try It online, go to the McGraw-Hill online resource.

Don't be afraid to get your message out there. The world is waiting to hear from you.

Advice Based on Writing, Presenting, and Striving Styles™

Leaders	You think you have enough time to write your report or expand your arguments when you don't. Have a time budget. Presenting can make you feel out of control, but you are a natural, so learn to relax and enjoy.
Socializers	Stay with facts when developing reports. Test the logic of your analysis with a trusted friend or teacher. Don't worry so much about being judged by others when you present.
Performers	Try not to get stuck creating the perfect report or exhausting yourself by over-delivering. Don't get so caught up in your enjoyment of presenting that you ramble or lose focus. Use cue cards or Microsoft PowerPoint.
Adventurers	Use a digital recorder to capture what you want to write instead of labouring over writing a report. You can entertain your audience during presentations but fail to make your points, so use PowerPoint or cue cards to stay focused.
Artists	Ask for help with the structure and analysis so you don't stall before you even begin. You can make yourself overly anxious about presenting when you can't separate what you are presenting from who you are.
Intellectuals	Don't focus so much on pursuing one argument that you fail to add breadth to a case or report. You can excel as a presenter when you are not afraid of engaging your audience.
Visionaries	Try not to go into information overload when preparing your report and business case. Keep your excitement about the content of your presentation in your voice when you present.
Stabilizers	Don't adhere so much to the literal instructions that you fail to provide a broader scope to your case analysis. When presenting, let your personality come through rather than just factually recounting information.

Time to Reflect: What **Did I Learn?**

1. Review the material in Chapter 1 on the four learning styles: read/write, visual/ graphic, auditory/verbal, and tactile/kinesthetic. Thinking about your own learning style, what approaches are likely to be most effective for you when you are generating ideas for a report or presentation?

2. When you are beginning work on a group report or presentation, and thinking again about your own learning style, what tasks should you volunteer to do?

3. When you are preparing a presentation for a diverse audience, what steps can you take to ensure that the content of your presentation will appeal to their learning styles?

Did You Know?

When Workopolis Canada examined its 60,000 or so job postings in 2015, it created a word cloud to show visually which skills were most sought after by Canadian employers. You can see from the image below that communication skills are in very high demand!

Communication skills are the number one skill appearing in Canadian job postings on Workopolis.[2]

© Workopolis

Looking Back

Why is communication so important?

> Virtually all course work at the post-secondary level relies on good communication skills.

> Without effective communication skills, you will not be able to maximize your impact on the world around you.

What do I need to do before I actually start writing a report?

> Research your topic thoroughly. Then use mind-mapping or brainstorming techniques to explore themes and possible subtopics for your report.

> Determine what your main thesis will be.

> Organize your arguments and research findings.

> Create a workback schedule to ensure you leave yourself enough time to rest, reread, and revise. (You can apply these concepts to the preparation of a presentation as well.)

How can I ensure that I get my message across in a report?

> Focus on a specific thesis and ensure you have a cohesive set of supporting arguments.

> Make sure your report is organized logically and that each section of the report flows readily into the next.

How can I avoid plagiarism?

> Cite all of your sources, both in the context of the report (in in-text citations) and in a bibliography or works cited page at the end.

How can I become a better presenter?

> Know your audience.

> Prepare your materials well ahead of time.

> Rehearse, preferably in front of a video camera.

> Invite audience feedback and take it to heart.

> Consider joining an organization like Toastmasters.

RESOURCES

ON CAMPUS

Contact your student association to find out if there is a Toastmasters (or similar) group operating on campus, and attend a meeting. You might also want to consider taking on volunteer positions that require you to write and/or present, such as the campus newspaper or various committees or clubs.

Colleges and universities will often sponsor a "Speaker Series." Take the time to attend and learn from these speakers.

Many colleges and universities have a writing centre or free tutoring available on campus. You can use these services to have a second pair of eyes proofread your reports before you submit them or to have someone watch a dry run of your presentations before you do them in front of the class.

And, remember, your instructors are also there to help!

IN PRINT

Nancy Duarte's book *Slide-ology: The Art and Science of Creating Great Presentations* is a wonderful resource to call upon when you are preparing a presentation (O'Reilly Media, 2008).

If you are interested in how to present data in a compelling way, you'll want to examine *The Wall Street Journal Guide to Information Graphics: The Do's and Don'ts of Presenting Data, Facts, and Figures,* by Dona M. Wong (W.W. Norton & Co., 2013).

Barcharts Publishing Inc. offers a three-panel laminated guide on MLA and APA citation styles that can be purchased for less than $10 at **chapters.indigo.ca.**

ON THE WEB

The following websites provide an opportunity to extend your learning about the material in this chapter:

> For an excellent site that outlines the process of writing in step-by-step fashion, using videos and exercises, you'll want to visit **groundsforargument.org/drupal/ sitemap.**

> For the top six grammar and proofreading apps, check out **appappeal.com/ apps/grammar-and-proofreading.**

> Garr Reynolds, author of the book *Presentation Zen* and its companion blog, has an excellent three-part series of tips on presentations that is divided into organizing and preparation, delivery, and slide tips. If you do nothing else before planning your presentation, check out this series at **garrreynolds.com.**

> For a funny take on "Life after Death by PowerPoint," check out manager-turned-stand-up-comedian Don McMillan's routine on YouTube at **youtube.com/ watch?v=IpvgfmEU2Ck.**

THERE'S AN APP FOR THAT

> **Grammarly** is an add-on to your Chrome browser that claims to "instantly fix over 250 types of errors, most of which Microsoft Word® can't find."[3]

> For a multi-platform mind-mapping app, check out Xmind at **www.xmind.net/.**

> **PowerPoint Keynote Remote** "turns your smartphone into a smart remote for PowerPoint and Keynote presentations. It uses Bluetooth or Wi-Fi to connect your phone and computer, then lets you use your phone to control your slideshow."[4]

TAKING IT TO THE WEB

1 After you have written a paper or report for one of your courses, copy and paste it into **paperrater.com.** This free site, which has been developed and is maintained by linguistics professionals and graduate students, will provide you with a detailed analysis of your report, including grammar suggestions, plagiarism detection, and writing suggestions. To top it all off, it will give you a "grade" for your paper, based on the analysis. While your instructor obviously gets the last word on your grade, this is still a good way to avail yourself of an artificial intelligence proofreader—at no cost to you!

THE CASE OF . . .
The "Creative" Presenter

Michelle Abellard was excited. She was going to get an opportunity to make a presentation to her psychology class on a topic that she'd recently researched for a report: creativity.

She immediately set to work, planning a grand entrance: She would enter the class dressed in a clown suit (last year's Halloween costume) with her dachshund, Soprano, at her side. She would open her presentation by asking the audience for their definition of creativity and bring candies to throw out to those who answered. To show just how creative she could be, she decided to develop a set of "wild and crazy" slides. She spent days lovingly designing the slides, each one with a different background and colour scheme. She experimented with several different-coloured fonts on each slide, although she decided on lavender for all the titles—it was, after all, her favourite colour. She ended up spending so much time designing the slides that she didn't have much time left over to think about what to put on them, but she came up with a creative solution, cutting and pasting paragraphs from her recently submitted report onto each slide. Her plan was to end the presentation with a bang by having her dog—who wasn't called Soprano for nothing—sing for the audience. What a splash she'd make … people would be talking about her presentation for the rest of the semester!

Well, Michelle did make her presentation, and people were certainly talking about it, but they were mainly commenting on the negative feedback Michelle received from the instructor, who decided to use the occasion to teach Michelle and the rest of the students what *not* to do.

1. How well did Michelle use her time to plan her presentation? What advice would you give her about the preparation stage of planning a presentation?

2. Clearly, Michelle was enthusiastic about the topic of creativity, and she tried hard to make it come alive for her audience. Where did she go wrong?

3. What was Michelle's priority when preparing this presentation? What *should* have been her priority?

4. Do you agree with Michelle's instructor's decision to provide feedback publicly? Why or why not?

CHAPTER 8
Making Decisions and Solving Problems

Learning Outcomes

By the time you finish this chapter, you will be able to

LO 8.1 Outline a framework for decision making.

LO 8.2 Discuss how critical thinking can be applied to the problem-solving process.

LO 8.3 Apply critical thinking to everyday problems.

Peter Visser had a tough decision coming up. In three weeks, he would earn his Construction Engineering Technician diploma. It had taken a great deal of effort and the sacrifice of a lot of free time, but he was almost there. It was what to do next, though, that was giving Peter problems.

All through college, he had worked for a local contractor, picking up construction jobs when the contractor needed an extra pair of hands. Now that Peter was graduating as a construction engineering technician, the contractor had offered to make him a permanent member of his construction crew. In short, he was being offered more work at a better salary.

Peter knew it was a great offer—but it was not his only option. A friend he had met in college wanted to start his own house inspection business, and he wanted Peter to be his partner. Working together, Peter's friend said, they could build the business quickly, and they would earn more and have more flexibility than if they worked for someone else.

As graduation approached, Peter knew he had to make up his mind. But he kept going around in circles. Was security more important than flexibility? How much was running his own business worth to him?

Peter knew he had to make up his mind. But how?

Looking Ahead

Like Peter, all of us face important life decisions at one time or another. How can we make the right decisions? The best way is to employ some basic techniques that can help improve the quality of our decision making.

This chapter begins by giving you a sense of what decision making is and is not, and it discusses a structured process that can help make your decisions the right ones. But what happens when you make the wrong decision or you fall victim to the law of unintended consequences (i.e., you make a decision but don't anticipate the fallout)? That's where the second and third sections of the chapter, which discuss problem-solving skills, come into play. Most students confront a variety of problems as they proceed through college or university and throughout their career. In this chapter, we'll look at a number of proven techniques that will help you find solutions to the problems you might face. We'll also examine some common problems that can affect our thinking and discuss several biases that can make us jump to the wrong conclusions.

LO 8.1 Making Better Decisions: A Framework

Neither making decisions nor solving problems is easy. Sometimes the best decision or solution to a problem is one that we don't see at first; we all have mental blind spots. The best problem-solvers and decision-makers use critical thinking to see around these blind spots. To use Robert Ennis's classic definition, "critical thinking is reasonable, reflective thinking that is focused on deciding what to believe or do."[1] In other words, it is the ability to reflect on your views and opinions about the world around you and on what gave rise to these views, i.e., *why* you think the way you do. An important part of critical thinking is knowing how to ask good questions.

Sometimes there seem to be too many options to choose from. For example, you may be wondering if you are in the right program. Rest assured—you are not alone in thinking this! It is far more common than you might think. Many college and university students enrol in a program not really knowing if it is for them, only to find as they progress through the program that they need to revisit their decision. The tips in this chapter can get you on the right path.

Decision making
The process of deciding among various alternatives

Decision making is the process of deciding among various alternatives. Whether you are trying to decide between a Ford and a Honda, between an apartment that is close to your job and one that is close to family, or simply between a hamburger and a pizza, every choice requires a decision. Some decisions are easily made and have few consequences, but others, such as whether to take one job or another, can involve the deepest examination of our beliefs and values.

Sometimes your need to make a decision or solve a problem has you in "crisis mode," and you feel as though your whole life will fall apart if you don't deal with the situation. In cases like these, it is critical that you compartmentalize the problem, isolating it so you can give it the thought it requires, while ensuring it doesn't have a negative impact on other aspects of your life.

Whatever you're deciding, you need to be focused and think critically to make a reasoned decision. You need to actively apply your past knowledge, synthesize and evaluate alternatives, and reason and reflect on a course of action. The greater your depth of thinking about the components of the decision, the more likely it is that you'll come up with the best choice.

To make a good decision, map out a strategy for making the choice that is best for you. Every decision can benefit from your thinking systematically through the options involved, based on the P.O.W.E.R. Plan illustrated below.

P Prepare
Examine your goals

O Organize
Consider and assess your alternatives

W Work
Make your decision and carry it out

E Evaluate
Consider the outcome

R Rethink
Reconsider your goals and options

P.O.W.E.R. Plan

P Prepare | Examine Your Goals

Every decision starts with the end you have in mind: the goals, both short and long term, that you wish to accomplish by making the decision.

For example, suppose you are trying to decide on something as simple as where to sit in a classroom. Your long-term goal is to make the Dean's List. You know that sitting near the front of the room means you'll probably pay attention more, the teacher will get to know who you are, and it will be easier to ask or answer questions. On the other hand, sitting at the back means you can sit with your friends, and if the class gets boring, you can text without the teacher noticing. Also, if you are at the back, it's unlikely that the teacher will call on you to answer questions. Your seat selection must be seen in light of your long-term goal: doing well enough to make the Dean's List. Where you sit in each classroom will very likely have an impact on your grade in each course: the closer you sit to the front, the more likely it is that you will be able to reach your goal.

In short, every decision should start with a consideration of what our short- and long-term goals are. Identifying the goals that underlie decisions ensures that we make decisions in the context of our entire lives and not just provide short-term answers to immediate problems.

⦿ Organize Consider and Assess Your Alternatives

Identifying Alternatives

Making a decision requires weighing various alternatives. Determining what those alternatives are, and their possible consequences, is often the most difficult part of decision making. It's important not only to think thoroughly about the obvious alternatives but also to consider alternatives that are less obvious. For many decisions, there are choices beyond the "this or that" alternatives that can dominate our thinking.

How can you be sure that you've considered all the possible alternatives? Do your research. What have others done in a similar situation? Investigate, either through reading about the life journeys of others in your situation, or by interviewing them personally. According to Charles Duhigg, author of *Smarter Faster Better: The Secrets of Being Productive in Life and Business*, "In theory, the ongoing explosion in information should make the right answers obvious. In practice, though, being surrounded by data often makes it harder to decide. This inability to take advantage of data as it becomes more plentiful is called 'information blindness.'"[2] When identifying alternatives, be careful to avoid information blindness.

You may wish to consider more-creative approaches to identifying alternatives. If you have a visual/graphic learning style, you might want to use the mind-mapping technique introduced in Chapter 7. If your learning style leans more toward read/write, using a technique called free writing may be the best way to go.

In **free writing**, you write continuously for a fixed period of time, perhaps 5 or 10 minutes. During this period, the idea is to write as many different ideas as possible without stopping. It makes no difference whether the alternatives are good or bad or even whether they make sense. All that matters is that you let yourself brainstorm about the topic for a while and get the ideas down on paper.

With free writing, evaluating the worth of the ideas you've generated comes later. After you have produced as many possibilities as you can, then you go back and sift out the reasonable ones from those that are unlikely or just plain wacky. It's OK if you have to delete quite a few alternatives from your list; the process is likely to have uncovered some reasonable alternatives that you might not otherwise have come up with. According to Eric Johnson, a cognitive psychologist who studies decision making at Columbia University, "our brains crave reducing things to two or three options,"[3] so once you've sifted through the ideas you've generated, try to reduce your list to two or three. Try this technique in **Try It! 1** "Use Free Writing."

Free writing
A technique involving continuous writing, without self-criticism, for a fixed period of time

Assessing Alternatives

Once you have generated a list of alternatives, assess them. You need to follow three key steps when assessing each alternative:

1. **Determine the possible outcomes for each alternative.** Some outcomes are positive, some negative. Try to identify as many outcomes as you can, whether positive or negative. "By pushing yourself to imagine various possibilities—some of which may be contradictory—you're

Use Free Writing

Part A: Use free writing to think of as many answers as you can to each of the following questions. The ground rules are that you should spend three minutes on each question, generating as many ideas as possible—regardless of whether they are feasible. To give yourself maximum freedom, write each answer on a separate sheet of paper.

1. How can you make room in your schedule to take one more course next term than you're taking this term?
2. Thinking about past relationships, what will you look for in future partners?
3. How can you make some extra money while going to school full time?
4. What activities can you participate in while in school that will make your resumé more attractive to potential employers?

Part B: After generating ideas, go back and evaluate them.

1. How many were actually feasible?
2. Do you think free writing led to the production of more or fewer ideas than you would have come up with if you hadn't used the technique?
3. Did the quality of your ideas change?

 CLASS DISCUSSION

After you have answered the questions above, compare your answers with those of others in your class. As a group, try to identify the best answers to each question.

To Try It online, go to the McGraw-Hill online resource.

better equipped to make wise choices."[4] For example, if you are considering ways of solving transportation problems, one alternative might be to purchase a car. That alternative produces several potential outcomes. For example, you know that it will be easier to get wherever you want to go, and you might even have a better social life—clearly positive outcomes. But it is also true that buying and owning a car will be expensive, and that it may be difficult to find convenient parking—both significant negative outcomes.

2. **Determine the probability that these outcomes will take place.** Some outcomes are far more likely than others. To take this into account, make a rough estimate of the likelihood that an outcome will come to pass, ranging from 100 percent (you are certain that it will occur) to 0 percent (you are certain that it will never occur). Obviously, the probabilities are just guesses, but going through the exercise of estimating them will make the outcomes more real and will permit you to compare the various alternatives against one another more easily.

3. **Compare the alternatives, taking into account the potential outcomes of each.** Systematically compare each of the alternatives. A simple pro/con list like the one shown in **Figure 8.1,** which examines the decision to get a tattoo, can help you make this comparison. Then ask yourself the key question: Which alternative, on balance, provides the most positive (and most likely) outcomes?

The Pros & Cons of Getting a Tattoo

Pros	Cons
1. It expresses my individuality.	1. My parents would be angry.
2. It would represent something special to me.	2. It's expensive to remove.
3. My friends all have one.	3. I don't like needles or pain.
4. It's the style these days to have a tattoo.	4. There's a risk of infection.
5. I think tattoos can be really pretty.	5. Will it still look good when I'm 60?
6. My style icon, Lady Gaga, has several.	6. It might not look good if I'm in a wedding dress or business attire.

Obviously, not every decision requires such an elaborate process. In fact, most won't. But when it comes to major decisions, those that could have a large impact upon you and your life, it's worthwhile to follow a systematic process.

Take a look at the **Career Connections** feature on page 212 for another process that you can follow to help you make a career decision.

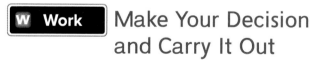

Make Your Decision and Carry It Out

Working through the previous steps will lead you to the point of decision: choosing one of the alternatives you've identified. Having carried out the steps will make the actual decision easier, but not necessarily easy.

Choosing among Alternatives

The reason that important decisions are difficult is that the alternatives you have to choose from carry both benefits and costs. Choosing one alternative means that you have to accept the costs of that choice and give up the benefits of the other alternatives. A decision can also mean a fork in the road: One decision can lead to a number of other decisions, and as you become more and more committed, you will find it almost impossible to go backward. A graphic representation of that process is captured by what is called a *decision tree*. Examine the decision tree in **Figure 8.2** (on page 214),

Career CONNECTIONS

Weighing Options

After choosing what type of education and career to pursue, one of the most important decisions you'll ever make is choosing how to apply this education in an employment setting that will stimulate you and that you will enjoy. Your long-term goals, as well as your personality, your Striving Style™, and your learning style, should all factor into this decision. Here's one method that can help you decide what might be best suited to you:

- Generate a selection of choices to consider. Include not only the obvious options that your current education prepares you for, but also alternative ideas such as pursuing a position in a different environment (e.g., dental hygienist in a public health setting), earning a degree, starting your own business, and so forth. Even if you doubt you'll select one of these other options, considering them will help you assess what you truly want to do.

- Determine life satisfaction considerations that are important to you. Generate a list of criteria to use in weighing the possibilities. For instance, you might want to consider the following:

  > Benefits (vacation, health insurance, etc.)
  > Salary
  > Spouse's/partner's opinion
  > Friends' opinions
  > Interest in the activity
  > Prestige
  > Job security
  > Flexible hours
  > Benefit to society
  > Practicality/attainability
  > Everyday working conditions
  > Clients you will be working with
  > Opportunities to learn
  > Opportunities to travel

- Determine how well a particular option fulfills each of the life satisfaction factors you consider important. By systematically considering how a potential path fulfills each of the criteria you use, you'll be able to compare different options. One easy way to do this is to create a chart like the one in **Table 8.1,** which shows an example of how job options for a massage therapist might fulfill the various criteria, using a scale of 1 to 10, where 1 means worst and 10 means best.

- Compare different choices. **Try It! 2** "Evaluate Alternative Careers" contains a blank template of Table 8.1 that you can fill in with your own set of choices and ratings. Using the chart, evaluate your possibilities. Keep in mind that this is just a rough guide and that it's only as accurate as (a) the effort you put into completing it and (b) your understanding of a given choice. Use the results in conjunction with other things you find out about the jobs—and yourself.

which shows a young woman who has already taken a fork in the road by deciding to get a tattoo. Now she must decide what the subject of that tattoo should be. She is torn between a text-based tattoo (either a song lyric or a line from a poem) or an illustration of a fish (goldfish or dolphin) or a flower (tulip or rose). As she moves through the decision process, she compares one alternative against the other, narrowing her preference down each time and finally coming to the conclusion that she will get a tattoo of a goldfish. While this decision tree is rather simple, consider what a similar tree might look like as you try to choose between five or six majors at college or university. To create your own decision tree in Microsoft Word, download the free template at **mywordtemplates .org/diagram/template1489.html.**

2 | TRY IT! POWER

Evaluate Alternative Careers

It may be too soon for you to choose a career. And, let's face it, unlike our parents and grandparents, most of us will have many careers over the course of our lifetimes. But that doesn't mean you shouldn't try to get some idea of where you'd like to begin. Using the blank template shown below, evaluate alternative careers of your own choice.

Evaluating Career Alternatives			
Life satisfaction considerations on a scale of 1–10	**Alternative A**	**Alternative B**	**Alternative C**
Benefits			
Income			
Spouse's/partner's opinion			
Friends' opinions			
Interest in the activity			
Prestige			
Job security			
Flexible hours			
Benefit to society			
Practicality/attainability			
Everyday working conditions			
Clients you will be working with			
Opportunity to learn			
Opportunity to travel			
Other			
Total			

To Try It online, go to the McGraw-Hill online resource.

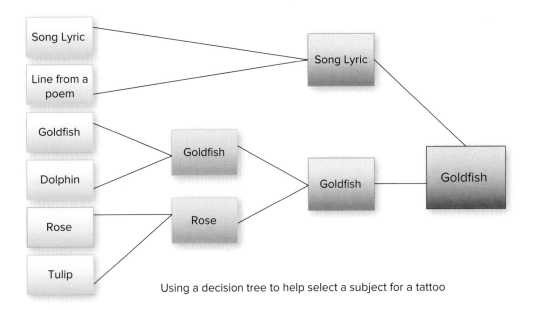

Using a decision tree to help select a subject for a tattoo

table 8.1 Making Career Decisions			
Life satisfaction considerations on a scale of 1 to 10	Massage therapist at a local spa	Sports massage therapist at a university	Massage therapist on a cruise ship
Benefits	4	8	5
Income	8	7	5
Spouse's/partner's opinion	8	6	1
Friends' opinions	4	7	7
Interest in the activity	5	6	8
Prestige	5	9	7
Job security	4	7	5
Flexible hours	8	5	6
Benefit to society	6	8	6
Practicality/attainability	9	4	2
Everyday working conditions	7	8	6
Clients you will be working with	5	7	8
Opportunity to learn	3	8	5
Opportunity to travel	1	5	10
Other			
Total	77	95	81

What if, after going through the steps of the process laid out here, you still can't make up your mind? Try these strategies:

> **Give the decision some time.** Sometimes waiting helps. Time can give you a chance to think of additional alternatives. Sometimes the situation will change, or you'll have a change in viewpoint.

> **Avoid decision fatigue.** Research has shown that "the more choices you make throughout the day, the harder each one becomes for your brain, and eventually it looks for shortcuts, usually in either of two very different ways. One shortcut is to become reckless: to act impulsively instead of expending the energy to first think through the consequences. (Sure, tweet that photo! What could go wrong?) The other shortcut is the ultimate energy saver: do nothing. Instead of agonizing over decisions, avoid any choice."[5]

> **Make a mental movie, acting out the various alternatives.** Many of us have difficulty seeing ourselves in the future and envisioning how various options would play out. One way to get around this difficulty is to cast yourself into a series of "mental movies" that have different endings depending on the decision you make. Working through the different scripts in your head makes potential outcomes far more real and less abstract than they would be if you simply left them as items on a list of various options.

> **Toss a coin.** This isn't as crazy as it sounds. If each alternative seems equally positive or negative to you, pull out a coin—make option A "heads" and option B "tails." Then flip it.

> The real power of the coin toss strategy is that it might help you discover your true feelings. It may be while the coin is in the air, or it may be when you see the result of the coin toss, that you won't like the outcome and will say to yourself, "No way." In that case, you've just found out how you really feel.

> **Ask for advice.** Although Western society teaches the virtues of rugged individualism, asking others for their advice is often an excellent strategy. Friends, instructors, parents, or a counsellor can provide helpful recommendations—sometimes because they've had to make similar decisions themselves. You don't have to take their advice, but it can help to listen to what they have to say.

> **Go with your gut feeling.** Call it what you like—gut feeling, intuition, hunch, superstition—but sometimes we need to go with our hearts and not our minds. If you've thought rationally about a decision and have been unable to determine the best course of action but have a gut feeling that one choice is better than another, follow your feelings.

Following a gut feeling does not mean that you don't need to consider the pros and cons of a decision rationally and carefully. In fact, generally our "intuition" is best when informed by the thoughtfulness of a more rational process.

If all else fails, toss a coin to decide which alternative to follow. Tossing a coin at least brings you to a decision. Then, if you find you're unhappy with the result, you'll have gained important information about how you really feel regarding a particular choice.

© Robert Dant/Getty Images

Carrying Out the Decision

Ultimately, decisions must move from thought to action—they have to be carried out. Consequently, the final stage in making a decision is to act upon it. You need to turn your decision into behaviour.

E Evaluate | Consider the Outcome

Did you make the right decision?

Even if you've spent time and mental effort in thinking through a decision, you still need to consider the results. Even well-considered decisions can end up being wrong, either because you neglected to consider an alternative or because something has changed: either you or the situation.

Remember, it's never too late to change your mind. Admitting that a decision was a mistake is often the wisest and most courageous course of action. You don't want to be so rigidly committed to a decision that you're unable to evaluate the consequences objectively. Give yourself permission to be wrong. Even major life decisions are often reversible. That's why it's so important to evaluate your choices. If you chose the wrong alternative, reverse course and reconsider your options.

R Rethink | Reconsider Your Goals and Options

We can get to most places by multiple routes. There's the fastest and most direct route, which will get us to our destination in the shortest time. Then there's the longer, more scenic route, where the trip itself provides pleasure. You can "take the long way home," as the Eagles song goes. Is one route better than the other? Often not. Both take us to our destination. However, the experience of reaching our goal will have been very different.

Decisions about how to achieve a goal are similar to travelling down different routes. There's often no single decision that is best, just as there's often no single road to a particular place. Consequently, it's important now and then to reconsider the major decisions that we've made about our lives.

Ask yourself these questions:

> Are my decisions still producing the desired consequences?

> Are my decisions still appropriate, given my circumstances and changes in my life?

> Are my decisions consistent with what I want to get out of life?

> Am I accountable for my own actions?

Periodically taking stock like this is the best way to make sure that your decisions are taking you where you want to go. Taking stock also helps you to be more effective in making future decisions.

Finally, whatever decisions you choose to make, recognize that you, and you alone, are responsible for making them. Choosing to drive with someone who is drunk, texting while driving, leaving your drink at the bar while you go to the washroom—these are all examples of actions that could have dire consequences. Don't be tempted to blame others if things go awry. Whether your decision was hurried or carefully planned, whether it was right or wrong, whether or not you are happy about the outcome, *you* are accountable for making the decision, and the adult thing to do is to take responsibility for your own actions.

LO 8.2 Problem Solving: Applying Critical Thinking to Find Solutions

> *Two trains are approaching one another, each moving at 100 kilometres an hour. If the trains continue moving at the same speed, how long will it be before ...?*

If this is what comes to mind when you think of problem solving, think again. **Problem solving** encompasses more than the abstract, often unrealistic situations portrayed in math texts. It involves everyday situations: How do we divide the restaurant bill so that each person pays a fair share? How do I keep my one-year-old from tumbling down the stairs when there seems to be no way to fasten a gate at the top? How can I stop a faucet from dripping? How do I manage to study for a test and do the laundry in the same evening?

Problem solving
The mental activity involved in generating a set of alternative courses of action to enhance decision making

While decision making is most focused on choosing among various alternatives, the central issue in problem solving is generating alternatives. Since many problems require that decisions be made regarding alternatives, decision making and problem solving are related.

What's the Problem?

The first step in solving any problem is to be as clear as you can about what the problem is. This may sound easy, but often it isn't. In fact, it may take some time to figure out just what is at stake. Some problems, such as mathematical equations or the solution to a jigsaw puzzle, are quite precise. Determining how to stop terrorism or finding peace in the Middle East, on the other hand, are big, ill-defined problems. Simply determining what information is required to solve such problems can be a major undertaking.

To determine what the problem is and set yourself on a course for finding a solution, ask yourself these questions:

> What is the initial set of facts?

> What is it that I need to solve? Which parts of the problem am I actually able to solve?

> Which parts of the problem appear to be most critical to finding a solution?

> Is there some information that can be ignored?

The more systematically you approach a problem, the better. For instance, you can apply the five P.O.W.E.R. steps to problems, similar to the way you can apply them to making decisions. When you consider a problem systematically and think through your options, your choices will become clearer to you.

As you clarify what the problem is, you may find that you have encountered similar problems before. Your experience may suggest the means to the solution of the current problem. For example, consider the problem of the trains rushing toward each other. If you have worked on this kind of problem before, you might know a fairly simple equation you can write to determine how long it will take before they meet. If someone asks you about the problem she has in keeping her toddler from tumbling down the stairs, you might offer your experience in keeping your own children from visiting an off-limits area of your home.

On the other hand, to solve many of the problems we face in our daily lives, we have to do more than reach into our memories of prior situations. Instead, we need to devise novel approaches. How do you do this? There are several strategies you might use.

Strategies for Solving Life's Messier Problems

> **Break the problem down into smaller, more manageable pieces, a process called "chunking."** Divide a problem into a series of sub-goals. As you reach each sub-goal, you get closer to your overall goal of solving the problem. For example, if your goal is to find a job in Montreal, a sub-goal should be to learn French. By reaching this sub-goal, you move closer to reaching your ultimate goal—a job in a city that interests you.

> **Work backward.** Sometimes you know the answer to the problem, but not how to get there. Then it's best to work backward. A workback strategy starts at the desired solution or goal and works backward, moving away from the goal. For example, if you have a project due in eight weeks, and you aren't sure how to start it, you might imagine the end result—the finished project—and then work backward to consider how to prepare it.

> **Use a graph, chart, or drawing to redefine the problem.** Transforming words into pictures can often help you devise solutions that would otherwise elude you. For ideas on how drawing pictures can help you solve problems, you'll want to take a look at the international bestseller *The Back of the Napkin: Solving Problems and Selling Ideas with Pictures*, as well as author Dan Roam's website **thebackofthenapkin.com.**

> **Consider the opposite.** You can sometimes solve problems by considering the opposite of the problem you're seeking to solve. For example, to define "good mental health," you might try to define "bad mental health."

> **Look at not only the short-term, but also the medium and long-term consequences.** Suzy Welch, in her book *10-10-10: 10 Minutes, 10 Months, 10 Years—A Life-Transforming Idea*, recommends that you think about how you will feel *after* making a particular decision. For example, if you are thinking about accepting a job, how will you feel about accepting it 10 minutes after you accept it, 10 months after you accept it, or 10 years after you accept it? In other words, think past the short term into how the decision fits in with your expectations and your values in the medium to long term. Will it take you where you want to go?

- **Use analogies.** Some problems can be solved through the use of an **analogy**, which is a comparison between concepts or objects that are alike in some respects, but dissimilar in most others. For instance, if you liken a disastrous family vacation to a voyage on the *Titanic*, you're using an analogy.

  Analogies may help us gain additional insight into the problem at hand, and they may provide an alternative framework for interpreting the information that is provided. For instance, the invention by 3M employee Spencer Silver of an adhesive that provided only a temporary bond was seen for several years as a "solution looking for a problem," until another 3M employee, Arthur Fry, recognized it could be used as a temporary bookmark for his hymnbook, and the Post-It note was born![6]

- **Take another person's perspective.** By viewing a problem from another person's point of view, it is often possible to obtain a new perspective on the problem that will make it easier to solve.

- **Forget about it.** Sometimes it's best to simply walk away from a problem for a while. Just a few hours or days away from a problem may give us enough of a break to jar some hidden solutions from the recesses of our minds. Sleeping on it also sometimes works; we may wake up refreshed and filled with new ideas.

- **Approach it in the spirit of trial and error.** Whether you are solving a problem or making a decision, recognize that what you choose to do is often reversible. You can dip your toe in by volunteering part time in a field that interests you. If it doesn't turn out the way you expected, you can always change gears later. If you research the requirements in advance, you can even try out a major in English, and later switch to psychology, without losing credits toward your degree.

- **Recognize that *not* making a decision *is* making a decision.** Keeping things as they are is as much a decision as choosing to change them, and the status quo can sometimes be a viable alternative. But don't let inaction be the result of procrastination, of letting time slip away without making a decision. Let it be a *true* choice.

Test these problem-solving strategies in Try It! 3 "Exercise Your Problem-Solving Skills."

Assess Your Potential Solutions

If a problem clearly has only one answer—a math problem, for example—this step in problem solving is relatively easy. You should be able to work the problem and figure out whether you've been successful. In contrast, messier problems have several possible solutions, some of which may be more involved and costlier than others. In these cases, it's necessary to compare alternative solutions and choose the best one. For example, suppose you want to surprise your best friend on her birthday. She is studying at a school about 100 kilometres from you, and you need to find a way to get there. You could rent a car, take a bus, or find some other way. Money is an issue. You will want to figure out how much each alternative costs before choosing one as your solution to the problem. Since every dollar you spend getting there is a dollar less that you will have to celebrate, you will want to weigh the options carefully.

Analogy
A comparison between concepts or objects that are alike in some respects but dissimilar in most others

3 | TRY IT! POWER

 CLASSROOM DISCUSSION

Exercise Your Problem-Solving Skills

Part A: Working in a group, try to solve these problems.[7] To help you devise solutions, a hint regarding the best strategy to use is included after each problem.

1. A college student has a flat tire on a dark, deserted stretch of country road. He pulls onto the shoulder to change it. After removing the four lug nuts and placing them into the hubcap, he removes the flat tire and takes his spare out of the trunk. As he is moving the spare tire into position, his hand slips and he upsets the hubcap with the lug nuts, which tumble off into the night, where he can't find them. What should he do? (*Hint:* Instead of asking how he might find the lug nuts, reframe the problem and ask where else he might find lug nuts.)

2. A construction worker is paving a walk and needs to add water quickly to the just-poured concrete. She reaches for her pail to get water from a spigot in the front of the house but sees that the pail has a large hole in it and cannot be used. As the concrete dries prematurely, she fumbles through her toolbox for tools and materials with which to repair the pail. She finds many tools, but nothing that would serve to patch the pail. The house is locked, and no one is home. What should she do? (*Hint:* When is a pail not a pail?)

3. What day follows the day before yesterday if two days from now will be Sunday? (*Hint:* Break it up, or draw a diagram.)

4. Sadia has four chains, each three links long. She wants to join the four chains into a single, closed chain. Having a link opened costs 2 cents and having a link closed costs 3 cents. How can she have the chains joined for 15 cents? (*Hint:* Can only end links be opened?)

5. What is two-thirds of one-half? (*Hint:* Reverse course.)

6. Toby has three separate large boxes. Inside each large box are two separate medium-sized boxes, and inside each of the medium boxes are four small boxes. How many boxes does Toby have altogether? (*Hint:* Draw it.)

Part B: After working together to solve these problems, consider these questions:

1. Which problems were the easiest to solve, and which were more difficult? Why?
2. Were the hints helpful?
3. Do you think there was more than one solution to any of the problems?
4. Did your initial assumptions about the problem help or hinder your efforts to solve it?

Note: Answers to the problems are found at the end of the chapter.

To Try It online, go to the McGraw-Hill online resource.

Finally, spend a bit of time seeing whether there's a way to refine the solution. Is the solution you've devised adequate? Does it address all aspects of the problem? Are there alternative approaches that might be better? Answering these questions, and refining your solution to address them, can give you confidence that the solution you've come up with is the best. For example, if you're trying to get to your friend's school, you might decide to use the ride board at your school to try to find a ride with someone going there that day. Maybe your friend's family is going to be driving in and could pick you up, or someone could even lend you a car for the trip.

Remember that not every problem has a clear-cut solution. Sometimes we need to be satisfied with a degree of uncertainty and ambiguity.

FoxTrot © 2009 Bill Armend. Reprinted by permission of Universal Press Syndicate. All Rights Reserved.

For some of us, such a lack of clarity is difficult, making us uneasy; it may push us to choose a solution—any solution—that seems to solve the problem. Others of us feel more comfortable with ambiguity, but this may lead us to let problems ride without taking steps to resolve the situation.

Either way, it's important to consider what your own problem-solving style is when you seek to identify solutions. And keep in mind that often there is no perfect solution to a problem—only some solutions that are better than others.

Reflect on the Process of Problem Solving

It's natural to step back and bask in the satisfaction of solving a tough problem. That's fine—but take a moment to consider your success. Each time you solve a problem, you end up a couple steps ahead, but only if you've thought about the process you went through to solve it.

Go back and consider what it took to solve the problem. Can the means you used to come up with your solution be applied to more complex kinds of problems? If you arrived at a solution by making a chart, would this work on similar problems in the future? Taking a moment to rethink your solution can provide you with an opportunity to become an expert problem solver and, more generally, to improve your critical-thinking skills. Don't let the opportunity slip away.

LO 8.3 Applying Critical Thinking to Everyday Problems

Being able to think clearly and without bias is the basis for critical thinking. As you have probably noticed already, the quality of the thinking you do regarding problems and decisions plays a crucial role in determining how successful you are.

Unfortunately, it is sometimes the alternative you *didn't* think of that can end up being the most satisfactory decision or solution. So how can we learn to think critically and avoid blind spots that hinder us in our decision making and problem solving? We can start by considering these common obstacles to critical thinking:

> **Don't assume that giving something a name explains it.** The mere fact that we can give an idea or problem a name doesn't mean we can explain it. Yet we often confuse the two.
>
> For instance, consider the following sequences of questions and answers:
>
> > Q. Why do I have so much trouble falling asleep?
> >
> > A. Because you have insomnia.
> >
> > Q. Why is he so unsociable?
> >
> > A. Because he's an introvert.
> >
> > Q. Why did the defendant shoot those people?
> >
> > A. Because he's insane.
> >
> > Q. How do you know he's insane?
> >
> > A. Because only someone who was insane would shoot people in that way.[8]
>
> It's clear that none of these answers are satisfactory. All use circular reasoning, in which the alleged explanation for the behaviour is simply the use of a label.

> **Don't accept vague generalities dressed up as definitive statements.** Read the following personality analysis and think about how well it applies to you:
>
> > *You have a need for other people to like and admire you and a tendency to be critical of yourself. You also have a great deal of unused potential that you have not turned to your advantage, but although you have some personality weaknesses, you are generally able to compensate for them. Nonetheless, relating to members of the opposite sex has presented problems to you, and while you appear to be disciplined and self-controlled to others, you tend to be anxious and insecure inside.*
>
> If you believe that these statements provide an amazingly accurate description of your unique qualities, you're not alone: Most college and university students believe that the description is tailored specifically to them.[9] But how is that possible? It isn't. The reality is that the statements are so vague that they are virtually meaningless. The acceptance of vague but seemingly useful and significant statements about oneself and others has been called the *Barnum effect*, after showman and circus master P. T. Barnum, who supposedly coined the phrase "there's a sucker born every minute" (it turns out it wasn't him, however; see **quoteinvestigator.com/2014/04/11/fool-born/,** for example).

> **Don't confuse opinion with fact.** Opinions are not facts. Although we may be aware of this simple formula, almost all of us can be fooled into thinking that someone's opinion is the same as a fact.
>
> A fact is information that is proven to be true. In contrast, an opinion represents judgments, reasoning, beliefs, inferences, or conclusions. If we accept some bit of information as a fact, we can use it to

build our opinions. But if we are presented with an opinion, we need to determine the facts on which the opinion is built to judge its reliability.

The difference between fact and opinion can sometimes be subtle. For instance, compare these two statements:

1. Every student needs to take a writing course during the first term of college or university.

2. Many students need to take a writing course during the first term of college or university.

The first statement is most likely an opinion, because it is so absolute and unqualified. Words such as "every," "all," and "always" are often evidence of opinion. On the other hand, the second statement is more likely a fact, since it contains the qualifier "many." In general, statements that are qualified in some way are more likely to be facts.

Complete **Try It! 4** "Distinguish Fact from Opinion" to see the difficulties sometimes involved in distinguishing between fact and opinion.

› **Avoid jumping to conclusions.** Read this riddle and try to answer it:

> *A father and his son were driving along the Trans-Canada Highway when the father lost control of the car, swerved off the road, and crashed into a utility pole. The father died instantly, and his son was critically injured. An ambulance rushed the boy to a nearby hospital. A prominent surgeon was summoned to provide immediate treatment. When the surgeon arrived and entered the operating room to examine the boy, a loud gasp was heard.*
>
> *"I can't operate on this boy," the surgeon said. "He is my son."*

How can this be?

If you find this puzzling, you've based your reasoning on an assumption: that the surgeon is a male. But suppose you had assumed that the surgeon was a female. Suddenly, the riddle becomes a lot easier. It's far easier to guess that the surgeon is the son's mother if we don't leap to embrace a faulty—not to mention sexist—assumption.

Why is it so easy to jump to conclusions? One reason is that we sometimes aren't aware of the assumptions that underlie our thinking. Another is our reliance on common sense.

› **Be skeptical of common sense.** Much of what we call common sense makes contradictory claims. For example, if you believe in the notion "Absence makes the heart grow fonder," you may assume that your girlfriend, now working at a job in another city, will arrive home at Christmas even more in love with you than before. But what about "Out of sight, out of mind," which suggests a less positive outcome? Common sense often presents us with contradictory advice, making it a less than useful guide to decision making and problem solving.

› **Don't assume that just because two events occur together one causes the other.** Just because two events appear to be associated with one another, we cannot conclude that one event has caused the other to occur. Suppose you read that a study showed that 89 percent of young offenders use marijuana. Does this mean that smoking marijuana *causes* youth crime?

No, it doesn't. It is pretty safe to say that close to 100 percent of young offenders grew up drinking water. Would you feel comfortable

Distinguish Fact from Opinion

Read the following statements and try to determine which are facts (put "F" on the line that follows the item) and which are opinions (put "O" on the line that follows the item). You'll find the answers at the end of the chapter.

1. College and university students should get at least seven hours of sleep every night. _____

2. The average college or university student sleeps less than seven hours a night. _____

3. Nike offers better styling and comfort than any other brand of shoe. _____

4. Two out of five athletes surveyed preferred Nike over Converse shoes. _____

5. Sidney Crosby is the most talented hockey player to ever step onto the ice. _____

6. Government figures show spending in Canada is much higher for health than for education. _____

7. The Government of Canada should spend more money on education. _____

8. The Liberal Party cares more about education spending than the Conservative Party. _____

9. Canadians are, by nature, polite. _____

10. Toronto is the most diverse city in the world.[10] _____

What are the main differences between opinion and fact?

To Try It online, go to the McGraw-Hill online resource.

saying that water causes youth crime? With the association between marijuana use and youth crime, it is very likely that there's some third factor—such as the influence of peers—that causes young people both to (a) try drugs and (b) engage in crime. The bottom line: We do not know that marijuana use is the cause of the crime just because young offenders often smoke marijuana.

In short, we need to be careful in assuming causality. Even if two events or other kinds of variables occur together, it is not necessarily true that one causes the other.

Apply Decision-Making and Problem-Solving Techniques to Everyday Life

In this chapter, you've learned about many tools and techniques that can help you with the problems you encounter and the decisions you have to make while pursuing your post-secondary education. You may be under the impression that it's only worth using these techniques to solve the *big* problems and make the *big* decisions—should you have children, should you change careers, or should you retire, for example—but they apply equally to the little decisions. And it doesn't stop there. Whether it's a pro/con list, a decision tree, a chart to help you weigh alternatives, or free writing, you will find that you will return to the techniques introduced in this chapter again and again, in all facets of your life, and through its many stages. For suggestions on the decision-making and

Course CONNECTIONS

Using Critical Thinking in Your Classes

Nowhere is critical thinking more important to use—and demonstrate to your instructors—than when you're in your classes. Here are some strategies to foster your skills as a critical thinker when you are in class:

- **Ask questions.** Most instructors welcome questions. Even if an instructor doesn't have time to provide a full response, the very act of formulating a question will help you think more critically about the course material.

- **Accept that some questions have no right or wrong answers.** Understanding that some questions have no simple answer is a sign of mental sophistication. Sometimes the best an instructor can do is present competing theories. Although you may want to know which theory is right, accept that sometimes no one knows the answer to that question—that's why they're theories, not facts!

- **Keep an open mind.** Your instructor and classmates have their own perspectives and opinions. Even if you disagree with them, try to figure out why they hold their views. It will help you see the multiple sides of different issues.

- **Don't deny your emotional reactions—manage them.** There may be times when an instructor or classmate says something that is bothersome or even makes you angry. That's OK. But be sure to manage your emotions so that they don't overwhelm your rational self. And use your emotional reactions to gain an understanding of what's important to you.

- **Don't be afraid of looking unintelligent.** No one wants to look foolish, especially in front of a roomful of classmates. But don't let self-defeating feelings prevent you from expressing your concerns. Take intellectual risks!

problem-solving techniques that best suit your Striving Style™, see the recommendations below.

Decision Making, Problem Solving, and Striving Styles™

Leaders	Approach problems logically, systematically, and objectively. Weigh options and alternatives. Can be reactive to problems when stressed.
Socializers	Use value judgments to decide (good/bad, right/wrong). Consider impact of decisions on people. Can ignore facts and details.
Performers	Approach problems as a challenge. Great at weighing pros and cons and arguing both sides. Can change their minds many times in the process and fail to conclude.
Adventurers	Prefer using instincts to decide. Don't like to delve into weighing options. Need to move to action to attempt to solve the problem.
Artists	Use subjective criteria for decision making. Value judgments (good/bad, right/wrong) influence approach. Problems that evoke emotion are challenging.
Intellectuals	Gather information to assess alternatives. Can spend too much time weighing options. Can come up with unique solutions and alternatives.
Visionaries	Arrive at a decision intuitively and then support it with facts and details. Generate lots of options. Try to make facts fit their decision even when they don't.
Stabilizers	Use a prescribed framework for making decisions. Like to decide quickly without too much consideration. Can get overwhelmed by too many alternatives.

Time to Reflect: What **Did I Learn?**

1. Generally speaking, how would you characterize your decision-making skills?

2. In what way(s) does your approach to decision making reflect your Striving Style™?

3. Based on what you learned about decision making in this chapter, what do you plan to do differently when making decisions in the future? Be specific.

Did You Know?

"Various internet sources estimate that an adult makes about 35,000 remotely conscious decisions each day (in contrast, a child makes about 3,000). This number may sound absurd, but, in fact, we make 226.7 decisions each day on just food alone according to researchers at Cornell University (Wansink and Sobal, 2007)."[11]

Looking Back

How can I improve the quality of my decisions?

> A structured process of decision making can clarify the issues involved, expand your options, and improve the quality of your choices.

> Good decision making begins with understanding your short- and long-term goals.

> Decision making is improved if you have a reasonable number of alternatives.

> For difficult decisions, strategies include taking time to make the decision, acting out alternatives, tossing a coin to test your feelings, seeking advice, and acting on gut feelings.

What strategies can I use for problem solving?

> Problem solving entails the generation of alternatives to consider.

> You need to first understand and define the problem and to determine the important elements in coming to a solution to a problem.

> Approaches to generating solutions include breaking problems into pieces, working backward, using pictures, considering the opposite, using analogies, taking another's perspective, and "forgetting" the problem.

> Problem solving ultimately requires the evaluation and refinement of the solutions that have been generated.

What are some problems that affect critical thinking?

> Labelling, using vague generalities, accepting opinion as fact, jumping to conclusions, mistaking common sense for logic, and assuming causation all pose threats to critical thinking.

RESOURCES

ON CAMPUS

Some colleges and universities offer courses in critical thinking, and they are a good bet to help increase decision-making and problem-solving skills. In addition, courses in logic and philosophy will help improve critical-thinking skills.

Never be afraid to ask for help. If you are facing a problem that you are finding difficult to solve, don't hesitate to turn to staff at the counselling centre at your college or university or to your local mental health centre. Trained counsellors and therapists can help you objectively sort through the different options. They may help you identify possibilities for solutions that you didn't even know existed. Even if the person you speak to initially is not the right one, they can direct you to someone who can help.

If you need additional information about choosing a career, your instructors can point you to staff at your campus counselling centre or career centre. They have access to a wide range of resources that can help you narrow down your career choices.

IN PRINT

Charles Duhigg's book *Smarter Faster Better: The Secrets of Being Productive in Life and Business* (William Heinemann Ltd., 2016) is a treasure trove of tips on how to make better decisions and become more productive.

Asking the Right Questions: A Guide to Critical Thinking, 11th edition (Pearson, 2013), by M. Neil Browne and Stuart M. Keeley, teaches readers how to effectively consider alternative points of view while making personal choices.

If you have trouble making good decisions, you'll want to check out *Learning to Think Things Through: A Guide to Critical Thinking across the Curriculum,* 4th edition (Pearson, 2011), by Gerald M. Nosich. It is an excellent, concise guide to improving your decision-making skills.

ON THE WEB

The following website provides an opportunity to extend your learning about the material in this chapter:

> "Guidelines to Problem-Solving and Decision-Making" (**managementhelp.org /prsn_prd/prob_slv.htm**), by Carter McNamara, PhD, provides seven steps to effective problem solving and decision making. This site is rich in links to comprehensive approaches to decision making, critical and creative thinking, time management, and organizing yourself.

THERE'S AN APP FOR THAT

> ChoiceMap for iOS allows you to replicate the process you used in Try It! 2. You can put in a decision, generate alternatives, create criteria and weight them, and input your scores to determine which is the preferred alternative.

> DecisionBuddy is a an app for Android that offers similar functionality to ChoiceMap.

ANSWERS TO TRY IT! 3 PROBLEMS

1. Remove one lug nut from each of the other three tires on the car and use these three to attach the spare tire. This will hold until four more lug nuts can be purchased.
2. Dump the tools out of the toolbox and use it as a pail.
3. Thursday.
4. Open all three links on one chain (cost = 6 cents) and use them to fasten the other three chains together (cost = 9 cents; total cost = 15 cents).
5. It is the same as one-half of two-thirds, or one-third.
6. 33 boxes (3 large, 6 medium, 24 small).

ANSWERS TO TRY IT! 4 PROBLEMS

Items 1, 3, 5, 8, and 9 are opinions; the rest are facts.

TAKING IT TO THE WEB

1 Mensa International is an organization that brings together people across the world who score within the top 2 percent in intelligence on a culturally unbiased test that is administered in a supervised setting. While 98 percent of us won't qualify, you can still have a little fun by completing Mensa's 30-question workout, which will test your ability to think critically. As you work your way through the test, take note of the strategies discussed in this chapter that you used. The test can be found at **mensa.org/workout.**

2 How good are you at problem solving? Go to the Mind Tools website (**mindtools. com/pages/article/newTMC_72.htm**) and take their short test to find out.

THE CASE OF . . .
The Missing Roommate

Alyssa Pearl had a problem.

In June, she and her cousin had rented a three-bedroom apartment near the university and had signed a lease for the two semesters from September to April. They had advertised for a third person on the university's website and had interviewed several applicants, finally settling on a young nursing student called Emily to be their third roommate. That wasn't the problem, though. The problem was that it was now the day after Labour Day and classes were starting, and Emily had still not shown up.

Concerned, Alyssa called her—and the nursing student brusquely told her she'd found a better place and wouldn't be sharing the apartment with Alyssa and her cousin after all. Then she hung up. Suddenly, Alyssa was left with an empty room, and without Emily's share of the rent money.

1. Of the problem-solving strategies outlined in this chapter, which would you use to approach this problem?

2. What alternatives does Alyssa have for dealing with the situation?

3. How should Alyssa go about evaluating the outcomes for each alternative?

4. Based on your analysis of the problem, what advice would you give Alyssa for dealing with the situation?

5. Is there anything Alyssa could have done to avoid this problem in the first place?

CHAPTER 9
Collaborating with Others

Learning Outcomes

By the time you finish this chapter, you will be able to

LO 9.1   Explain why the ability to work well as part of a group is an essential skill, and describe how groups evolve into well-functioning teams.

LO 9.2   Describe how agendas and minutes can be used to facilitate group meetings.

LO 9.3   Discuss ways of communicating openly with other group members.

LO 9.4   Describe approaches that can be used to resolve conflicts.

LO 9.5   Identify the various types of diversity, and discuss how to build the kind of cultural competence that facilitates working with people who are different from you.

His parents immigrated to Canada from Tanzania. He was born in Toronto and moved to Calgary as an infant. He attended public schools in northeast Calgary and went on to graduate with a Bachelor of Commerce degree in 1994 from the University of Calgary, where he also served as President of the Student Union. By 1998, he had obtained a Master's degree in public policy from Harvard University and had jump-started his career at highly respected global consulting firm McKinsey & Company. By the age of 30, he became a Board member and eventually Chair of the Board of the EPCOR Centre for the Performing Arts in Calgary, the largest performing arts centre in western Canada. He was one of 190 people chosen from a pool of nearly 5,000 candidates for the World Economic Forum's list of Young Global Leaders (YGLs) for 2011. Bill Graveland of the Canadian Press described him as "young, funny, educated, a visible minority and a Muslim." Supporters on his election website, **Purple Revolution**, referred to him as "a real people person," "a team player," and "willing to listen to people's ideas." His grassroots election campaign was built from the ground up, using the power of collaboration and the leverage of social media. He led the recovery efforts after one of the costliest natural disasters in Canadian history: the June 2013 Calgary flood, which resulted in the evacuation of 80,000 residents and 32 communities. To top it all off, in 2014, he was awarded the prize for the world's top mayor.[1]

He is Naheed Nenshi, who at age 38 became the first Muslim mayor of a major Canadian city.

Looking Ahead

Whether you are Catholic or Muslim or Hindu, have a Stabilizer or a Visionary Striving Style™, were born in India or China or Lethbridge, are physically challenged or not—whatever your background, post-secondary education presents a world of new opportunities for you to encounter people with very different backgrounds and perspectives from your own. If you take the opportunity to work with and form relationships with a variety of individuals, you will increase your understanding of the human experience and greatly enrich your life. This will also benefit you enormously in your career, because, whatever your field, you will inevitably find yourself in situations where success will depend on your ability to collaborate effectively with people different from you.

In this chapter, we address the issue of teamwork as an essential life skill. We examine how groups are formed and how they evolve into smoothly functioning teams. We put forth practical strategies for communicating with others and working well in a group environment. We look at how diversity can enhance your academic and life experience and the importance of being receptive to others based on their own merits. Finally, the chapter addresses the conflicts that can arise between people and what you can do to resolve them.

LO 9.1 Working Productively in Groups

Naheed Nenshi's story is not remarkable because he is Muslim. Nor is it remarkable because he is a visible minority. It isn't even particularly remarkable because he was only 38 years old when he became mayor. What is remarkable about Nenshi's story is that his faith was never an election issue. What got him elected was Nenshi's passion for his city; his drive to get things done; and his power to leverage his contacts and social networks like Facebook, LinkedIn, and Twitter—and his ability to work collaboratively with others resulted in his re-election as Calgary's mayor for a second term. In our increasingly connected and interconnected world, Nenshi has shown by example that learning to work collaboratively is now, more than ever before, an essential life skill.

No matter where you end up—whether in a lab working on a cure for cancer or in a classroom teaching six-year-olds—you cannot get there without working with and learning from other people. "Plays well with others" is a comment commonly found on elementary school report cards, so it may come as a surprise to you that years later, in college and university and even on the job, your ability to work well with others continues to have a significant impact on your success. Take a look at your course outline or syllabus. It is increasingly common to find that a significant portion of your course grade is related to group work. In some schools, group work has become so important that figuring out whom to work with, how to communicate within a group, and how to move toward a common goal can make the difference between getting a B grade and achieving an A. Building a well-functioning team proceeds in several steps, outlined in the P.O.W.E.R. Plan.

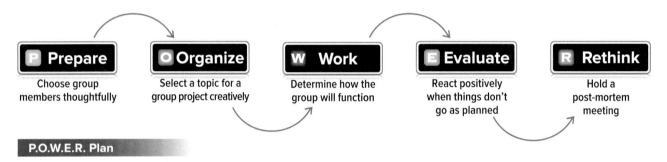

P.O.W.E.R. Plan

| P Prepare | O Organize | W Work | E Evaluate | R Rethink |
| Choose group members thoughtfully | Select a topic for a group project creatively | Determine how the group will function | React positively when things don't go as planned | Hold a post-mortem meeting |

P Prepare Choose Group Members Thoughtfully

In some courses, you may not have the luxury of picking your own group members, but if you do, think very carefully about whom you want to work with and why. Left to their own devices, students will often make the mistake of working with their friends or will seek out the students with the highest GPAs. While it is important that the people you choose to work with have a similar end goal in mind—for example, you all want a minimum B grade—and that you have compatible schedules to allow for meetings, you don't all have to be super smart!

In fact, a study published in *Science* magazine found that the most important variables for optimal group performance were these: the average social sensitivity of the group's members, the degree to which each person in the group was allowed to speak in turn, and the proportion of females in the group.[2] The emphasis on social sensitivity and speaking in turn is consistent with the notion advanced by author Daniel Goleman that **emotional intelligence**, or EQ, is a better predictor of success in life than the traditional measure known as IQ, or intelligence quotient. There are five dimensions of EQ: self-awareness, self-regulation, motivation, empathy, and social skills. For a short survey that measures *your* EQ, go to **mindtools.com/pages/article/ei-quiz.htm**.

Emotional intelligence

According to Daniel Goleman, the quality of possessing "abilities such as being able to motivate oneself and persist in the face of frustrations; to control impulse and delay gratification; to regulate one's moods and keep distress from swamping the ability to think; to empathize and to hope."

In any group, there will be a leader and there will be followers. Some group members will be smarter than others. There will be people who enjoy doing research, and others who prefer to write up the results. There will be people who understand the content deeply, and others who excel at presenting it in a simple manner that their classmates will understand. The various Striving Styles™ approach collaboration differently. While all styles can and do work well together, there are some that work together better than others.

Approaches to Collaboration and Striving Styles™

Leaders	Always willing to do more than their share, including taking the lead and dividing the work. Will make sure the group creates the outcome the Leader wants. Take over when others don't meet their timelines. Give lesser roles if they don't feel confident others will work to their standards. Frustrated with others who don't take projects as seriously as they do. Work best with other Leaders or Visionaries. May not work well with Artists or Intellectuals.
Socializers	Prefer to be in charge of distributing work. Hard-working and supportive of overall goals. Want everyone to contribute equally to make things fair. Like the social aspect of group projects and frustrate others by spending too much time talking. Take on more than their share helping others and making sure everyone is included. Can fail to do their own work because of over-commitment. Work best with Visionaries or Stabilizers. May not work well with Intellectuals or Leaders.
Performers	Enjoy working with others who recognize them as talented and valuable. Want to be recognized for their own contribution and can be unduly competitive. Will take on more than they can handle at times so that others will recognize and appreciate them. If not recognized, can be negative about the work of others. Can miss timelines, holding projects up by doing what they thought was best instead of what was agreed upon. Work best with Leaders or Visionaries. May not work well with Stabilizers or Artists.
Adventurers	Contribute energy and enthusiasm, especially at the beginning of a project. Enjoy the social side of collaborative projects and use others to stay motivated. Excellent at problem solving and figuring out what needs to be done to make everything work. Easily distracted if their part of the project doesn't make sense. Will make the team process fun, but won't always meet commitments. Work best with Leaders or Performers. May not work well with Artists or Stabilizers.
Artists	Creative and imaginative. Work hard to do their best work as they want their contribution to be perfect. Working with others can make them feel inadequate, and they may compensate by doing more than their share. Can also miss timelines because they fear their work isn't good enough. Take a low-key role on teams and contribute what is expected. Prefer to work independently. Work best with Visionaries or Socializers. May not work well with Leaders or Intellectuals.
Intellectuals	Prefer to work independently or in the role of researcher in a group. Don't think about what others are doing; focus on their objective. Like a role that no one else has expertise to do. If they aren't interested in the subject or can't be the expert, they won't contribute freely. Can spend too much time collecting information or procrastinating and fail to deliver. Don't need the social interactions. Work best with Adventurers or Performers. May not work well with Socializers or Leaders.
Visionaries	Envision what the project should look like and what everyone needs to do. Will take charge. Prefer to work alone but enjoy working with like-minded people. Can be overly ambitious about what can be achieved. Can think others are more competent and trustworthy than they are. Get angry when people are lazy or only want to do the minimum. Need their ideas and insight to be used. Work best with Performers or other Visionaries. May not work well with Socializers or Stabilizers.
Stabilizers	Need clear expectations of what others require of them. Wait to be told what they should do. Will volunteer for the difficult parts of the project that others don't want to do. Will deliver precisely what is expected and not be concerned with what others are doing. Frustrated by others who miss timelines and will take responsibility for doing their work for them. Work best with Leaders or Socializers. May not work well with Artists or Visionaries.

What *is* important when selecting group members is to ensure that you have a *mix* of the Striving Styles™, that you respect one another and are willing to listen to each other, and that you are sensitive to each other's needs.

Finally, and on a more practical note, be sure to take into consideration the following when choosing group members:

> Do your school and work timetables allow for time to meet?

> Do you live close to one another, or can everyone easily get to a central meeting spot?

> Do you have a mix of the required skill sets to do the project well?

> Are you committed to the same type of outcome, e.g., an A or a B?

Brainstorming
A process whereby ideas are generated by a group following a specific set of rules that do not permit censoring or critiquing of ideas as they are generated

⊙ Organize Select a Topic for a Group Project Creatively

If your group is given an opportunity to select the topic of the group report, you may want to consider holding a **brainstorming** session to allow everyone in the group an opportunity to contribute ideas. A brainstorming session is a structured process whereby group members generate as many ideas as they can within a specific time frame; no censoring of ideas is permitted, no matter how inane the idea might seem at first. The process allows everyone to contribute and is designed to make everyone feel that any idea is a good idea. Once the session is over, ideas can be categorized and weeded out, as required, to come up with the best of the best. See **Try It! 1** "Organize a Brainstorming Session" for specific guidelines on how to hold a brainstorming session.

Analyzing the results of a brainstorming session.
© stevecoleimages/Getty Images

---

1 | TRY IT! [POWER]

Organize a Brainstorming Session

Task: Your marketing instructor would like your group to come up with ideas for a new smartphone app.

1. Explain the rules of brainstorming:
   a. Don't censor your own ideas before stating them. Allow every thought to come out as you are thinking it. Feel free to suggest your wildest, craziest ideas.
   b. Every idea is a good idea. Don't critique anyone else's ideas.
   c. Build on the ideas of others. You are going for quantity, not quality.

2. Assign someone to capture every idea. They can write the ideas on a flip chart, or record them on individual sticky notes and stick them to a wall. Keep generating ideas until no one can think of any more. When everyone runs out of steam, the brainstorming part of your session is over.

(continued)

(continued)

3. Either with the same group, or with a different group, develop a set of criteria against which you can assess the ideas that have been generated, e.g., can implement immediately, cheap to do, interesting to all/most members of group.

4. Go back through each idea, assessing it against your set of criteria, eliminating some and creating a list in order of priority with the others.

To Try It online, go to the McGraw-Hill online resource.

 Determine How the Group Will Function

Some years ago, psychologist Bruce Tuckman proposed that a highly functioning team, whether set up for a temporary purpose or as a permanent group, would pass through five stages: He called these the **stages in a group's evolution**: forming, storming, norming, performing, and adjourning. Recognizing this evolution and adjusting to what happens at each stage can help you and your group members understand how groups evolve and how to become a high-performing group.

Stages in a group's evolution
According to psychologist Bruce Tuckman, all well-functioning groups go through five stages: forming, storming, norming, performing, and adjourning

The Forming Stage

In the forming stage of a group's evolution, which may last only as long as the very first group meeting, group members usually feel one another out, trying to determine how the group will work and what role each person will play. Some members may want to jump right in and get to work, but an upfront investment in planning will pay off later on. At the forming stage, list your goals and ground rules upfront:

> What are members' grade expectations, and the time commitment they are willing to make to achieve it (if these have not already been determined during the group selection stage)?

> When, where, and how often will the group meet? Exchanging timetables and detailed contact information is critical at this stage, as is identifying a time and meeting spot that is convenient to all group members.

> How will the workload be divided up? You may want to get your instructor's guidance on this to ensure that some group members are not shouldering a heavier load than others.

> Who will be responsible for what? This includes responsibilities for the actual functioning of the group, such as who will lead meetings, plan agendas, and take minutes. As for the actual project, try to allocate the work to leverage group members' individual strengths. If someone is good with Microsoft Excel, for example, they should be assigned the section on spreadsheets and graphs.

> What will be the consequences when a group member fails to meet the expectations set out by the group? Will that person be given a second chance? Fired from the group? Given a lower grade than the rest of the group? Given a low grade on the peer evaluation? You will need your professor's guidance on what the consequences can be. For example, some professors do not allow group members to be fired but will allow grades to differ by group member.

figure 9.1 | A Team Charter

Sample Team Charter

Group members will attend all group meetings.

1. Group meetings will be held every Friday from 12:30 P.M. to 2:30 P.M. in Room B-416.
2. We will start and end group meetings on time.
3. All meetings will have an agenda, and a set of minutes will be taken by a designated group member.
4. Group members will use Google Docs as the repository for all of their work.
5. We will focus on problems, not personalities, when conflicts arise.
6. Conflicts will be resolved during the meeting in which they are raised to allow us to move forward.
7. Each member of the group is responsible for getting their work completed by the agreed-upon time.
8. Group members that fail to submit their work on time will receive a zero grade on their peer evaluation.

Team charter

A set of written guidelines that outline the rules, roles, and responsibilities of team members and set out how a team plans to operate to achieve its goals

A group that wants to function well should draw up a **team charter** that puts rules, roles, and responsibilities for the group and its project into writing. A sample charter is shown in **Figure 9.1**. For detailed guidelines on how to draw up a team charter, see "On the Web" in the **Resources** section at the end of this chapter.

 **Evaluate** React Positively When Things Don't Go as Planned

The Storming Stage

It is normal and natural in the evolution of a team for disagreements and conflict to arise. These might involve who should be the leader, or how the work should be done, or even what the work should entail. Many groups disintegrate at this point, with some members giving up entirely and deciding not to do the work they'd promised. During this stage, it is useful to evaluate where team members stand with respect to their ongoing commitment to the team and its objectives. Keeping lines of communication open, ensuring everyone has an opportunity to contribute, and dealing with situations as soon they arise are important to moving to the next stage. For information on how to resolve conflicts, see the section called **Managing and Resolving Conflicts**.

How might your Striving Style™ affect how you collaborate with others? You'll want to examine the table on page 237 for suggestions. Specific suggestions for communicating with other team members and resolving conflicts are also provided in this chapter.

The Norming Stage

At this stage of a group's evolution, the group is beginning to gel: Members have settled into their roles and accepted their responsibilities, and there

Leaders	Organize and lead groups. Create rules, roles, and structure and hold others accountable. Will take over when others don't contribute.
Socializers	Do best cooperating and working on teams. Try to get others to work together, managing conflict and helping with work of others.
Performers	Enjoy working on teams, but want to be recognized for their own contribution. Project must reflect their abilities even if it means doing the work of others.
Adventurers	Need to work with others to stay motivated. Will make the team process fun, but won't always meet commitments.
Artists	Take a low-key role on teams and contribute what is expected. Prefer to work independently. Expectation of others creates anxiety.
Intellectuals	Prefer to work independently or in the role of researcher on the team. Can procrastinate and fail to deliver. Play devil's advocate.
Visionaries	Independent thinkers who prefer to work alone. On a team, will encourage people to think outside the box. Need ideas and insight they contributed to be used.
Stabilizers	Need clear roles and rules on the team. Will deliver precisely what is expected. Frustrated by others who don't follow rules.

is palpable commitment to achieving the group's objectives. There may be an occasional lapse back into the storming stage, but for the most part, the foundation work of getting the team to move in one direction has been accomplished.

During the norming stage, the focus is on collaboration. Many applications are available to help you create and integrate your work product. With Google Docs, for example, a group of people can share and edit documents. Learning management systems also offer group workspaces. Sites that are designed to facilitate collaboration among students or employees have many benefits. Aside from the obvious—anyone can access the site, anywhere, at any time—these online workspaces play an important role in ensuring the accountability of those who participate in them.

The Performing Stage

Once groups have reached the performing stage, most of the friction has gone out of the equation. The focus has shifted to working together to get the task done. Unfortunately, in the case of groups who tend to procrastinate, this stage is reached far too close to the project deadline, and quality suffers as a result.

 Hold a Post-mortem Meeting

The Adjourning Stage

Unless there is another project in the offing, the adjourning stage is usually reached once the group disbands, after having received a grade on the project they have submitted. One of the most important things a group can do at this stage is hold a post-mortem meeting, where they discuss what worked and what didn't, and how to do things differently the next time.

Unfortunately, student groups rarely bother with this stage, and it is often left up to the individual—that's you!—to reflect on what they have learned from the process.

Over the course of your post-secondary education, you will undoubtedly collaborate with many, many people, some of whom you will want to stay in touch with after your group project has ended. Snapchat and Instagram are *not* the place to stay in touch with these people. Instead, you'll want to use a more "professional" site; the most popular networking site out there by far is LinkedIn, and if you aren't on it yet, you need to be. You'll learn more about LinkedIn in Chapter 11, but for now, what is important is to recognize that networking is absolutely key to your future, and LinkedIn is one way to keep in touch with professional, as opposed to social, contacts. When your group has adjourned, send LinkedIn invitations to those group members you would like to stay in touch with. You never know when they might come in handy!

LO 9.2 Facilitating Group Meetings

Group projects are assigned often in colleges and universities, which means that group meetings to discuss those projects are also frequently held. But with group meetings come issues to discuss, decisions to take, and promises to make.

Drawing up an agenda for each meeting you have is key. For example, your first meeting might include tackling the following questions: What topic will you choose? Who will work on what? How will it all come together in time for the due date?

An agenda sets out the following:

> Date and time of the meeting
> The topics up for discussion
> Who will lead each discussion
> How much time will be devoted to each discussion

Interested in using a template for your agenda? Visit **templatelab.com /meeting-agenda-templates/**, where you'll find over 40 templates.

During the meeting, keeping track of what is going on is also critical:

> How will you recall which group members attended which meetings?
> How will you recall the decisions made by the group?
> How will you recall who will be responsible for which deliverables?
> How will you recall when deliverables are due?

This is where meeting minutes, that is, notes about the meeting, come into play. These notes or minutes serve not only as a reminder of what was discussed but also as a record of accountability. Did the group agree to focus the project on Toyota's Lexus brands? Did Priya attend only 10 percent of the meetings? Did Jan promise she would have the research part completed by February 10? Did Mohammed promise he would do the final edit? When good meeting minutes are taken, it is a lot easier to hold group members accountable for doing what they promised or agreed to do, because there is a written record of those promises or agreements.

So how does one take good meeting minutes?

To start, you should note the date and purpose of the meeting and the name of each attendee. Then, you should include the following:[3]

> What was achieved since the last meeting, using the previous meeting's minutes as a reference

> Current business (whatever is on your agenda)

> Decisions made during the current meeting

> Any actions that were agreed to in the current meeting, whom they were assigned to, and the date they should be completed by

> Any items on the agenda that need to be deferred to the next meeting

> The agreed-upon date for the next meeting

For Word templates to help you organize your meeting minutes, **visit vertex42.com/WordTemplates/meeting-minutes.html**.

LO 9.3 Communicating Well with Others

While texting may be your go-to way of communicating with your friends about your plans for the weekend, communicating well with others when you are trying to work as a group on a complex project or assignment is best done the old-fashioned way: face-to-face. Face-to-face interaction has several advantages over electronic communication: You have the opportunity to see and react to someone's body language, group members can express themselves in a more detailed fashion, and there is a chance to clarify misunderstandings more quickly and move on to the task at hand.

Communicating well in a group setting is a blend of talking and listening. Not only does it help to do both well, but it is also important to know when it's time to listen and when it's time to speak up. Listening is an often underrated skill. When working closely with others, we may be so busy trying to communicate our opinions and perspective that we overlook the need of others to be heard. As you work collaboratively with others toward a common goal, doing all the talking simply isn't enough. Knowing when to talk and when to stop talking and listen, and knowing how to express yourself, especially in moments of difficulty, can be very important to getting your message across.

What you *don't* say also matters. Good teamwork is often built on good listening skills.

© Onoky/SuperStock

Be a Good Listener

Supportive silence is very powerful. When it comes to working with others on a group project, how you listen is sometimes more important than what you say. The silence involved in listening is a powerful force, one that can bind us more closely to others.

We've already discussed the art and science of listening as it applies to academic success in Chapter 4. The same principles that promote learning about lecture topics also promote learning about the people we work with in an academic setting and in our future career. You can't call yourself a team player without knowing what others are like and what they are thinking. Good listening is one of the ways to enhance your understanding of others.

When we feel we are heard, we get the message that our listeners care about our opinions, not just their own. Similarly, when we listen, we show that we have respect for those who are speaking, that we are interested in their ideas and beliefs, and that we are willing to take the time to pay attention to them.

There are several ways you can improve your ability to listen:

> **Stop talking!** Are you the kind of person who revels in giving your opinions on every subject? Do you wait eagerly for others to finish what they are saying so that you can jump in with your perspective? Do you accidentally cut other people off or finish their sentences while they are still speaking?
>
> No one likes to be interrupted, even in casual conversation. People who are more introverted, or whose first language is not English, may need more time to organize and present their thoughts. Ensure that all group members are given an opportunity to voice an opinion. And when they do, don't interrupt—you may be amazed by what you learn.

Conversational markers
Non-verbal indications that we are listening to what someone else is saying

> **Demonstrate that you are listening.** Linguists call them **conversational markers**—those non-verbal indications that we're listening. They consist of head nods, eye contact, and other signs that we're keeping up with the conversation. Listening this way shows that we're paying attention and are interested in what the other person is saying.
>
> When you are listening, *truly* listening, you should not be multitasking. If you're having a serious conversation, turn off your cellphone. If your phone rings, don't look at the caller ID. Even glancing at your phone for a moment shows you're not paying full attention.

Reflective feedback
A technique of active listening in which a listener rephrases what a speaker has said, trying to echo the speaker's meaning

> **Use reflective feedback.** Carl Rogers, a respected therapist, developed a very useful way to lend support to someone and draw them out. In **reflective feedback**, a listener rephrases what a speaker has said, trying to echo the speaker's meaning. For example, a listener might say, "If I understand what you're saying, …" or "You seem to feel that …" or "In other words, you believe that …."
>
> In each case, the summary statement doesn't just play back the speaker's statements literally. Instead, it is a rephrasing that captures the essence of the message in different words.
>
> Reflective feedback has two big benefits. First, it provides speakers with a clear indication that you're listening and taking what they're saying seriously. Second, and equally important, it helps ensure that you have an accurate understanding of what the speaker is saying.

> **Ask questions.** Asking questions shows that you are paying attention to a speaker. Questions permit you to clarify what the speaker has said, so they can move the conversation forward. Further, people feel valued when others ask them about themselves.

> **Deal with distractions.** We've all had those moments: Something is bothering you and you can't get it out of your mind, or you've simply

2 | TRY IT! [POWER]

The Role of Body Language in Active Listening

Non-verbal communication plays an important role in active listening. In this role-play exercise, the instructor will divide the class into groups of three, each group comprising a speaker, a listener, and an observer. Each group will complete the following three role-plays, with the group members maintaining the *same* role each time.

1. The first role-play will involve the speaker talking to the listener about having had a very hard time finding a parking spot that morning.

2. The second role-play will involve the speaker talking about how their significant other has just learned they have been accepted into a program at a prestigious educational institution 1,500 kilometres away.

3. The third role-play will involve the speaker talking about their dog, who has just died.

Each time, the observer should make notes regarding both the speaker's and the listener's body language. Observations can then be shared in the small group or within the larger class.

To Try It online, go to the McGraw-Hill online resource.

---

got to finish something and don't really have time to chat. If at the same time someone wants to engage you in conversation, your distraction will undoubtedly show, making the other person feel you are not interested.

The way to deal with this situation is to admit that you're distracted. Simply say, "I'd love to talk, but I've got to finish reading this chapter." That should be enough to explain the situation to a classmate who just wants to chat.

You should work to avoid distractions during a planned group meeting. Don't hold your meeting in a busy student centre, or where the smell of coffee or food, or the presence of people outside your group, can distract you.

In **Try It! 2** "The Role of Body Language in Active Listening," you have the opportunity to participate in a role-play that will illustrate just how important a role body language plays in active listening.

LO 9.4 Managing and Resolving Conflicts

Group work is an unavoidable part of the academic experience, and, for many students, it is often the most frustrating. Group members don't show up for meetings, or they don't do what they said they'd do, or they drop out of the class you share midway through the semester and don't tell anyone. Disagreements may arise through cultural misunderstanding. When conflicts of any type occur—as they will from time to time—communication can fall apart. These situations test your ability to communicate effectively. Using the active listening strategies discussed earlier will be helpful. Here are some other approaches that will help you resolve conflict in your group. (These approaches will also serve you well at work and in personal relationships.)

Use "I" Statements to Defuse Anger

Suppose a group member says something you disagree with, such as, "All you guys are the same—you always expect to get everything your way!" You might respond by directing anger at the other person, directly or indirectly accusing the person of some imperfection. "You're always looking for something to complain about!" Such responses (and, as you will notice, the initial statement) typically include the word "you." For instance, consider these possible responses to indicate disagreement: "*You* really don't understand," "*You're* being stubborn," and "How can *you* say that?"

These types of statements cast blame, make accusations, express criticism, and make assumptions about what's inside the other person's head. And they inevitably lead to defensive replies that will probably do little to move the conversation forward: "I am *not*!" "I do so understand," "I'm *not* being stubborn," and "I can say that because that's the way I feel."

"I" statements

Responses spoken in terms of oneself and one's individual interpretation, rather than casting blame on the other person

A far more effective approach is to use "I" statements. **"I" statements** cast responses in terms of yourself and your individual interpretation. Instead of saying, for example, "You really don't understand," a more appropriate response is, "I think we're misunderstanding each other." "You're being stubborn" could be rephrased as "I feel like you're not really listening." And "Why don't you call when you're going to be late?" becomes "I worry that something has happened to you when you don't call if you are going to be late." In each case, "I" statements permit you to state your reaction in terms of your perception or understanding, rather than as a critical judgment about the other person. Practise using "I" statements in **Try It! 3** "Switch 'You' to 'I.'"

---

3 | TRY IT!

CLASS DISCUSSION

Switch "You" to "I"

Turn the following "you" statements into less aggressive "I" statements. For example, a possible "I" statement alternative to "You just don't get it, do you?" is, "I don't feel I'm making my feelings clear."

1. You just don't get it, do you?
2. You never listen to what I say.
3. You don't see where I'm coming from.
4. You don't really believe that, do you?
5. You never try to see my point of view.
6. Please stop interrupting me and listen to what I'm saying for a change.
7. Stop changing the subject!
8. You're not making sense.
9. You keep distorting what I say until I don't even know what point I'm trying to make.
10. You use too many "you" statements. Use more "I" statements when you're talking to others.

To Try It online, go to the McGraw-Hill online resource.

Create a Win–Win Proposition

Even with careful attention to putting our own feelings forward instead of making accusations, whenever people share their thoughts, concerns, fears, and opinions with each other, chances are that sooner or later some sort of conflict will arise.

Conflict is not necessarily bad; in fact, it is often necessary to achieve progress.

Often, people are upset simply by the fact that they are having a conflict. It is as though they believe conflicts don't occur in a "good" group. But the opposite is true. Conflict can be helpful in some very important ways: It can force us to say what is really on our minds, it can encourage us to clear up misconceptions and miscommunications before they begin to undermine the team, it can lead to creative solutions, and it can even give us practice at resolving conflicts with others outside the group.

Outside the context of academic group work, conflict is not necessarily a bad thing, either. In the working world, conflict is often inevitable. Yet as with school, conflict on the job can be beneficial. Inefficiencies can be removed, misconceptions cleared up, and new processes devised when co-workers engage in honest, passionate discussion.

Like anything else, though, there are good ways to resolve conflict, and there are bad ways. Good ways move people forward, defining the problem and promoting creative problem solving. Bad ways make the situation worse, driving people apart rather than bringing them together. The following are some fundamental principles of conflict resolution that you can use when conflict occurs in academic, professional, and personal relationships:

> **Stop, look, and listen.** In the heat of an argument, all sorts of things that otherwise would go unsaid get said. If you find yourself making rash or hurtful statements, stop, look at yourself, and listen to what you and the other person are saying.
>
> Stopping works like a circuit breaker that prevents a short circuit from causing a deadly fire. You've probably heard about counting to 10 to cool off when you're angry. Do it. Take a break and count to 10 … or 20 … or more. Whether you count to 10 or 100, stopping gives you time to think and not react rashly. You don't want to say things you will regret later.

> **Defuse the argument.** Anger is not an emotion that encourages rational discourse. When you're angry or annoyed with someone, you're not in the best position to logically evaluate the merits of various arguments others may offer. It may feel exhilarating to get our fury off our chests in the heat of an argument, but you can bet it isn't taking anyone any closer to resolving the problem.
>
> Don't assume that you are 100 percent right and the other person is 100 percent wrong. Make your goal to solve the problem rather than to win an argument.

> **Admit personal responsibility.** Perhaps you've heard others suggest that you shouldn't get personal in an argument. In one sense that's true: Accusing people you're arguing with of having character flaws does nothing to resolve real issues.
>
> At the same time, you should be willing to admit personal *responsibility* for at least part of the conflict. The conflict would not exist

without you, so you need to accept that the argument has two sides and that you are not automatically blameless. This creates some solid ground from which you and the other person can begin to work on the problem.

> **Listen to the real message.** When people argue, what they say is often not the real message. There's typically an underlying communication—a subtext—that is the actual source of the conflict.

It's important, then, to dig beneath what you're hearing. If someone accuses you of being selfish, the real meaning hidden in the accusation may be that you don't give anyone else a chance to make decisions. Remember, arguments are usually about behaviour, not underlying character and personality. What people *do* is not synonymous with who they *are.*

If you rephrase the person's statement in your own mind, it moves from an insult ("You're a bad person") to a request for a change of behaviour ("Let me participate in decision making"). You're much more likely to respond reasonably when you don't feel that the essence of your being is under attack.

> **Show that you're listening.** It's not enough to listen only to the underlying message that someone is conveying. You also need to acknowledge the *explicit* message. For example, say something like "OK, I can tell you are concerned about sharing the burden on our group project, and I think we should talk about it." This acknowledges that you see the issue and admit that it is worthy of discussion. This is a far more successful strategy than firing back a countercharge each time someone makes a complaint.

> **If you are angry, acknowledge it.** Don't pretend that everything is fine if it isn't. Ultimately, teams that have members that bottle up their anger may suffer more than those in which the group members express their true feelings. If you're angry, say so and explain why.

> **Ask for clarification.** As you're listening to another person's arguments, check your understanding of what is being said. Don't assume that you know what's intended. Saying something like "Are you saying …" or "Do you mean that …" is a way of verifying that what you think someone means is really what they mean.

> **Make your requests explicit.** If you're upset that a team member isn't providing you with the quality of work you'd expected, remarking that they are stupid shows more than that you are angry: It also shows that your intent is to hurt rather than to solve the problem.

It's far better to be explicit in your concerns. Say something like "I feel like the group would get a higher mark overall if you could find time to put more effort into your submission." Couching your concern in this way changes the focus of the message from your group member's personality to a specific behaviour that can be changed.

> **In an argument, there doesn't have to be a loser.** Many of us act as if life were a **zero-sum game**, a situation in which when one person wins, the other person automatically loses. A zero-sum game is what happens when you make a bet: If one person wins the bet, the other person loses.

Life is not like that. If one person wins an argument, it doesn't mean that others automatically have to lose it. And if someone loses an

Zero-sum game
A situation in which when one person wins, the other person automatically loses

argument, it doesn't mean that others have automatically won. In fact, all too often conflict escalates so much that the argument turns into a lose–lose situation, where everyone ends up a loser.

However, life can be a win–win situation. The best resolution of conflict occurs when both parties walk away with something they want. They may not have achieved *every* goal, but at least they have enough to feel satisfied.

When Group Members Simply Don't Deliver

Not every situation that arises in a group involves conflict. Sometimes, group members simply don't do what they say they will do, or don't do it to an acceptable standard, or deliver so late that their work doesn't fit with what has already been done. What then?

To prevent this from happening in the first place, agree on internal deadlines, where group members need to show their in-process work. This will allow group members to provide feedback to one another and ensure that work is done to the acceptable standard. Remind team members of the consequences of not delivering, as per your team charter. If there is no change in the group member's behaviour, escalate your concerns to the instructor.

What if it's too late for prevention? If a peer evaluation is part of the project, use it to reflect your group member's lack of contribution. If there is no peer evaluation, ask your instructor if the person's grade can be adjusted to reflect their lack of contribution. Some instructors will allow you to remove the person's name from the project's cover page, signalling that they did not contribute, and will then give that person a zero on the project.

What if none of these strategies are available to you and the person who did not contribute still gets the grade that everyone else in the group received? How is that fair? Well, it isn't. But that's life. There will always be people out there who get away with doing the least possible and are only too happy to ride the coattails of others. They rarely achieve the heights others can, although that is little solace. You have no choice but to chalk this up to experience and do your best, in future, to learn how to identify who they are and, if possible, avoid working with them.

LO 9.5 Living in a Diverse World

No matter where we live, our contacts with others who are different from us are increasing. The Web is bringing people from across the globe into our homes, as close to us as the computer sitting on the desk in front of us. Businesses now operate globally, so co-workers are likely to come from many different countries and cultures. Being comfortable with people whose backgrounds and beliefs differ from our own is a necessity, not only socially, but also for career success.

As you can see in the Diversity Wheel in **Figure 9.2**, diversity encompasses characteristics such as ethnicity, gender, sexual orientation, and age; it also includes mental and physical characteristics and even work style. Layer on top of all that factors such as language, religion, and income level, and the complexity of others—and ourselves—becomes apparent.

figure 9.2 | Diversity Wheel

Diversity is composed of many different characteristics, as exemplified by the Diversity Wheel.[4]

© Loden Associates, Inc.

Ethnicity, Culture, and Values

Are you Québécois? Italian? South Asian? Chinese? Aboriginal?

The language we use to describe our ethnic membership, and those of other people, is in constant flux. And what we call people matters. The subtleties of language affect how people think about members of particular groups, and how they think about themselves.

Ethnicity refers to shared national origins or cultural patterns. In Toronto, North America's most multicultural city, half the city's residents were born outside of Canada. According to the city's website, 160 languages and dialects are spoken there, and 45 percent of Toronto residents have a first language other than English or French.[5]

Culture comprises the learned behaviours, beliefs, and attitudes that characterize an individual society or population. But it's more than that: Culture also encompasses the products that people create, such as architecture, music, art, and literature. Culture is created and shaped by people, but at the same time it contributes to people's behaviour.

Ethnicity and culture shape each of us and our values to an enormous degree. They profoundly influence our view of others, as well as who we are. They affect how others treat us, and how we treat them in turn. They determine whether we look people in the eye when we meet them; how early we arrive when we're invited to dinner at a friend's house; and even, sometimes, how well we do in school or on the job. If many ethnic backgrounds are represented in your class and you'd like to learn more about them, ask your instructor to consider devoting a class to a potluck, where students bring in a dish that in some way reflects their ethnicity. Then,

Ethnicity
Shared national origins or cultural patterns

Culture
The learned behaviours, beliefs, and attitudes that characterize an individual society or population, and the products that people create

during the potluck, have each person deliver a short presentation, for example, "five things I love about being Korean."

One example of cultural differences is related to the decade of your adolescence. The 1960s brought us the hippie culture, a subculture within a larger group that became known as the Baby Boomers. The 1970s ushered in the "Me Generation." Then came Gen X and later Gen Y; members of the latter are commonly referred to as millennials. There was a time in the not-too-distant past when college and university students were drawn from a relatively homogeneous population. These days, universities and colleges are a mosaic of students coming straight out of high school, people returning after a few years off, and those in middle age who've been laid off and are now returning to post-secondary institutions to prepare for a new career. In spite of their different experiences and the fact that they may have grown up in very different times, these students may find themselves collaborating with one another, studying together, and working on group projects. They bring different skill sets to the table, and often they also bring different expectations that can affect group dynamics, as can be seen in **Table 9.1**.

table 9.1 Different Generations View Work Differently

	WORKPLACE CHARACTERISTICS			
	Veterans (1922–1945)	**Baby Boomers (1946–1964)**	**Generation X (1965–1980)**	**Generation Y (1981–2000)**
Work ethic and values	Hard work Respect authority Sacrifice Duty before fun Adhere to rules	Workaholics Work efficiently Crusading causes Personal fulfillment Desire quality Question authority	Eliminate the task Self-reliance Want structure and direction Skeptical	What's next Multi-tasking Tenacity Entrepreneurial Tolerant Goal-oriented
Work is …	An obligation	An exciting adventure	A difficult challenge A contract	A means to an end Fulfillment
Leadership style	Directive Command-and-control	Consensual Collegial	Everyone is the same Challenge others Ask why	TBD*
Interactive style	Individual	Team player Loves to have meetings	Entrepreneur	Participative
Communications	Formal Memo	In person	Direct Immediate	Email Voice mail
Feedback and rewards	No news is good news Satisfaction in a job well done	Don't appreciate it Money Title recognition	Sorry to interrupt, but how am I doing? Freedom is the best reward	Whenever I want it, at the push of a button Meaningful work
Messages that motivate	Your experience is respected	You are valued You are needed	Do it your way Forget the rules	You will work with other bright, creative people
Work and family life	Ne'er the twain shall meet	No balance Work to live	Balance	Balance

*As this group has not spent much time in the workforce, this characteristic has yet to be determined.

Because some of us grow up in neighbourhoods that are not ethnically diverse, we may have little or even no experience interacting with people who are different from us. Depending on where your college or university is located, some campuses don't have much diversity either, and, consequently, even in college or university, your exposure to people who have different backgrounds may be limited. But as you move to the larger urban centres, you will quickly realize that Canada is a country of astonishing diversity, and it's not a matter of *if* you will be exposed to people who have profoundly different backgrounds from your own, but *when*. Whether in the workplace or in your neighbourhood, living in a diverse environment will be part of your life. You can examine the diversity around you by completing **Try It! 4** "How Diverse Is Your Community?"

We've talked about the diversity that comes with Canada being a multicultural nation, but it is also important to examine what unites us—those values that are the cornerstone of our shared destiny as Canadians. We first introduced the concept of values in Chapter 1, where we indicated that your values are influenced by your upbringing, your culture, your education, and so forth. So you won't be surprised to learn that identifying the values that Canadians share depends on whom you speak with. The Canadian Index of Wellbeing (CIW) is a framework developed through research and consultations with Canadian leaders that distilled the essence of Canadian values into the following eight core values: fairness, diversity, equity, inclusion, health, safety, economic security, democracy, and sustainability.[6] A website for Durham Region (**durhamimmigration .ca/creating%20community/Pages/WhatareCanadianValues.aspx**), located just east of Toronto, offers a list of Canadian values, including respect for cultural differences and a commitment to social justice, equality, freedom, peace, and law and order. Take a minute to reflect on the differences in these values and ask yourself: What do *I* think are *typical* Canadian values—and what in my past may have influenced me to think that way?

4 | TRY IT! POWER

How Diverse Is Your Community?

Try to assess the degree of diversity that exists in your community. "Community" can be a loosely defined term, but for this **Try It**, think of it as the group of people you encounter and interact with on a regular basis. When thinking of diversity, remember to include the many different ways in which people can be different from one another, including ethnicity, culture, gender, sexual orientation, physical challenges, and so on.

1. Overall, how diverse is your community? Why do you say that?

2. Which organizations in your community promote diversity? Are there organizations that work to raise the visibility and understanding of particular groups within your community?

3. What is the nature of your university or college's student diversity in terms of statistics regarding membership in different ethnic or cultural groups? (You may be able to find these statistics on your university or college's website.)

4. Is your student community more or less diverse than your community at large? Why do you think this might be?

To Try It online, go to the McGraw-Hill online resource.

Accept Diversity as a Valued Part of Your Life

We're not born knowing how to drive a car or cook. We have to learn how to do these things. The same is true of developing a basic understanding of other ethnic groups and cultures. Called **cultural competence**, this knowledge of the customs, perspectives, background, and history of others can teach us a great deal about others and about ourselves. Cultural competence also provides a basis for civic engagement, permitting us to act with civility toward others and to make the most of our contributions to society.

In the title of her book on social diversity, psychologist Beverly Tatum asks, "Why are all the black kids sitting together in the cafeteria?"[7] She might just as well have asked a similar question about the white kids, the Asian kids, and so forth. It often appears as if the world comes already divided into separate ethnic and cultural groups.

It's more than appearances: We form relationships more easily with others who are similar to us than with those who are different. It's more comfortable to interact with others who look the same as we do, who come from similar backgrounds, and who share our ethnicity and culture; we can take for granted certain shared cultural assumptions and views of the world.

But that doesn't mean that "easy" and "comfortable" translate into "good" or "right." We can learn a great deal more, and grow and be challenged, if we seek out people who are different from us. If you look beyond surface differences and find out what motivates other people, you can become aware of new ways of thinking about family, relationships, earning a living, and the value of education. It can be liberating to realize that others may hold very different perspectives from your own and that there are many ways to lead your life.

Letting diversity into your own life also has very practical implications: As we discuss in **Career Connections**, learning to accept and work with people who are different from you is a crucial skill that will help you in whatever job you hold.

Cultural competence
Knowledge and understanding about other ethnic groups, cultures, and minority groups

Workplaces are increasingly diverse.
© monkeybusinessimages/Getty Images

Career **CONNECTIONS**

Diversity in the Workplace

Diversity, and issues relating to it, are a part of today's workplace. Employers must deal daily with issues ranging from whether time off for religious holidays should count as vacation time to whether the same-sex partner of a worker should be covered by the worker's medical insurance.

The gulf in the workplace between people with different cultural backgrounds may be wide. For instance, an immigrant from Japan might consider it the height of immodesty to outline his or her accomplishments in a job interview. The explanation? In Japan, the general cultural expectation is that people should stress their incompetence; to do otherwise is considered highly immodest and inappropriate.

The increasing diversity of the workplace means that increasing your cultural competence will serve you well. It will help you perform on work teams of people of different ethnic backgrounds, it will help you supervise people whose first language and customs are different from yours, and it will help you work for a boss from another country and cultural background.

Equally important, gaining cultural competence will help you respond to the legal issues that surround diversity. It is illegal for employers to discriminate on the basis of ethnic background, gender, age, gender identity, or physical disability. Cultural competence will help you not only to deal with the letter of the law but also to understand why embracing diversity is so important to getting along with others in the workplace.

Explore Your Own Prejudices and Stereotypes

South Asian. Gay. Female. Disabled. Overweight.

Quick: What comes into your mind when you think about each of these labels? If you're like most people, you don't draw a blank. Instead, a collection of images and feelings comes into your mind, based on what you know, have been told, or assume about the group. The fact that we don't draw a blank when thinking about each of these terms means that we already have a set of attitudes and beliefs about them and the groups they represent. Acknowledging and then examining these pre-existing assumptions is a first step toward developing cultural competence: We need to explore our own prejudices and stereotypes.

Prejudice refers to evaluations or judgments of members of a group that are based primarily on their membership in the group, rather than on their individual characteristics. For example, the auto mechanic who doesn't expect a woman to understand auto repair or the job supervisor who finds it unthinkable that a father might want to take a leave for child care is engaging in gender prejudice. *Gender prejudice* is evaluating individuals on the basis of their gender and not on their own specific characteristics or abilities. Similarly, prejudice can be directed toward individuals because of their ethnic origin, sexual orientation, age, physical disability, or even physical attractiveness.

Prejudice leads to discrimination. **Discrimination** is behaviour directed toward individuals on the basis of their membership in a particular group. Discrimination can result in exclusion from jobs and educational opportunities. It may also result in members of particular groups receiving lower salaries and benefits.

Prejudice and discrimination are maintained by **stereotypes**, beliefs and expectations about members of a group. For example, do you think that women don't drive as well as men? Do you believe that people raised in developing countries are less intelligent than those raised in Western society? Do you think that people on welfare are lazy? If you answered yes to any of these questions, you hold stereotypes about the group being referred to. It is the degree of generalization involved that makes stereotypes inaccurate. It may be true that some women are bad drivers. But the fact is, women can be good drivers and men can be bad drivers—the stereotypes ignore this diversity.

To develop cultural competence, it's important to identify our prejudices and stereotypes and to fight them. Sometimes they are quite subtle and difficult to detect. For instance, a wealth of data taken from observing elementary school classrooms shows that teachers are often more responsive to boys than to girls. The teachers don't know they're doing it; it's a subtle, but very real, bias.

Why does this happen? In part it's because we're exposed to stereotypes from a very young age. Parents and relatives teach them to us, sometimes unwittingly, sometimes deliberately. The media illustrate them constantly and often in very subtle ways. For instance, men in the movies are often portrayed as action heroes, career women like Claire Underwood in *House of Cards* are seen as strident, and gay men are frequently depicted as effeminate.

But it's not only stereotypes that lead us to view members of other groups differently from those of our own. For many people, their own membership in a cultural or ethnic group is a source of pride and self-worth. There's nothing wrong with this. However, these feelings can lead to a less desirable outcome: the belief that their own group is superior to others. As a result, people inflate the positive aspects of their own group and belittle groups to which they do not belong. The bottom line is continuing prejudice.

Prejudice
Evaluations or judgments of members of a group that are based primarily on membership in the group and not on the particular characteristics of individuals

Discrimination
Behaviour directed toward individuals on the basis of their membership in a particular group

Stereotypes
Beliefs and expectations about members of a group that are held simply because of their membership in the group

To fight prejudice and to overcome stereotypes, work to develop cultural competence. Identify and conquer your own prejudices.

Develop Cultural Competence

Although it's neither easy nor simple to increase your understanding of and sensitivity to other cultures, it can be done. Several strategies are effective:

> **Study other cultures and customs.** Take an anthropology course, study religion, or learn history. If you understand the purposes behind different cultural customs, attitudes, and beliefs, you will be able to understand the richness and meaning of other people's cultural heritage.

> **Become more aware of your own culture.** We tend to believe that the way our culture does things is the way everyone does things. But this is not the case. Look at some of your own celebrations to raise your awareness of practices that you take for granted but that people from other cultural backgrounds might find strange.

> **Travel.** There is no better way to learn about people from other cultures than to see those cultures firsthand. Investigate student exchange programs at your college or university. Volunteer for study or work terms in other areas of Canada or overseas. If you have some time off in the summer or between semesters, consider buying a cross-Canada student pass for the bus or the train. If you are short on time or money, focus on exploring the different neighbourhoods in the city or town you live in. No matter where you go, just finding yourself in a new context can aid your efforts to learn about other cultures.

Travel provides us with an opportunity to become immersed in very different cultures and to see the world—and ourselves—through different eyes.

© Design Pics Inc / Alamy Stock Photo

> **Participate in community service.** By becoming involved in community service, such as tutoring middle-school students, volunteering to work with the homeless, or working on an environmental cleanup, you get the opportunity to interact with people who may be very different from those you're accustomed to.

> **Don't ignore people's backgrounds.** None of us are blind to ethnicity. Or to culture. It's impossible to be completely unaffected by people's ethnic and cultural backgrounds. So why pretend to be? Cultural heritage is an important part of everyone's identity, and to pretend that someone's background doesn't exist and has no impact on them is unrealistic at best and insulting at worst. It's important, though, to distinguish between accepting the fact that other people's backgrounds affect them and pigeonholing people, expecting them to behave in particular ways.

> **Don't make assumptions about who people are.** Don't assume that someone is heterosexual just because most people are heterosexual. Don't assume that someone with an Italian-sounding last name is Italian. Don't assume that a Filipino has two Filipino parents.

> **Accept differences.** Different does not mean better. Different does not mean worse. Different just means different—not looking, acting, or believing exactly the same as you. We shouldn't attach any kind of value to being different; it's neither better nor worse than being similar.

In fact, even people who seem obviously different on the surface probably share many similarities with you. Like you, they have commitments to family or loved ones; they have fears and anxieties like yours; and they have aspirations and dreams, just as you do.

The important point about differences is that we need to accept and embrace them. Think about how different you may be even from people who are similar to you in culture and upbringing. Perhaps you really can't stand baseball, yet one of your childhood friends has followed the game since they were five and loves it. Chances are you both accept that you have different tastes and see this difference as part of who you are.

Check Your Progress in Attaining Cultural Competence

Because you will often meet and work with people from other cultural groups, developing cultural competence is an ongoing process. To evaluate where you stand, ask yourself the following questions:

> Do I make judgments about others based on external features, such as skin colour, ethnic background, cultural customs, gender, weight, or physical appearance?

> Who are my friends? Do they represent diversity, or are they generally similar to me?

> Do I openly express positive values relating to diversity? Do I sit back passively when others express stereotypes and prejudices, or do I actively question their remarks?

> Am I educating myself about the history and varying experiences of different ethnic and cultural groups?

> Do I give special treatment to members of particular groups, or am I even-handed in my relationships?

> Do I recognize that, despite surface differences, all people have the same basic needs and desires?

> Do I feel so much pride in my own ethnic and cultural heritage that it leads me to look less favourably upon members of other groups?

> Do I seek to understand events and situations through the perspectives of others and not just my own?

Understand How Your Own Ethnic and Cultural Background Affects Others

If you are a member of a group that has traditionally been the target of prejudice and discrimination, you probably don't need to be told that your ethnicity and cultural background affect the way that others treat you. But even if you are a member of a traditionally dominant group in society, how others respond to you is, in part, a result of others' assumptions about the group you are a part of.

In short, both how we view others and how we ourselves are viewed are affected by the groups to which we—and others—belong. But keep this in mind: No matter how different other students, co-workers, or community members are from you in terms of their ethnicity and cultural background, they undoubtedly have many of the same concerns you do. Like all of us, they question themselves, wonder whether they will be successful, and fret about making ends meet. Bridging the surface difference between you and others can result in the development of close, lasting social ties. (See **Course Connections** for more insights related to diversity in your college or university.)

Course CONNECTIONS

Diversity in the Classroom

The increasing diversity of classrooms presents both opportunity and challenge. The opportunity comes from the possibility of learning on a first-hand basis about others and their experiences. The challenge comes when people who may be very different from us call into question some of our most fundamental beliefs and convictions.

Here are some ways that you can be better equipped to deal with the classroom challenges involved in diversity:

- **Present your opinions respectfully.** Don't get annoyed or angry when others disagree with your point of view. Be tolerant of others' perspectives and thinking.

- **Don't assume you can understand what it's like to be a member of another ethnicity, cultural group, or gender.** Talk about your own experiences, and don't assume you know what others have experienced.

- **Don't treat people as representatives of the groups to which they belong.** Don't ask someone how members of their ethnic or cultural group think, feel, or behave with respect to a particular issue. No single individual can speak for an entire group. Group members are likely to display little uniformity on most issues and in most behaviours. Consequently, this type of question is ultimately impossible to answer.

- **Seek out students who are different from you.** If you are assigned a group project, volunteer to work with students who are different from you. You may learn more working with them than with those who are like you.

- **Don't be afraid to offer your opinion out of concerns for political correctness.** If you offer an opinion in a respectful, thoughtful, and tolerant manner, you should feel free to voice your opinion. Even if your views are minority opinions, they deserve to be considered.

Time to Reflect: What **Did I Learn?**

1. Generally speaking, do you prefer doing individual work or group work? Why?

2. Thinking about the eight Striving Styles™ outlined in Chapter 1, which do you think is most amenable to doing group work? Which is least amenable? Why?

3. If you had to put together a group of four people to work on a research/analysis project, which Striving Styles™ would you most want represented? Why? Would your answer be different if you were working on a creative project? In what way?

Did You Know?

You will also need to rely on conflict resolution skills in your career: "Office workers spend more than two and a half hours per week trying to resolve conflict, which translates into $359 billion in losses for U.S. companies every year, according to task management software firm AtTask."[8]

Looking Back

Why is learning to work well as part of a team an essential life skill?

> There are very few jobs out there where you can operate as a lone wolf. Most organizations today are complex, and the projects they undertake often require combining the talents of many people from different backgrounds and/or with different perspectives. Whether it's a group project in college or university or a job-related challenge, learning to work well with other people is an investment that will pay positive dividends and help lead to success in many areas of your life.

What can I do to facilitate group meetings?

> Ensure you have a detailed agenda for each meeting.

> Designate a group member to write minutes.

How can I communicate openly with other group members?

> Rely on face-to-face communication whenever possible.

> Be a good listener and let others have their say.

> Provide conversational markers that demonstrate that you are listening.

> Use reflective feedback, ask questions of the person who is speaking, and deal with distractions so you can concentrate on what your group members have to say.

How can I deal with conflict?

> Listening is an important skill for team building, demonstrating that the listener really cares about the views of other group members.

> Conflict is an inevitable part of the evolution of a team, and sometimes it is useful because it permits us to clear up misconceptions and miscommunication before they escalate.

How can I become more at ease with differences and diversity?

> Being aware of diversity can allow you to accept the challenge and opportunity of living and working with others who are very different.

> Cultural competence begins with accepting diversity by seeking out others who are different, as well as by exploring your own prejudices and stereotypes.

> Joining clubs or student associations can bring you into contact with people from different backgrounds.

> Reading about or joining organizations that fight against injustice and discrimination can help you develop a better understanding of the issues faced by those who are different from you.

> You can learn about other cultures by travelling to other countries and geographic areas. It also helps to accept differences simply as differences.

RESOURCES

ON CAMPUS

Anyone who feels they are facing discrimination based on gender, ethnic background, sexual orientation, or national origin should contact a university or college official immediately. Often there is a specific office that handles such complaints. If you don't know which campus official to contact, speak to your instructor, your academic adviser, or someone in the dean's office, and you'll be directed to the appropriate person. The important thing is to act and not to suffer in silence. Discrimination is not only immoral; it is against the law.

IN PRINT

In Betsy R. Rymes's book *Communicating beyond Language: Everyday Encounters with Diversity* (Routledge, 2013), the author examines how the way we speak, the way we dress, the nicknames we use, and our pop culture references influence our identity and how we communicate in increasingly multicultural settings.

Beverly Daniel Tatum's *"Why Are All the Black Kids Sitting Together in the Cafeteria?" And Other Conversations about Race*, revised edition (Basic Books, 2017), explores race, racism, and the everyday impact of prejudice.

ON THE WEB

The following websites provide an opportunity to extend your learning about the material in this chapter:

> Visit the Mind Tools website at **mindtools.com** for more information on working in groups, team charters, and conflict resolution.

> To measure your own level of emotional intelligence, or EQ, visit **verywell.com /how-emotionally-intelligent-are-you-2796099**.

> The Conflict Resolution Network website at **crnhq.org** offers free training materials and self-study guides on the subject of conflict resolution.

THERE'S AN APP FOR THAT

> **Dropbox** is a multi-platform app that allows your group members to keep all files in one place and allows any group member to access any file. Dropbox makes it easy to look at in-process work or determine if someone in the group is failing to deliver.

> **Trello**'s multi-platform app has a user-friendly card-based interface that lets you plan a project, assign tasks, and manage a project, all from your smartphone.

TAKING IT TO THE WEB

1 Dealing with difficult people is never easy. For a step-by-step process on how to deal with them, see **chopra.com/articles/7-steps-for-dealing-with-difficult -people**. Now see if you can find other articles on the Web that deal with the same topic.

2 Using Google, find three examples of team or project charters and use them as the basis to develop one for your project team. Where can you start? Take a look at Ryerson University's suggested approach at **ryerson.ca/content/dam/lt/ resources/handouts/GroupWorkConflict.pdf**.

THE CASE OF . . .
Keeping Your Mouth Shut

Fidel Azar immigrated with his parents to Canada from the Dominican Republic when he was 11 years old. Although Fidel has become fluent in English, he still speaks with an accent. Fidel has never felt self-conscious about it before. He's lived most of his life in Toronto, surrounded by dozens of different accents.

Now, though, Fidel has relocated to a small city located several hours outside of Toronto. He's enrolled in university to earn his degree in software engineering. Sitting in a classroom in which he is the only Hispanic, Fidel suddenly feels too nervous to open his mouth. He is sure that no matter what he says, his classmates will disregard it because of his accent. Despite graduating from high school at the top of his class, Fidel has been struck dumb at the idea of answering the questions his instructors are asking.

One day, Fidel can't avoid the problem any more. In one of his programming classes, his instructor has called on him by name to explain a technical term. Fidel knows what the term means and how to explain it ... but he is afraid that as soon as he speaks, he'll be laughed at. As the moments tick by and the class waits for Fidel's response, Fidel starts to wonder why he's enrolled in university in the first place.

1. Can you identify with Fidel's situation? Are there aspects of yourself that you feel self-conscious about?

2. What assumptions does Fidel fear his classmates will make?

3. What assumptions about his classmates is Fidel making?

4. What advice would you give Fidel to help him feel more comfortable, not just speaking in class but in university in general?

5. Have you ever judged someone based not on what they say, but on how they say it? What did you learn from this incident, and how could you avoid it in the future?

CHAPTER 10
Managing Stress and Money

Learning Outcomes

By the time you finish this chapter, you will be able to

LO 10.1 Define stress, recognize that it is common, and analyze its effects on your life.

LO 10.2 Identify practical ways of managing stress.

LO 10.3 Differentiate between needs and wants, and prepare and explain how to stick to a budget.

LO 10.4 Discriminate between good and bad debt, discuss how student loans and credit cards work, and explain how to use credit wisely.

I t had been a long day for Alexandra Isaacs—and now, lying in bed, she couldn't fall asleep.

The many stresses and worries of her day kept repeating in her mind. She'd received a call from a collection agency that morning, demanding that she pay off her credit card bill, which was several months overdue. Alexandra was already having trouble paying her other bills: utilities, rent, car insurance, tuition, books, and everything else. Her paycheque from her job as a bank teller was already stretched thin. And given that she worked full time and was going to college, she didn't think she could find time to take on a new job or even additional shifts.

Alexandra reassured herself that she could figure out a way to save a little more money. She told herself that at the moment what she really needed was sleep. She had to get up at 5:00 A.M. to exercise, then go to work, then go to class. But all she could do was toss and turn, worrying about all the many challenges she had to face in the morning.

Looking Ahead

Do you ever feel like Alexandra? Do you ever stay awake wondering how you'll meet the demands of college or university, work, bills, and family? Then you're no stranger to stress, and you are definitely not alone. All of us experience stress from time to time, and studying at a post-secondary institution can often exacerbate it. It isn't easy to be a student on top of being a parent, a spouse, an employee, and so forth.

Coping with stress is one of the challenges that virtually all college and university students face at one time or another. In 2012, almost a third of U.S. first-year college students reported feeling that, as high-school seniors, they were frequently overwhelmed with all they needed to do.[1] The many demands on your time can make you feel that you'll never finish what needs to get done. This pressure produces wear and tear on your body and on your mind, and it's easy to fall prey to ill health as a result.

However, stress and poor health are not inevitable outcomes. In fact, by following simple guidelines and deciding to make health a conscious priority, you can maintain good physical and mental health. It's not easy to balance the many responsibilities of study, work, and family, but it is possible, and in this chapter, we discuss how this delicate balance can be achieved.

Perhaps the greatest source of stress for college and university students, if not for people in general, is money. Even under the best of circumstances, our finances present us with many challenges. But money stress is not inevitable, either. In the second part of this chapter, we address the basics of managing your money. We begin by discussing how to distinguish your needs from your wants, and then we examine how to track your spending and prepare a realistic budget for the coming year—the basis for sound money management. The chapter then goes on to look at the difference between good and bad debt, and how to discriminate between smart and stupid borrowing. We take a close look at how credit cards work and why credit card companies target college and university students, and we examine how to manage your student loans. Finally, we address the role of credit-reporting agencies and discuss why you need to build up a good credit rating and how to use credit effectively to do just that.

PARDON MY PLANET (I NEED HELP) ©2011 Vic Lee. Dist. By King Features Syndicate, Inc.

LO 10.1   Living with Stress

Stressed out? Tests, papers, job demands, family problems, volunteer commitments …. It's no surprise that these can produce stress. But it may be a surprise to know that stress can also result from positive life events, such as graduating from high school, starting your dream job, falling in love, getting married, and even winning the lottery.

Virtually anything—good or bad—is capable of producing stress if it presents us with a challenge. **Stress** is the physical and emotional response we have to events that threaten or challenge us. It is rooted in the primitive fight or flight response wired into all animals. You see it in cats, for instance, when confronted by a dog or other threat: Their backs go up; their fur stands on end; their eyes widen; and, ultimately, they either attack or take off. The challenge stimulating this revved-up response is called a *stressor*. For humans, common stressors can range from a first date or losing a wallet to driving in a winter storm. Your Striving Style™ and the way you experience stress are related.

Stress

The physical and emotional response to events that threaten or challenge us

Experience of Stress and Striving Styles™

Leaders	Feel stress when unable to have control over their time and commitments or when they have to work with an inefficient or disorganized group or when planning or organizing doesn't help the situation. Become increasingly inflexible, withdrawn, and emotionally detached. May lose control of emotions, leading to increased anger, frustration, and irritability.
Socializers	Feel stress when working with others who won't cooperate; when they overextend themselves helping and doing for others; or when they are devalued, misinterpreted, or criticized. Become increasingly judgmental and critical of others. Focus on faults of others and blame them for problems. Are aloof and cool toward people and stop seeing friends and family.
Performers	Feel stress when they are restricted or confined by rules or directives, when they find things boring or not worthwhile, or when they aren't recognized or approved of for their competence and contribution. Will absent themselves from situations and avoid others. Increased worry and anxiety lead to overindulgence in food, drink, sleep, or exercise.
Adventurers	Feel stress when they are expected to conform to structure and deadlines; when their freedom to choose and act is limited; and when they have to plan, discuss, or prioritize their work. Become negative and withdrawn from others. Can't focus their attention and are easily distracted, impeding progress toward goals. Become insecure and anxious.
Artists	Feel stress when there are strict deadlines, excessive rules, and competing priorities; when they are dealing with autocratic, challenging, or aggressive people; or when they have to disclose personal information, thoughts, or work before ready. Become depressed, anxious, and unhappy. Are perfectionists and are hypercritical of their work, leading to missed deadlines.

Intellectuals	Feel stress when others are excessively illogical or emotional, when they feel they have to follow instructions to the letter, or when they are expected to participate in group activities and projects. Become increasingly critical of self and others. Withdraw, becoming uncommunicative and unavailable to others. Procrastinate and lose track of timelines.
Visionaries	Feel stress when they fail to achieve, when they have to work with others whom they perceive to be not as smart or competent, or when they don't have enough information to see what they need to do. Experience stress physically with increased muscle tension, fatigue, or sleeplessness. Become irritable, angry, and easily frustrated. Escape into TV, video games, and so forth.
Stabilizers	Feel stress when there is frequent change or uncertainty, when instructions or information is too broad or theoretical, or when the work of others is deficient and has a negative impact on their own work. Become anxious and catastrophize, worrying excessively about dire negative outcomes. Focus excessively on details, losing perspective.

How Common Is Stress?

Because our everyday lives are filled with events that can be interpreted as threatening or challenging, stress and anxiety are common in most people's lives. How common? Data from the Spring 2016 ACHA National College Health Assessment (Canadian Reference Group) of close to 44,000 Canadian university students puts it into perspective. The students were asked how they had been feeling in the past 12 months.[2] Here are some of their answers—the numbers clearly show that if you've been feeling stressed and anxious, you are *far* from being alone:

> 89.5 percent of students surveyed felt overwhelmed by all they had to do.
> 88.2 percent of those surveyed described themselves as feeling exhausted (not from physical activity).
> 73.7 percent said they felt very sad.
> 66.6 percent described themselves as feeling very lonely.
> 64.5 percent said they felt overwhelming anxiety.
> 59 percent felt things were hopeless.
> 44.4 percent felt so depressed that it was difficult to function.

What Causes Stress?

There are three main types of stressors:

Cataclysmic events
Sudden, powerful events that occur quickly and affect many people simultaneously

Personal stressors
Major life events that produce stress

Daily hassles
The minor irritants of life that, individually, produce little stress, but can add up and produce more stress than a single, larger-scale event

1. **Cataclysmic events** are events that occur suddenly and affect many people simultaneously. Avalanches, tornadoes, and plane crashes are examples of cataclysmic events.

2. **Personal stressors** are major life events that produce a negative physical and psychological reaction. Failing a course, losing a job, and ending a relationship are all examples of personal stressors. Helping others deal with stress can, in and of itself, be stressful. Positive events—such as getting married or starting a new job—can also act as personal stressors. Although the short-term impact of a personal stressor can be difficult, the long-term consequences may decline as people learn to adapt to the situation.

3. **Daily hassles** are the minor irritants of life that, singly, produce relatively little stress. Waiting in a traffic jam, receiving a tuition bill riddled with mistakes, and being interrupted by noises of major construction while trying to study are examples of such minor irritants. However, daily hassles add up, and cumulatively they can produce

figure 10.1 | Daily Hassles

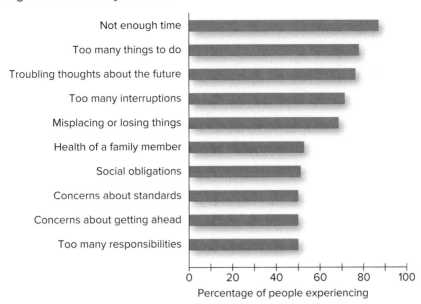

figure 10.1 | Daily Hassles

Not enough time
Too many things to do
Troubling thoughts about the future
Too many interruptions
Misplacing or losing things
Health of a family member
Social obligations
Concerns about standards
Concerns about getting ahead
Too many responsibilities

0   20   40   60   80   100

Percentage of people experiencing

even more stress than a single larger-scale event. (**Figure 10.1** indicates the most common daily hassles in people's lives.[3])

Data from the 2016 ACHA study (see **Figure 10.2**) also shed light on the types of stressors Canadian students have been dealing with over the past 12 months.

figure 10.2 | Events That Have Been Traumatic or Difficult to Handle in the Last 12 Months

Within the last 12 months, have any of the following been traumatic or very difficult to handle?			
Percent (%)	Male	Female	Total
Academics	48.3	62.0	58.1
Career-related issue	30.1	34.9	33.7
Death of family member or friend	12.6	18.2	16.6
Family problems	22.9	35.9	32.3
Intimate relationships	30.2	35.1	33.8
Other social relationships	23.5	32.1	29.8
Finances	34.0	42.8	40.4
Health problem of family member or partner	18.3	26.9	24.4
Personal appearance	22.6	37.7	33.4
Personal health issue	19.9	29.5	27.0
Sleep difficulties	32.3	38.8	37.1
Other	11.2	13.9	13.6
Students reporting none of the above	24.5	14.5	17.4
Students reporting only one of the above	13.6	10.1	11.1
Students reporting 2 of the above	13.2	11.6	12.0
Students reporting 3 or more of the above	48.7	63.8	59.6

© ACHA-NCHA

finds that eating fast foods just a few times a week leads to significant weight gains over the long run.[8]

> **If you want to lose weight, follow a sensible diet.** There's really only one proven way to lose weight: Control your food portions, eat a well-balanced diet, and increase the amount of exercise you get. Fad, quick-fix diets are not effective and will eventually lead to regaining any weight you might have lost.

Make Exercise a Part of Your Life

Exercise produces a variety of benefits: Your body will run more efficiently, you'll have more energy, your heart and circulatory system will run more smoothly, and you'll be able to bounce back from stress and illness more quickly.

> **Choose a type of exercise that you like.** Exercising will be a chore you end up avoiding if you don't enjoy what you're doing.

> **Incorporate exercise into your daily activities.** Take the stairs instead of the elevator. Leave your car at home and walk to campus or to work. When you're on campus, take the longer way to reach your destination.

> **Make exercise a group activity.** Exercising with others brings you social support and turns exercise into a social activity. You'll be more likely to stick to a program if you have a regular exercise date with a friend.

> **Vary your routine.** You don't need to do the same kind of exercise day after day. Choose different sorts of activities that will involve different parts of your body and keep you from getting bored. For example, for cardiovascular fitness, you might alternate between running, swimming, biking, and using a cardio training machine.

One note of caution: Before you begin an exercise program, it is a good idea to have a physical checkup, even if you feel you're at the peak of health. This is especially true if you're starting an exercise program after years of inactivity. You might also consult a personal trainer at the gym to set up a program that gradually builds you up to more vigorous exercise.

Get a Good Night's Sleep

Do you feel as if you don't get enough sleep? You probably don't. Most college and university students are sleep deprived, a condition that causes them to feel fatigued, short tempered, and tense. Sleep deprivation makes staying alert in class nearly impossible (see the **Course Connections** feature on page 276).

Ultimately, insufficient sleep leads to declines in academic, work, and physical performance. You can't do your best at anything if you're exhausted, or even tired.

Often the solution to the problem is simply to allow yourself more time to sleep. Most people need around eight hours of sleep each night, although there are wide individual differences. In addition to sleeping more, you can make some relatively simple changes in your behaviour to help you sleep better:

> **Exercise more.** Regular exercise will help you sleep more soundly at night, and it will help you cope with stress that might otherwise keep you awake.

Course CONNECTIONS

Staying Alert in Class

If you're having trouble staying alert or, even worse, if you're falling asleep in class, the best solution is to get more sleep. Short of that, you can try the following strategies to help stay awake:

- Throw yourself into the class. Sit near the front, pay close attention, take notes, ask questions, and generally be fully engaged in the class. You should do this anyway, but making a special effort when you're exhausted can get you through a period of fatigue.
- Sit up straight. Pinch yourself. Stretch the muscles in different parts of your body. Fidget. Any activity will help you thwart fatigue and feel more alert.
- Eat or drink something cold in class. If your instructor permits it, the mere activity of eating a snack or drinking can help you stay awake.
- Avoid heavy meals before class. Your body's natural reaction to a full stomach is to call for a nap, the opposite of what you want to achieve.
- Stay cool. Take off your coat or jacket and sit by an open window. If it's warm, ask your instructor if there's a way to make the classroom cooler.
- Take off one shoe. This creates a temperature difference, which can be helpful in keeping you awake.

> **Have a regular bedtime.** By going to bed at pretty much the same time each night, even on weekends, you give your body a regular rhythm and make sleep a habit.

> **Use your bed for sleeping and not as an all-purpose area.** Don't use your bed as a place to study, read, eat, or watch TV. Let your bed be a trigger for sleep.

> **Banish electronics 15 to 30 minutes before you hit the pillow.** According to **WebMD**, the blue glow of the screen revs up your brain and makes it harder for you to get to sleep. Apple now offers a feature called "Night Shift" on its mobile devices. The feature shifts the display's colour from a blue spectrum to a yellow spectrum after sunset[9] to address the finding that "perhaps the single biggest contributor to our collective sleep problems is the use of artificial lighting and electronics at night."[10]

> **Remove your phone from your bedroom before going to bed.** Waking up in the middle of the night to return a text is not going to help you sleep.

> **Avoid caffeine after lunch and dinner.** The stimulant effects of caffeine (found in coffee, tea, energy drinks, and some soft drinks) may last as long as 8 to 12 hours after you have consumed the drink.

> **Drink a glass of milk at bedtime.** Drinking a glass of milk before you go to bed will help you get to sleep. The reason: Milk contains a natural chemical that makes you drowsy.

> **Steer clear of sleeping pills and pills that keep you awake.** Although these pills may be temporarily effective, in the long run they

impair your ability to sleep because they disrupt your natural sleep cycles. Some are also addictive.

> **Don't try to force sleep on yourself.** Although this advice sounds odd, it turns out that one of the reasons that we have trouble sleeping is that we try too hard. Consequently, when you go to bed, just relax, and don't even attempt to go to sleep. If you're awake after 10 minutes or so, get up and do something else. Only go back to bed when you feel tired. Do this as often as necessary. If you follow this regimen for several weeks—and if you don't take naps or rest during the day—eventually getting into your bed will trigger sleep.

When we have more responsibilities than time, sleep is often the first thing to suffer. Getting an appropriate amount of sleep can actually help you get more done in the time you do have.

© Rob Melnychuk/Getty Images

LO 10.3 Managing Your Money

When it comes to addressing the stress in our lives, it's probably hard to overstate the impact of money. Few things command the attention—and worry—that money does. Indeed, in a 2013 study published in *Science* magazine,[11] researchers discovered that strained finances can actually impede your brain's ability to function. And a 2013 BMO study found that while 44 percent of students relied on parental support for school in 2013, that was down significantly from 52 percent only a year earlier.[12] More students are paying their own way. That's why it's essential to learn to manage your money effectively while you are attending college or university, and to keep doing so throughout your life. Not only are many of your choices and opportunities influenced by money, but so too is your mental well-being. Take a look at **Try It! 3** "Test Your Knowledge of Personal Finance" before reading on.

Do you know where your money goes? Do you spend more than you think you should? Do you never have quite enough money to buy the things you want? Does the arrival of your credit card bill send you into a tailspin?

Understanding the role money plays in your life is the first step toward wise money management. If you have money problems—and there's virtually no one who doesn't have some concerns about finances at some point in life—there are a number of different things you can do. We discuss solutions in the remainder of this chapter. Let's start by taking a look at what is often at the root of money problems: mistaking a want for a need.

Distinguish Needs from Wants

If you are living on your own for the first time, one of the first things you'll probably notice is that your **disposable income**—money you used to be able to spend on clothing or electronics or partying—is now needed for other things: feeding yourself, keeping a roof over your head, buying books, and paying for tuition. Those of you who've always worked part

Disposable income
The amount left over after payment of taxes and contributions to social insurance plans (such as the Canada Pension Plan and Employment Insurance) and other fees

3 | TRY IT! POWER

Test Your Knowledge of Personal Finance

Understanding the basics of personal finance is the key to living within your means and building a solid financial future. Use this **Try It** to get started.

1. What is the average Canadian family's *largest* annual expenditure?
   a. Food
   b. Shelter
   c. Taxes
   d. Communications (phone, cable, Internet)

2. What is the average amount of student debt outstanding after graduation for a student graduating with a four-year bachelor's degree from a Canadian university?
   a. $11,506
   b. $22,370
   c. $16,781
   d. $26,819

3. You have a $3,000 balance on your credit card, which charges 19 percent on outstanding balances. If you make only the minimum payment each month (usually 2.5 percent of the outstanding balance), how many months will it take you to pay off the entire balance (assuming you don't use your card again)?
   a. 239 months (almost 20 years)
   b. 125 months (a bit more than 10 years)
   c. 62 months (a bit more than 5 years)
   d. 35 months (almost 3 years)

4. Using the credit card example in question 3, how much interest will you have paid on that $3,000 balance if you make the minimum payment monthly until it is paid off?
   a. $2,190
   b. $1,575
   c. $4,504
   d. $3,120

5. If you graduate from college with a two-year diploma, how much more money will you earn in total over a 37-year working life than someone who has only a high-school diploma?
   a. $38,925
   b. $58,825
   c. $96,825
   d. $173,825

6. The average Canadian couple invited 129 guests to their wedding in 2015. How much does the average couple spend for this size of wedding?
   a. $19,456
   b. $13,382
   c. $30,717
   d. $11,992

The answers to these questions are supplied at the end of the chapter.

 CLASS DISCUSSION

Compare your answers to the following questions with those of your classmates.

1. What surprised you the most?
2. What misconceptions about personal finance did most of you share?

To Try It online, go to the McGraw-Hill online resource.

time in high school and considered shopping a harmless pastime are in for a shock: What you used to think was a "need"—the latest iPad, for instance—is actually a "want," something that you can do without. You may *need* winter boots, but you *don't* need a $200 pair of UGGs. You may *need* transportation to and from school, but there are many ways to address this need and a shiny new Mazda3 isn't one of them for most students. And on a day-to-day basis, you may *need* a coffee, but you *don't* need a Starbucks Venti Non-Fat Caramel Macchiato.

How do you make distinguishing needs from wants a part of your daily life? It starts with asking yourself a simple question. With every expenditure you make, no matter how small, ask yourself this: Is this a need or a want? If you experience even the slightest hesitation, it's probably a want.

How do you stop yourself from spending excessively on wants? One way is to postpone the purchase. It is amazing how many things we think we want are just fleeting desires that go away when we are no longer in the mall. A week later, you probably won't even remember what it was that you wanted. Another way is to replace the want with a cheaper substitute: A serviceable pair of winter boots does *not* have to cost $200. And a final strategy to avoid overspending, which will probably cause the fashionistas among you to recoil in horror, is simply this: Avoid shopping unless you have a real need. Daily notifications on your smartphone of the latest "Hot Buy" from your favourite shopping site, Groupon email offers, or strolling through your local mall just to pass the time are surefire ways to uncover items that you didn't know existed, let alone think you needed. Don't do it. While you are in college or university, stay away from shopping as a way to pass the time. Try studying instead!

As a student attending an institution of higher learning, you are probably not in a position to entertain having several lofty financial goals. But you are at a point in your life where you should definitely have one overriding financial goal: graduating from college or university with as little debt as possible. Let's now discuss how strategies like budgeting and the wise use of credit can help you get there.

What Is a Budget?

A **budget** is a formal plan that accounts and plans for the money that comes into your life (income) and the money that goes out (expenditures). Taking your needs into account, a budget helps you determine how much money you should be spending each month, and on what. Budgets can also help you prepare for the unexpected, such as the loss of a job that would reduce your income, or for sudden, unanticipated expenses, such as a major car repair, by giving you a sense of the financial impact on the rest of your expenses.

Although all budgets are based on an uncomplicated premise—expenditures should not exceed income—budgeting is not simple. There are several times during the year when you can incur especially large expenses, including the start of each semester, when you must pay your tuition and purchase books. Furthermore, your income can be erratic; it can rise and fall depending on overtime, on whether another member of your family starts or stops working, and so forth. But a budget will help you deal with the ups and downs in your finances, smoothing the bumps and extending your view toward the horizon. Learning budgeting skills can also help you at work, as discussed in **Career Connections**.

Budget
A formal plan that accounts for income and expenditures

Career CONNECTIONS

Budgeting on the Job

If you've ever held a job, the salary you received was determined, in part, by your employer's budget.

Although an employer's financial statements or annual budget may not always be accessible to every employee, budgets are part of the world of work. Regardless of who the employer is—be it a small dry-cleaning business or the federal government—there is a budget outlining anticipated income and expenditures. Managers are expected to keep to the budget, and if their expenditures exceed what is budgeted, they are held accountable.

For this reason, the ability to create and live within a budget is an important skill to acquire. Not only will it help keep your own finances under control, but it will also prepare you to be financially responsible and savvy on the job—qualities that are highly valued by employers.

Most of all, a budget provides security. It will let you take control of your money, permitting you to spend it as you need to without guilt, because you have planned for the expenditure. It also makes it easier to put money aside because you know that your current financial sacrifice will be rewarded later, when you can make the purchase that you've been planning for.

Budgeting is very personal: What is appropriate for one person doesn't work for another. For a few people, keeping track of their spending comes naturally; they enjoy accounting for every dollar that passes through their hands. For most people, though, developing a budget—and sticking to it—does not come easily. In this chapter's P.O.W.E.R. plan, we take you through the process of developing a budget and provide you with tips that will help you stick to it.

Prepare | Track the Money Coming In and Going Out

Do you open your wallet for the $10 that was there yesterday and find only a loonie? Spending money without realizing it is a common affliction. There's only one way to get a handle on where your money is going: Keep track of it.

To get an overview of your income for the coming year, take a look at your paycheques from work, and focus on the bottom line—your take-home pay.

As you can see from the *Dilbert* cartoon, what your employer tells you is your salary is not the last word. In Canada, deductions for Canada Pension Plan, Employment Insurance, income taxes, and so on will reduce the amount that ends up in your bank account. There is no point whining about it—just be aware that, when looking at incoming sources of cash, you have to look at them after deductions and after tax. And if you plan to reduce your hours while attending college or university, ask your employer to help you estimate how this will impact your take-home pay.

Aside from job-related income, you'll also want to get a sense of other sources of funds you can count on for the coming year. This might include money from family members, bursaries or scholarships, and financial aid from the government in the form of grants and student loans. According to the 2015 Canadian University Survey Consortium survey,[13] students required $15,798 to finance their current year of education. Forty-one percent of students financed some portion of this with government student loans and/or bursaries.

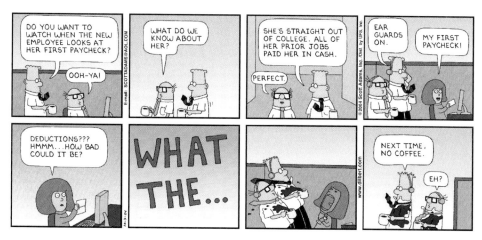

DILBERT © 2004 Scott Adams. Used By permission of UNIVERSAL UCLICK. All rights reserved.

To get an overview of your expenditures for the coming year, the first thing you should do is go through any records you've kept to identify where you've spent money over the last year. If, like most Canadians, you prefer to bank and pay bills online, the easiest way to do this is to bring up your account summary and look at it on a month-by-month basis. Otherwise, you'll have to rely on cancelled cheques, rent and utility receipts, and tuition and book receipts from past years to help you estimate what you spend.

To track all of the little items that you tend to pay for with cash, the best thing to do is for one week, keep track of everything you spend. *Everything.* When you spend $1.25 for a chocolate bar from a vending machine, write it down. When you buy lunch for $6.99 at a fast-food restaurant, write it down. When you buy a double-double at Tim Hortons, write it down. Record your expenditures in a small notebook that you carry with you all the time. It may be tedious, but you're doing it for only a week. And it will be eye-opening: People are usually surprised at how much they spend on little items without thinking about it.

⦿ Organize Prepare a Budget

Once you have the information you need to put your budget together, it's time to categorize it and list it in an organized fashion, putting the sources of income together, and separating them from the uses of income.

How Much Money Do I Have Coming In?

You probably have a pretty good idea of how much money you have each month. But it's as important to list each source of income as it is to account for everything you spend.

Add up what you make from any jobs you hold. Also list any support you receive from family members, including occasional gifts you might get from relatives. Finally, include any government aid or financial aid, such as bursaries, student loans, or scholarships you receive from your college or university. Use **Table 10.2** to record this information. When you do, be sure to list the amounts you receive in terms of disposable income.

table 10.2 Estimated Income, Next 12 Months

Category	The next 4 months	5–8 months from now	9–12 months from now
Take-home pay			
Family support (e.g., RESPs)			
Financial aid			
Bursaries			
Grants			
Scholarships			
Student loans			
Gifts of $ (birthday, etc.)			
Other			
TOTAL			

How Much Money Do I Have Going Out?

Make a list of everything you think you'll need to spend over the next year. Some items are easy to think of, such as rent and tuition payments, because they occur regularly and the amount you pay is fixed. Others are harder to budget for because they can vary substantially. For example, the price of gasoline changes frequently. If you have a long commute, the changing price of gasoline can cause substantial variation in what you pay each month. Use **Table 10.3** to estimate your expenditures for the coming year. For a template of this form online, go to the McGraw-Hill online resource.

table 10.3 Estimated Expenditures, Next 12 Months

Category	The next 4 months	5–8 months from now	9–12 months from now
Personal Necessities			
Groceries & eating out			
Shelter			
Utilities (e.g., heat, hydro)			
Cellphone & Internet			
Clothing			
Personal care (haircuts, toiletries, medication, etc.)			
Transportation (car payments, gas, car repairs, bus tickets, etc.)			
Loan and credit card payments			
Child-care expenses			
Savings fund			
Other			
Educational Necessities			
Tuition and fees			
Books			
School supplies			
Computer expenses			
Other			
Social Needs			
Relationships			
Clubs and teams			
Charitable contributions & gifts			
Other			
Entertainment			
Movies and concerts			
Trips			
Recreation and sports			
Other			
TOTAL			

Always Include Some Savings in Your Budget

When you are listing your upcoming expenditures, be sure to include an amount that you will routinely put aside in a savings account, a way of paying yourself first. The best way to do this is to automate the process, so it is out of sight, out of mind. Ask your financial institution to set up an automatic withdrawal, where a specific amount is taken out on a regular basis from your main account and moved to an interest-bearing savings account. For obvious reasons, this is best scheduled to coincide with the day you normally get paid. Some online banking services, like the one offered by Tangerine, allow you to set up specific savings goals and create your own automatic savings program. For instance, if you are planning to buy a car in a few years, start socking away a regular amount in your "Car Account," so you'll have a down payment when the time comes. If you are planning to travel to Mexico during study week next year, estimate the amount you'll need, divide it by the number of pay periods between now and study week, and start putting that amount into an account every time you get paid. Most money stress comes from poor choices or poor planning. Saving regularly is a very potent way to ward off financial stress. Knowing you have savings to fall back on should something unexpected come up is like having an umbrella on a rainy day!

W Work | Balance Your Budget, and Stick to It!

If you've prepared and organized your income and expenditures, actually constructing your budget is as easy as adding 2 + 2. Well, not exactly; the numbers will be larger. But all you need to do is transfer your total income and total expenses for each time period to a table like **Table 10.4**. Then, subtract the expenses from the income. In a perfect world, the result will be zero, or there will be some money left over.

But most of the time, the world is not perfect: Most of us find that our expenditures are larger than our income, and we are left with a shortfall. If you find you are expecting to spend more than you make, there is only one thing to do: Find places in your budget either to decrease your spending or to increase your income. This is where the real work of balancing your budget begins. It's often easiest to decrease expenditures, because they tend to be more under your control. For instance, you can do many things to save money, including the following:

> **Control impulse buying.** If you shop for your groceries, read your weekly grocery flyer ahead of time (most are online), plan your menus around sale items, always take a list with you (and stick to it), and don't shop when you're hungry.

table 10.4 Budget, Next 12 Months

Category	The next 4 months	5–8 months from now	9–12 months from now
Money coming in (income)			
Money going out (expenditures)			
Leftover or shortfall (+ or −)			

- **Make and take your own lunch.** Brown-bag lunches can save you a substantial amount of money over purchasing your lunches, even if you go to a fast-food restaurant or snack bar.

- **Plan major purchases to coincide with sales.** When making major purchases, like a new laptop, plan to buy when these items are usually on sale. Take advantage of price-matching policies by doing your research first.

- **Shop at consignment stores and thrift stores.** Stores like the Salvation Army Thrift Store and Value Village sell household goods like dishes, small appliances, and furniture, as well as clothing, at deep discounts.

- **Buy used rather than new.** Check out your school's "buy and sell" web page, your local Kijiji site, or eBay for items like used textbooks, bicycles, and electronics.

- **Share, barter, and trade.** Pool your resources with friends. Offer to babysit your friend's child in exchange for help painting your apartment. Carpool, share computers, and trade clothes.

- **Move out of residence and back in with your parents.** If you are living in an apartment or on-campus residence and your parents live within commuting distance of the educational institution you attend, ask them if you can move back in. This simple move can save you a lot of money.

- **Live more simply.** Is it really necessary to subscribe to the premium cable TV package? Do you absolutely *have* to have an iPad? Is it really necessary to eat out once a week? Do you buy clothes because you need them or because you want them? It always goes back to needs and wants. Because you are forgoing a full-time income to go to school, and you are probably borrowing to attend school, this is a time in your life when it is critical that you keep your expenses low. Living simply really is your best strategy.

There are as many ways to save money as there are people looking to save it. But keep in mind that saving money should not necessarily be an end in itself. Don't spend hours thinking of ways to save a dime, and don't get upset about situations where you are forced to spend money. The goal is to bring your budget into balance, not to become a tightwad who keeps track of every nickel and feels that spending money is a personal failure. To help you get started, get a sense of your current style of saving money in **Try It! 4** "Determine Your Saving Style" on page 286.

Finally, it's important to remember that budgets may be brought into balance not only by decreasing expenditures, but also by increasing income. The most direct way to increase income is to get a job if you don't already have one, or to work more hours at the job you have.

E Evaluate Review Your Budget Regularly

Budgets are not meant to be set in stone. You should review where you stand financially, preferably at the end of each month, but, at the very least, at the end of each semester. Only by monitoring how closely actual expenditures and income match your budget projections will you be able to maintain control of your finances.

4 | TRY IT! [POWER]

Determine Your Saving Style

Read each of the following statements and rate how well it describes you, using this scale:

1 = That's me
2 = Sometimes
3 = That's not me

	1	2	3
1. I count the change I'm given by cashiers in stores and restaurants.			
2. I always pick up all the change I receive from a transaction in a store, even if it's only a few cents.			
3. I don't buy something right away if I'm pretty sure it will go on sale soon.			
4. I feel a real sense of accomplishment if I buy something on sale.			
5. I always remember how much I paid for something.			
6. If something goes on sale soon after I've bought it, I feel cheated.			
7. I have money in at least one interest-bearing bank account.			
8. I rarely lend people money.			
9. If I lend money to someone repeatedly without getting it back, I stop lending it to that person.			
10. I share resources (e.g., books, magazines) with other people to save money.			
11. I'm good at putting money away for big items that I really want.			
12. I believe most generic or off-brand items are just as good as name brands.			

Add up your ratings. Interpret your total score according to this informal guide:

12–15: Very aggressive saving style
16–20: Careful saving style
21–27: Fairly loose saving style
28–32: Loose saving style
33–36: Non-existent saving style

1. What are the advantages and disadvantages of your saving style?
2. How do you think your saving style would affect your ability to keep to a budget?
3. If you are dissatisfied with your saving style, how might you be able to change it?

To Try It online, go to the McGraw-Hill online resource.

You don't need to keep track of every penny you spend to evaluate your success in budgeting. As you gain more experience with your budget, you'll begin to get a better sense of your finances. You'll know when it may be possible to consider splurging on a gift for a friend, and when you need to operate in penny-pinching mode.

R Rethink Revisit Your Budget When Circumstances Change

Reviewing your budget on a regular basis is one thing, but most budgets should be revisited whenever your personal circumstances change in a significant way. Perhaps you've decided to move in with a friend and you plan to share expenses. Maybe the funds from your Registered Education Savings Plan (RESP) have run out and you still have a year of university to finish. Maybe you have to move and your rental costs are about to take a major jump. Or maybe the store where you work is closing and you are losing your job. Whatever the change in circumstances, you need to take immediate steps to rethink and revise your budget accordingly.

LO 10.4 Using Credit Wisely

The first thing to learn about borrowing and credit is that there is good debt and there is bad debt. When you borrow money to invest in your education, it is considered good debt. Why? Because graduating from college or university is an investment in your future, one that can add well over $100,000 to your lifetime earnings, as you learned in Try It! 3. Bad debt is the kind that stems from borrowing to buy something you don't really need and can't really afford, like taking a trip to Florida during spring break and putting it on your credit card, knowing full well that you don't have the money to pay for it now and won't have the money to pay for it when the bill comes due. You are left with $1,500 on your credit card and you can barely make the minimum payment.

While the return on your investment in education is generally very good, the upfront outlay of money is high; for most students, borrowing is the only answer. But just as there is good debt and bad debt, there is also smart borrowing and stupid borrowing.

Smart borrowing is getting a loan that will provide you with the funds you need at the lowest possible interest rate and with the most flexible payment terms and then paying it off as quickly as you can.

Stupid borrowing is putting a major purchase on a department store credit card that charges 28 percent interest and then making only the minimum payment every month. Or buying something on the basis of "no money down, no interest, no payments for a year," paying a $99 fee for the privilege of doing so (read the fine print!), and then not having the money available a year down the road, so you end up paying a year's worth of accrued interest and then some—at a horrifying interest rate—plus the $99 fee. All on top of the initial purchase price.

Credit does have a purpose, and there are ways to use it without getting in over your head. We'll discuss some of them in the next section.

How Credit Cards Work

You see them in the campus cafeteria: a couple of students, sitting at a table, with a poster behind them advertising a free T-shirt, a free Frisbee, free tickets to a basketball game. All free—just for signing up for ABC credit card. By now, you've learned that there is no such thing as a free lunch. So what's the catch? It's simple. Credit card companies make their money from cardholders who have difficulty making their payments every month, and students just happen to be one of the groups that fit that description perfectly. Now, you may consider yourself different from the average student, and maybe you are. Maybe you *will* be the exception to the rule, using your card only for emergencies, spending only what you can pay back when the bill arrives, paying every bill in full on the due date. But the hugely profitable credit card companies are betting against you—and their profits suggest they know their market rather well.

So how do credit cards work, and how can you make them work for you? Used properly, credit cards are tools that can help you manage your money. Here's how they work. When you use a credit card to make a purchase, you are essentially being given an interest-free loan for a period of up to 21 days (known as a "grace period"), after which you will have to pay the credit card company the amount of the original purchase in full, or begin paying interest on the amount they lent you.

A 2016 survey by Abacus data found that 58 percent of households pay their credit card balance in full each month.[14] Those households have had the use of someone else's money for 21 days, while their own money was hopefully collecting interest in a bank account somewhere. That's smart borrowing.

But that means 42 percent of households don't pay off their balance in full—and it is a safe bet that, given their limited incomes, many students are in that group. With interest rates for major credit cards usually hovering around 19.5 percent, and department store credit cards charging an obscenely high 28 percent, it doesn't take long for the interest charges to start to pile up. That's what we call stupid borrowing. Even stupider than that is using that same credit card to take out a cash advance, where you get no grace period and the interest starts being charged immediately, often at a higher interest rate than for a purchase, and with a transaction fee tacked on for good measure. A credit card cash advance should *never* be used unless there is truly a dire emergency. And while we're on the subject, ditto for a payday loan.

So why even bother getting a credit card in the first place? There are a few good reasons:

1. Credit cards are one of the most accepted forms of payment worldwide.
2. Sometimes there is no other payment alternative—try booking a hotel room or renting a car without one.
3. You need to start building up your credit rating.

Credit rating
A judgment by a credit-reporting agency about your creditworthiness

What is a credit rating? A **credit rating** is a judgment about your creditworthiness given to you by an external agency called a credit-reporting agency. Equifax and Trans Union are the two credit-reporting agencies currently operating in Canada. These companies monitor and record every aspect of your credit history: when and where you've applied for credit, how much credit you can currently access, whether you've been paying your bills on time, and whether any of your payments are in arrears and by how much. The data they collect are reproduced in a credit *report* and summarized in a credit *score* that establishes your overall creditworthiness.

While no one can access a report of your credit history without your express permission, you'll find that something as simple as renting an apartment will be difficult to do without giving a potential apartment owner that permission. If you have already built up a credit history and would like to see your credit report, you can obtain it free of charge by mail. However, if you need immediate online access to your credit report or you want access to your credit score, you will be charged. Visit **equifax .ca** or **transunion.ca** for details.

Once you receive a credit report, you'll want to know how to interpret it. This link, provided by the Government of Canada's Financial Consumer Agency, offers information on how to interpret the letters and numbers that appear in your credit report: **canada.ca/en/financial-consumer-agency /services/credit-reports-score/understand-credit-report.html**.

The information contained in a credit report is summarized in a credit score, which is a score that summarizes your creditworthiness. That score affects what you will pay for loans: The more creditworthy you are, the higher your credit score. The higher your credit score, the lower your interest rate.

In 2009, the Financial Consumer Agency published an excellent brochure that is still available on the Internet today at **publications.gc.ca /collections/collection_2009/acfc-fcac/FC5-8-25-2008E.pdf**. The brochure uses plain language to help you understand what to look for on a credit report, and how to interpret your credit score. Here's an illustration to help you interpret your credit score:

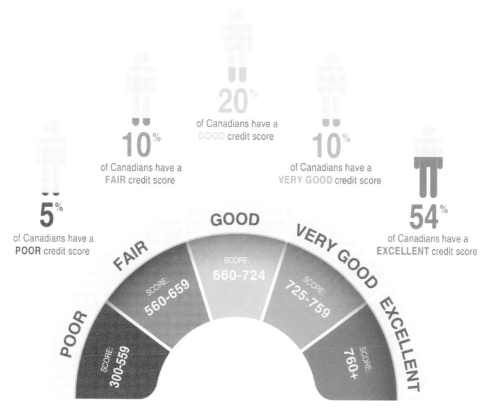

Percentages as of March, 2017.

Companies like Mogo and Borrowell offer you free online access to your credit score. To access your score, go to **mogo.ca/free-credit -score** or **borrowell.com/**

How Student Loans Work

Because the student loan programs in Canada vary from province to province, you will need to visit the website for your province to get specific details. That said, there are several things you need to know about student loans. First and foremost, for many students, while they provide you with a very good return on your investment, they are a significant financial liability. Based on figures from Statistics Canada and Université de Sherbrooke,[15] the projected total cost of education for a student living at home and entering a four-year university program in 2013 was $34,321. This climbed to $59,599 if you chose to live away from home. That is a *lot* of potential debt. It is, therefore, not surprising that according to a survey conducted for BMO by Léger Marketing, more than two-thirds of Canadians are concerned about the cost of post-secondary education.[16]

When do you have to start making payments on your student loan? In the case of Canada Student Loans, they are interest-free while you are pursuing your education, but *they begin accumulating interest as soon as you complete your program.* While there is a six-month grace period before you have to start making payments, don't be fooled: If you wait six months, you will have an additional six months of interest tacked on to your overall payment, so start making payments as soon as you can. And graduation from your program is not the only condition for repayment of your loan to begin. The requirement to repay your loan also kicks in if you switch to part-time studies or stop going to school altogether. You need to stay in regular contact with your loan provider to ensure that they know you are still a student; otherwise, you may find yourself being asked to repay a loan when you simply chose to take six months off to make some money. If you are unable to make the payments, you will want to look into the Repayment Assistance Plan (**canada.ca/en/employment-social-development /services/student-financial-aid/student-loan/student-loans/student -loans-repayment-assistance-plan.html**), which can provide you with some relief until your circumstances change.

What payments can you expect to have to make? Taking the projected average of $34,321 for a student in a four-year program living at home, and assuming you decide to take advantage of the six-month grace period (when interest on the loan continues to accumulate and adds $1,373 to your overall liability), you would find yourself paying $448/month for 120 months—that's 10 years! If you elected to live away from home and paid the projected average of $59,599 over four years, you'd find yourself making payments (following the six-month grace period) of $778/month for 10 years. The grace period alone would tack on $2,384 to the overall payment due. By the time you'd finished paying off this loan, you would have paid a total of $88,688—and $26,705 of that is interest! To obtain your own estimate, go to the Government of Canada site **tools.canlearn.ca/cslgs-scpse/cln-cln /rae-ear/rae-ear-1-eng.do** and use their Repayment Assistance Estimator.

How can you pay a student loan off sooner? Live simply, and borrow only as much as you absolutely need. Start paying it back as soon as you finish school, make lump sum payments whenever you can, and increase the amount you pay whenever you get a raise or your circumstances allow you to increase your payment.

If You Get in over Your Head

All of us face financial difficulties at one time or another. Sometimes it happens suddenly and without warning. Other times people sink gradually into financial problems, each month accumulating more debt until they reach the point where they can't pay their bills.

However it happens, finding yourself with too little money to pay your bills requires action. You need to confront the situation and take steps to solve the problem. The worst thing to do is nothing. Hiding from those you owe money makes the situation worse. Your creditors—the institutions and people you owe money—will assume that you don't care, and they'll be spurred on to take harsher action.

There are several steps to take if you do find yourself in financial difficulty (see also **Table 10.5**):

> **Assess the problem.** Make a list of what you owe and to whom. Look at the bottom line and figure out a reasonable amount you can put toward each debt. Work out a specific plan that can lead you out of the situation.

> **Contact each of your creditors.** Start with your bank, credit card companies, and rental property owner, and if necessary continue through other creditors. It's best to visit personally, but a phone call will do.
>
> When you speak with them, explain the situation. If the problem is due to illness or unemployment, let them know. If it's due to overspending, let them know that. Tell them what you plan to do to pay off your debt, and show them your plan. The fact that you have a plan demonstrates not only what you intend to do, but also that you are serious about your situation and capable of financial planning.
>
> If you've had a clean financial record in the past, your creditors may be willing to agree to your plan. Ultimately, it is cheaper for them to accept smaller payments over a longer time than to hire a collection agency.

> **See a credit counsellor.** If you can't work out a repayment plan on your own, visit a credit-counselling service. These are non-profit organizations that help people who find themselves in financial trouble. They can advise you on whether you need to consider a consumer proposal. They can explain to you what bankruptcy involves and show you how to dig yourself out of debt. To locate one near you, visit **creditcounsellingcanada.ca/**.

> **Stick to the plan.** Once you have a plan to get yourself out of debt, follow it. Unless you diligently make the payments you commit to, you'll find your debt spiralling out of control once again. It's essential, then, to regard your plan as a firm commitment and stick to it.

table 10.5　Steps to Help You Deal with Financial Difficulties

Assess the problem.	Make a list of what you owe and to whom. Figure out a reasonable amount you can put toward each debt. Work out a specific plan.
Contact each of your creditors.	Start with your bank, credit card companies, and rental property owner. Explain the situation. Show them your plan to pay off debt.
See a credit counsellor.	If you cannot work out a repayment plan on your own, visit a credit-counselling service. Your bank or creditor can help you identify a credit counsellor.
Stick to the plan	Once you have a plan, make a commitment to stick to it.

Time to Reflect: What **Did I Learn?**

1. Generally speaking, how would you characterize your money management skills?

2. Research has shown that although winning the lottery or other large sums of money brings an initial surge in happiness, a year later the winners' level of happiness returns to what it was before.[17] Why do you think this is true in general, and do you think it would be true for you?

3. Based on what you learned about money management in this chapter, what changes do you plan to make in the way you handle your money in the future? Be specific.

Did You Know?

According to **MoneySense.ca**, in 2015 the average cost of raising a child to age 18 is a whopping $253,947.[18] Break down that number, and that's $13,366 per child, per year—or $1,113 per month. And that's before you send them off to college or university!

Perhaps it's time to give your parents a call and say thank you?

Looking Back

What is stress, and how can I manage it?

> Stress is a common experience. Three main types of stressors are cataclysmic events, personal stressors, and daily hassles. Excessive stress is not only unpleasant and upsetting, but it also has negative effects on the body and mind.

> Stress is common among college and university students. You are not alone.

> Coping with stress involves becoming prepared for future stress through proper diet and exercise, identifying the causes of stress in your life, taking control of stress, seeking social support, practising relaxation techniques, training yourself to redefine and reinterpret stressful situations, and keeping your promises.

> Poor ways of coping with stress include overeating, cigarette smoking or vaping, and turning to alcohol or drugs.

What is involved in keeping fit and healthy, and why is it important for me to do so?

> For all people, keeping fit and healthy is both essential and challenging. Balance your responsibilities by identifying your priorities and using time management techniques.

> Eating properly means eating a variety of foods on a regular schedule and restricting your intake of sugar, fat, and salt.

> Exercise is valuable because it improves health and well-being. Choosing exercises that you like, making everyday activities a part of exercise, and exercising with others can help form the habit of exercise.

> The third key element of good health is sleeping properly. Good exercise and eating habits can contribute to sound sleep, as can the development of regular sleeping habits and the use of sleep-assisting practices.

What are reasons for keeping to a budget, and how can I prepare and stick to one?

> Concerns about money can be significantly reduced through the creation of a budget by which spending and income can be planned, accounted for, and aligned with your goals.

> Budgets provide security by helping you control your finances and avoid surprises.

> The process of budgeting involves identifying sources of income, keeping track of current expenses, estimating future expenses, and making the necessary adjustments to keep income and spending in balance.

What is the difference between good and bad debt, and how do I ensure I use credit wisely?

> Good debt involves borrowing for the purpose of investing in your future earnings; it promises a future financial return. Bad debt involves borrowing for immediate consumption, with no possibility of future gain.

> Credit cards, when used wisely, are a very convenient payment instrument. To use them wisely, get a no-fee card, use it sparingly, and always pay the amount outstanding in full and on the due date.

> If financial difficulties relating to credit do arise, contact your creditors and arrange a plan for paying off the debt. If you need help in designing a repayment plan, non-profit credit counsellors can help.

RESOURCES

ON CAMPUS

Many post-secondary institutions have mental health counsellors who can help you deal with emotional problems. If you are depressed, have trouble sleeping, or have other problems coping with the challenges of life, speaking with a counsellor can be extremely helpful. Ask your instructor where to find the school's counselling centre or health centre. There you will find someone appropriate to speak to.

If you are receiving financial aid, there is usually an on-campus office devoted to the complexities of scholarships, loan processing, and other forms of aid. The personnel in the office can be very helpful in maximizing your financial aid package as well as in solving financial problems related to your schooling. If you have a problem with your finances, see them sooner rather than later.

IN PRINT

Coping with Anxiety: Ten Simple Ways to Tame Tension and Start Enjoying Your Life (New Harbinger Publications, 2016), by Edmund Bourne, provides 10 techniques for coping with anxiety and its effects on your health and your life.

Emotional Intelligence: Achieving Academic and Career Excellence, 2nd edition (Pearson, 2010), by Darwin B. Nelson and Gary R. Low, is an interactive book that takes the theory of emotional intelligence and applies it to your academic life and career.

YOU: The Owner's Manual, Updated and Expanded Edition: An Insider's Guide to the Body That Will Make You Healthier and Younger (Harper Collins, 2013), by Mehmet C. Oz and Michael F. Roizen, is an engaging and comprehensive book that provides practical information on how the body works and also offers hundreds of pointers on how to live healthier, resist disease, and maintain a high quality of life.

Stop Overthinking Your Money!: The Five Simple Rules of Financial Success (Portfolio, 2014), by Preet Banerjee, is a no-nonsense guide to what it takes to manage your money.

Murray Baker's national bestseller *The Debt-Free Graduate*, revised edition (Money$marts Publishing, 2009), is a must-read for any student enrolled in a post-secondary institution. You can also visit the website at **debtfreegrad.com**.

ON THE WEB

The following websites provide an opportunity to extend your learning about the material in this chapter:

> You can learn more about maintaining variety in your diet by visiting Health Canada's website (**hc-sc.gc.ca**), where you can download *Canada's Food Guide*, which is available not only in English and French, but also in Arabic, Chinese, Farsi, Korean, Russian, Punjabi, Spanish, Tagalog, Tamil, and Urdu. On the website, you can also construct a personalized food guide that involves choosing

from a large list of ingredients, including many commonly used in cooking by various ethnic groups—such as bok choy, paneer, couscous, bannock, lentils, and tortillas.

> Visit **mindfullivingprograms.com/mbsr_online.php** to learn more about Mindfulness-Based Stress Reduction (MBSR) programs.

> The Government of Canada's Student Financial Assistance website at **canada .ca/en/employment-social-development/services/student-financial-aid.html** is an excellent online resource, offering videos, quizzes, and plenty of information on funding your post-secondary education. The site also provides you with interactive tools, such as a budget planner, a student financial assistance estimator, and a loan repayment estimator.

> For budget trackers, credit and savings calculators, and other financial tools, check out the websites of the major Canadian banks, or try **getsmarteraboutmoney.ca.**

> Need credit counselling? Take a look at the Canadian registered not-for-profit organization called the Credit Counselling Society at **nomoredebts.org.**

THERE'S AN APP FOR THAT

> **MyFitnessPal** is the most popular health and fitness app in the world. The multi-platform app allows you to track the impact of what you eat and how much you exercise.

> **Strava** is a social networking app designed for the runner or cyclist who wants to keep track of where they've been and how far they've gone. Available for iOS or Android.

> **Mint** is a money management, finance, and budgeting app that allows you to see all your financial accounts in one place and tracks the transactions that occur within them. You can also set up bill reminders and alerts. Available for iOS and Android.

> **YNAB**, an abbreviation for "You Need A Budget," is a user-friendly and millennial-friendly cloud-based budgeting site that is free to use for 12 months for college and university students. The site connects to your bank account for seamless transaction downloading, allows you to track where your money is going, shows you ways to reduce debt, and teaches you how to save money. The site is also connected to a mobile app.

> **Wally** is a user-friendly multi-platform budgeting app that tracks your income and expenses and projects your savings each month.

ANSWERS TO QUIZ IN TRY IT! 3

1. c. According to the Fraser Institute's Canadian Consumer Tax Index study, a Canadian family earning $79,010 in 2014 would have spent 42.1 percent of income on total tax bills compared to 21 percent of income on shelter, 11 percent on food, and 5 percent on clothing.[19]

2. d. The Canadian University Survey Consortium surveyed more than 18,000 graduating university students from 36 Canadian universities for its 2015 annual report. The average debt-ridden student owed $26,819.[20]

3. a. See table below—try it with your own balance![21]

4. c. See table below.

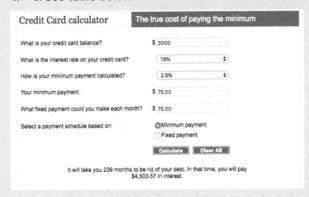

Credit Card calculator | The true cost of paying the minimum

What is your credit card balance? $ 3000

What is the interest rate on your credit card? 19%

How is your minimum payment calculated? 2.5%

Your minimum payment: $ 75.00

What fixed payment could you make each month? $ 75.00

Select a payment schedule based on: ●Minimum payment
○Fixed payment

Calculate   Clear All

It will take you 239 months to be rid of your debt. In that time, you will pay
$4,503.57 in interest.

5. d. Colleges Ontario[22]
6. c. Weddingbells.com[23]

TAKING IT TO THE WEB

1 Some of the most interesting research ever done on humans and their ability to succeed in the face of life's stressors comes from a longitudinal study done some time ago by psychologist Walter Mischel, which came to be known as "The Marshmallow Experiment." Find a video related to this experiment, and after watching it, research some of Mischel's findings from this seemingly simple but very powerful study.

2 Discover three new ways to save money. Using the search engine of your choice, enter the phrase "ways to save money." Examine the sites for tips and tricks to help you hold on to what you earn.

THE CASE OF . . .
The Breaking Point

Staring at the balance in his chequing account on the computer screen, Mario Gagliardi thought to himself, *It's all over.*

"It" was his college career. For three semesters, Mario had worked two jobs to pay his way through school. He'd been careful with his money, only rarely indulging in major new purchases, such as a new computer and a refurbished car stereo.

Now, though, financial events beyond his control had taken their toll. His brother had broken his leg on a construction site and couldn't return to work for months. While details of compensation were being worked out, Mario had helped support his brother and his young niece.

Staring at his chequing account, Mario realized that supporting his brother had added up to a lot more than he thought. Now his tuition was due—and Mario simply did not have the money. Mario had never felt the sinking sensation he now experienced: After everything he'd done, he believed his college career was finished.

1. Is Mario's college career really over? What should his next steps be if he wants to stay in college?

2. What can Mario do in the long term to make sure he doesn't face a similar crisis down the road?

3. Is there anything Mario could have done to have avoided this situation in the first place?

4. Do you think Mario was right to support his brother while he was injured? Would you have done the same thing in a similar circumstance in your own life?

5. Have you ever had a moment when you thought your financial plans had been ruined? In the end, was the situation as bad as it first appeared?

Glossary

Academic honesty Completing and turning in only one's own work under one's own name

Acronyms Words or phrases formed by the first letters of a series of terms

Acrostic A sentence in which the first letters of the words correspond to material that is to be remembered

Active listening The intentional act of focusing on what is being said, making sense of it, and thinking about it in a way that permits it to be recalled accurately

Advance organizers Broad, general ideas or materials related to what is to about to be read or heard, which pave the way for subsequent learning

Analogy A comparison between concepts or objects that are alike in some respects but dissimilar in most others

Anxious Experiencing anxiety, or the feeling of worry, nervousness, or unease, typically about an imminent event or something with an uncertain outcome

Arguments Facts, research findings, or other evidence used to support a thesis

Attention span The length of time that attention is typically sustained

Auditory/verbal learning style A style that favours listening as the best approach to learning

Blended (or hybrid) courses Courses in which instruction is a combination of traditional face-to-face classroom interaction and a significant amount of online learning

Blog A Web-based public diary in which a writer provides written commentary, ideas, thoughts, and short essays

Brainstorming A process whereby ideas are generated by a group following a specific set of rules that do not permit censoring or critiquing of ideas as they are generated

Budget A formal plan that accounts for income and expenditures

Career portfolio A dynamic record that documents your skills, capabilities, achievements, and goals and provides a place to keep notes, ideas, and research findings related to careers

Cataclysmic events Sudden, powerful events that occur quickly and affect many people simultaneously

Concept mapping A method of structuring written material by graphically grouping and connecting key ideas and themes

Conversational markers Non-verbal indications that we are listening to what someone else is saying

Coping The effort to control, reduce, or tolerate the circumstances that lead to stress

Cornell method of note-taking A method of structuring one's written notes into three categories: main notes, cues and questions, and a summary

Cramming Hurried, last-minute studying

Credit rating A judgment by a credit-reporting agency about your creditworthiness

Critical thinking A process involving reanalysis, questioning, and challenge of underlying assumptions

Cultural competence Knowledge and understanding about other ethnic groups, cultures, and minority groups

Culture The learned behaviours, beliefs, and attitudes that characterize an individual society or population, and the products that people create

Daily hassles The minor irritants of life that, individually, produce little stress, but can add up and produce more stress than a single, larger-scale event

Daily to-do list A schedule showing the tasks, activities, and appointments due to occur during the day

Decision making The process of deciding among various alternatives

Discrimination Behaviour directed toward individuals on the basis of their membership in a particular group

Disposable income The amount left over after payment of taxes and contributions to social insurance plans (such as the Canada Pension Plan and Employment Insurance) and other fees

Distance or online learning A form of education in which students participate via the Web or other kinds of technology

Dry run A rehearsal for a presentation in its entirety, from beginning to end, with all visuals and audio effects

Educated guessing The practice of eliminating obviously false multiple-choice answers and selecting the most likely answer from the remaining choices

Emoticons Symbols used in email messages and other online communication that provide information on the emotion that the writer is trying to convey

Emotional intelligence According to Daniel Goleman, the quality of possessing "abilities such as being able to motivate oneself and persist in the face of frustrations; to control impulse and delay gratification; to regulate one's moods and keep distress from swamping the ability to think; to empathize and to hope."

Ethnicity Shared national origins or cultural patterns

Evaluation An assessment of the match between a product or activity and the goals it was intended to meet

Flash cards Index cards that contain key pieces of information to be remembered

Free writing A technique involving continuous writing, without self-criticism, for a fixed period of time

Frontmatter The preface, introduction, and table of contents of a book

Hearing The involuntary act of sensing sounds

"I" statements Responses spoken in terms of oneself and one's individual interpretation, rather than casting blame on the other person

Information competency The ability to determine what information is necessary, and then to locate, evaluate, credit, and effectively use that information

Learning disabilities Difficulties in processing information when listening, speaking, reading, or writing, characterized by a discrepancy between learning potential and actual academic achievement

Learning style One's preferred manner of acquiring, using, and thinking about knowledge

Long-term goals Aims relating to major accomplishments that take some time to achieve

Master calendar A schedule showing the weeks of a longer time period, such as a term or semester, with all assignments and important activities noted on it

Meditation A technique for refocusing attention and producing bodily relaxation

Meta-message The underlying main ideas that a communicator is seeking to convey; the meaning behind the overt message

Mind mapping A visual technique that involves writing a central idea in the middle of a sheet of paper and then drawing "branches"—i.e., subtopics or themes that stem from the central idea. These subtopics can then be used to form a new thesis

Mnemonics Formal techniques used to make material more readily remembered

MOOCs Massive Online Open Courses

Netiquette Guidelines for demonstrating civility and respect in an online environment

Online database An electronic, organized body of information on a related topic, or dealing with related media

Outline A framework that sets out a logical progression or flow of ideas, prepared before the writing process begins

Outline method of note-taking A method of taking notes that summarizes ideas in short phrases and indicates the relationship among concepts through the use of indentations

Overlearning Studying and rehearsing material past the point of initial mastery to the point at which recall becomes automatic

P.O.W.E.R. Learning A system designed to help people achieve their goals, based on five steps: Prepare, Organize, Work, Evaluate, and Rethink

Personal stressors Major life events that produce stress

Plagiarism Taking credit for someone else's words, thoughts, or ideas

Podcast An audio or video recording that can be accessed on the Internet and viewed on a computer or downloaded to a mobile device

Prejudice Evaluations or judgments of members of a group that are based primarily on membership in the group and not on the particular characteristics of individuals

Presentation anxiety Fear related to speaking in public

Priorities The tasks and activities that one needs and wants to do, rank-ordered from most important to least important

Problem solving The mental activity involved in generating a set of alternative courses of action to enhance decision making

Procrastination The habit of putting off tasks that need to be accomplished

Read/write learning style A style that involves a preference for written material, favouring reading over hearing and touching

Reflective feedback A technique of active listening in which a listener rephrases what a speaker has said, trying to echo the speaker's meaning

Rehearsal The process of practising and learning material to transfer it into memory

Short-term goals Relatively limited steps toward the accomplishment of long-term goals

SMART approach to goal setting A framework for goal setting that emphasizes that goals should be specific, measurable, achievable, realistic, and time-bound

Social support Assistance and comfort supplied by others in times of stress

SQ3R approach A model for reading and comprehension based on these five steps: Survey, Question, Read, Recite, and Review

Stages in a group's evolution According to psychologist Bruce Tuckman, all well-functioning groups go through five stages: forming, storming, norming, performing, and adjourning

Stereotypes Beliefs and expectations about members of a group that are held simply because of their membership in the group

Stress The physical and emotional response to events that threaten or challenge us

Striving Style™ A mode of thought and behaviour driven by a predominant need that directs how we seek satisfaction from our lives

Study groups Small, informal groups of students whose purpose is to help members work together and study for a test

Study notes Notes taken for the purpose of reviewing material

Tactile/kinesthetic learning style A style that involves learning by touching, manipulating objects, and doing things

Team charter A set of written guidelines that outline the rules, roles, and responsibilities of team members and set out how a team plans to operate to achieve its goals

Test anxiety A temporary condition characterized by fears and concerns about test-taking

Thesis A closely related set of ideas that suggest an angle or way of approaching a topic

Time log A record of how one spends one's time

Values What you judge to be important in life

Visual/graphic learning style A style that favours material presented visually in a diagram or picture

Visualization A memory technique by which images are formed to help recall material

Vlog A video-based version of a blog

Weekly timetable A schedule showing all regular, prescheduled activities due to occur in the week, together with one-time events and commitments

Workback A plan of when to start an assignment, report, or project set up by working your way back from its due date

Zero-sum game A situation in which when one person wins, the other person automatically loses